ART AS REVELATION

BY THE SAME AUTHOR

Art into Life
Art as Understanding
Alchemy as a Way of Life
Nature Regained
Crystal and Cosmos

ART AS REVELATION

The Role of Art in Human Existence

Frank Avray Wilson

CENTAUR PRESS LTD

381 PARK AVENUE SOUTH • NEW YORK, N.Y. 10016

First published 1981 by Centaur Press Ltd., Fontwell, Sussex

British Library Cataloguing in Publication Data
Wilson, Frank Avray
Art as Revelation
1. Art and society
I. Title
700 N72.S6

ISBN 0-900000-96-1

Distributed in the United States by
Universe Books
381 Park Avenue South
New York, N.Y. 10016

ISBN (USA) 0-87663-359-9

Designed by Quill Design Limited, Cross Street,
Padstow, Cornwall

Photoset and printed by Photobooks (Bristol) Limited,
28 Midland Road, St. Philips, Bristol, England

CONTENTS

List of illustrations

Unless otherwise stated details used to illustrate certain points are from the author's own work

Acknowledgements

I am grateful to my son, Jason, for helpful comments on reading the first typescript, and to Ruth Lumley-Smith for her perseverance in finding light in the darker passages and for so often finding the nerve of communication in my scattered dissections. If the book has a togetherness, it is thanks to her. I am as ever grateful to Jon Wynne-Tyson for his encouragement and support, with so many ideas shared over the long years.

The fact that the aesthetic response is useless and purposeless, and that we know nothing about its motivations, if indeed there are any in the ordinary sense, should indicate to us only the poverty of our official psychology.

A. H. Maslow *Motivation and Personality*.
Harper, New York 1970.

INTRODUCTION

This is an account of my search for the relevance of the arts in nature and in human existence. It deals particularly with an experience that is derived from communion with beauty and harmonious order through all the arts and in the wonders of the natural world. Its particular significance lies in the fact that whereas other levels of enjoyment in the arts can be accounted for by accepted beliefs, this 'high' or 'peak' experience defies explanation because of its intensity and total otherness from ordinary human experience.

Because it is rare in modern civilisation it may not seem to justify the attention I am giving it, but we know that it has been a part of human experience since the beginning of man's recorded history, and is still a frequent occurrence among other races from the most primitive to the most sophisticated. Most people, at some time or other, mostly in youth, have had some intimation of the peak experience in communion with the arts or nature or through loving, but because it fails to fit into the generally accepted view of what is real or important, they seldom speak of it.

Those who are well acquainted with it will be so convinced by its supernal power and the sense of hyper-reality it gives them, that they will not feel that any explanation is needed. But, because I believe that such a powerful phenomenon must have an important part to play in the schemes of nature, and the role of man in those schemes, and because furthermore I am convinced that the loss of this significant area of experience not only deprives the arts of their proper place in a humanly controlled cosmology, but also impoverishes every aspect of modern living, I have long felt challenged to attempt to reinstate it.

The concepts I have been obliged to call on in discussing my thesis will seem strange to some; they are certainly remote from common experience, being mostly derived from advanced ideas in physics and biology, but they deserve consideration even by those with little or no practice in the further reaches of scientific speculation, for their relevance to life and art is truly great.

My approach to the arts in this book depends on a view of reality that I have adopted from very recent concepts in physics. Human art could not have arisen without a long evolutionary antecedent; indeed human sensitivity to music, and colour, as well as to the beauty of the human form and face, suggest a prolonged and elaborate evolutionary expertise which, in biological terms indicates their importance in the process of humanisation. Nature does not waste such effort for inconsequential activities. Aesthetic sensitivity is therefore likely to be as much a human characteristic as our upright gait.

Why, then, has science so neglected the relevance of art in nature and in humanisation? One finds no mention of it in hundreds of books on general biology, and those few authors who have ventured to touch on the subject usually avoid its more profound aspects. It is my belief that the explanation for this lies in the fact that the arts are instinctively felt to be a threat to the scientific world view.

I have explored the possibilities for a natural history of art in other books, but I will return to the subject because it is a necessary stepping stone to the much wider view of art that I want to deal with—a view which I hope will emphasise the relevance of aesthetic process in the creativity of the universe—thus opening up the possibility of a cosmology of art.

Although it is most frequently manifested in the arts, the hyperaesthetic experience is generally ignored by art historians as well as by psychologists and scientists. This is indeed a great loss, for here is the one phenomenon that could have been used to challenge the cultural monopoly of science. In the past every system of philosophy worthy of the name possessed its aesthetic. This is no longer true. The impoverishment brought about by the scientific view is demonstrated in Marx, whose system barely possesses an aesthetic. Perhaps the tide is beginning to turn for one finds an increasing number of people critical of this specific aspect of science, even though they may have immense respect for its cultural contribution. These are people too well aware of the humanities and the arts to accept their total rejection by science. This is well expressed in Theodore Roszak's recent book *Person Planet. The Creative Disintegration of Industrial Society* (Gollancz 1980). Until the hyperaesthetic experience is reinstated, the arts will remain a peripheral activity commonly regarded as irrelevant to the real world, and the vast majority of people, at least in Western industrial countries, will thus be deprived of a profoundly important source of inspiration and reassurance.

Combined with this cultural impoverishment goes the desecration of the natural world which is such a dominant feature of modern society. Sadly this means that much of the aesthetic value of nature is unavailable to large numbers of people. Before the materialistic values of recent western civilisation interfered, all societies from the most primitive to the most sophisticated judged the peak experience to be of the utmost importance to existence. Today Western man dismisses the evidence of its genetic significance and arrogantly relegates it to the category of the outworn or outgrown, superseded, he choses to believe, by the rationality of the scientific world view.

The scorn of the materialist for the arts can also be found in the challenge of the symbolic. A *sign* summarises an event occurring in the material world, whereas a *symbol* reveals an event occurring in another world which cannot therefore be compared to any experience in the material world. Such a concept has always been intolerable to the scientific mind. Nevertheless, here too, the first exciting gleams of a future reconciliation of these opposing views is in sight. Recently it has become evident that in pursuing its own logical progress, science has been obliged to deal increasingly with the symbolic, in the most abstract mathematical systems, which provide the only way of expressing non-material, non-mechanical aspects of physical reality.

By temperament artists are not investigators but instinctive believers. A close acquaintance with the life of many artists reveals some sort of belief in another world, even if this is unavowed, and not properly realised. It is probably true that if creative people lose their belief in this other dimension they cease to be able to create anything of importance. Fortunately, in a world increasingly discarding its formal religious beliefs and in spite of the present worship of materialism, there are still many both in the arts and elsewhere, for whom the evidence of an immaterial dimension is beyond doubt.

Until about the middle of the nineteenth century, the most learned people, among them many scientists, retained some belief in another world, even if it meant a contradiction in the materialistic world view which was then becoming popular. This resistance to materialism was due to something more than religious indoctrination and could be found as much among those who had emancipated themselves from unquestioning obedience to the church as it was in those still professing the faith of their ancestors. This instinctive belief may have been the reason why Charles Darwin hesitated for so many years before he published his theory. Did he, perhaps, sense the inadequacy of the purely mechanistic explanation of evolution offered by random natural selection? In his early career Darwin was sensitive to the creative exuberance and fantasy in nature, which defies a completely utilitarian explanation. As his theory gained acceptance Darwin himself seems to have lost his own sense of wonder and pagan reverence for nature.

It is the purely random mechanistic explanation of evolution offered by the theory of natural selection that accounts for its immense popularity, for the mystery of life has long been a thorn in the flesh of materialists. However it is now quite evident that while natural selection does account for evolutionary change—and much of evolution is nothing but change—it fails to explain genuine creative advances, the vital creativity and forward leaps that we call inspiration, which can only emanate from another immaterial and timeless world.

The intransigent denial of any possibility of this other world has had a calamitous effect on the modern mind, adding, through its rigid attitude, to the soaring dementia in every advanced industrial society. By its assumption that visions of a transcendental world are nothing but manifestations of mental instability in those professing them, it has contributed to the misery of generations of creative people, for the belief that life has meaning and that the transcendental world exists is central to the well being of the artist and indeed to all those sensitive to the arts.

Knowledge of the transcendental world is as old as man. The Buddhist cosmology is of particular relevance for it embraces a non-theological religious, and totally rational philosophy with a naturalistic concept of another world, and at the same time underlines one factor in our disarray—our wrong thinking about the role of the natural world. However the solution to our present situation is not likely to be found in reviving the past or indeed by borrowing from other cultures and civilisations fundamentally different from our own. Whether we like it or not it seems probable that we are committed to going forward in a world conditioned by science and technology. Therefore, although science must bear some of the responsibility for the part it has played in bringing about the present crisis of unmeaning, and for the tragic situation in the arts, it is never the less to a change in science's present limited world view, that we must look for a quite new formulation of meaningfulness.

To achieve this we need a minimal model or paradigm of nature which will meet the facts we wish to reconcile with a self-sustaining reality—the peak experience in the arts—and in communion with the arts of nature. Although models of this kind have been made in the past, they could not be checked against any scientific evidence. However, in the last two decades this situation has changed dramatically. The most matter-involved of the sciences, physics, has produced much of the new evidence.

The simplest model I have found which meets the above needs, rests on the theory that matter is a form of energy. For well over a century classical physics has accepted that energy is insubstantial and eternal. So here is the basic requirement—what is needed now is to understand how it can be put to work to create another non-material, atemporal aspect in nature. If the unity and consistency of the universe is to be preserved such a transcendental aspect must be capable of being seen as arising out of matter.

One can suppose that as matter exists, functions and evolves, so a purely energetic functional replicate of all its changes is automatically registered in a non-material atemporal aspect of nature. For this to be possible the atom has to be a reciprocating mechanism, the tangible expression of organised energy in space and time, and the means of creating parallel but purely functional replicas of all atomic activity in the non-material core of nature. Furthermore, atoms have to retain the potential of playing back this replicate in space and time.

Such a replicate world, formed by matter and yet not material once it has been created has many advantages over a one-level material world. All the experience of matter, in the course of its evolution, can be recorded and played back into the world of space and time, providing it with a self-constituted direction and consistency. Only some such system can account for the marvellous co-ordination in nebulae and stars—and, as we are at the point of discovering—for the humanly congenial functioning of the world.

With the evolution of living matter this ability to direct events in the material world is raised to incomparably more versatile levels. Nervous function, and the mind in particular, with its clear manifest of an irreducible difference from matter can be accounted for. Furthermore the pool of experience in the replicate level of reality, made available to the material world, explains the startling leaps in evolution and spurts in creative achievement not accounted for by Darwin's theory. Such a source of other-worldly information has a true revelatory quality, not found in ordinary experience, for it incorporates the quite distinctive qualities of the replicate world. Thus the irreducible characteristics of life, although apparently made entirely of matter, and the qualities of mind—the product of the material brain—are explained as the accumulation of vital neural and cerebral experiences in a transcendental level of nature; the source of inspiration in the arts and the hyper-reality, the unutterable joy and reassurance of the peak experience, can be understood as a participation in the universal pooling of mind activity.

This view of a transcendental level in nature is consistent with modern science's need for a naturalistic explanation. Such a need is an article of faith, nurtured by every scientist and the product of long scientific influence, which rules out the tendency of the untrained mind to dabble in the supernatural, (which a consistent scientific outlook rightly sees as confusion). So virtually anything is possible in science, so long as it has a naturalistic origin.

Until very recently science has insisted on a mechanical model of the mind; it is this model that now has to be changed since physics has itself produced proof of a non-mechanistic core to matter which has been experimentally demonstrated. If there is another world then it has to be the product of the world that has preceded it in evolutionary time—that is to say our material world.

The main difficulty in accepting the irreducible reality of the arts, of what they reveal, is the difficulty that the rationalising mind has always had in accepting any order radically different from that of the visible world. The replicate model accounts for this by the playback of sur-reality in moments of the peak experience, during which the individual mind of the artist actually participates in surreality. This means that art, both in its creation and the experience of it, cannot be a continuous or sustained phenomenon, but must perforce be intermittent. At its truly creative moments, all nature operates in this way. Evolution is not a continuous process—its periods of creativity are unpredictable and interspersed with long periods when only uninspired change occurs, human existence is itself a ceaseless oscillation between the world of common understanding and the world of dreams and splendour, of communion with nature and the inspiration of the arts.

That another level exists in nature is demonstrated in the phenomena of radiation and wireless which exist in a matter-free environment and are well understood and therefore accepted by the most materially oriented minds. Such an elemental level is but a poor shadow of that achieved by the human brain. This fantastic achievement —the creation of the replicate model of the mind by the brain is unique—no computer has as yet managed to create such a highly organised and potentially independent entity.

The search for scientific evidence for the replicate model should, one might reasonably suppose, be the business of biology and psychology, but there is as yet no natural history of the mind, and only a rudimentary understanding of the brain—the complexities of the subject seem to have driven most biologists into an evermore materialistic and mechanistic position, and the kind of revolutionary concepts which biologists and psychologists should be searching for are instead being pursued by physicists and also by non-scientists such as Arthur Koestler (see for example *Janus: A Summing Up* Hutchinson 1978). The new physics, one feels, is on the verge of explaining non-mechanical qualities inherent in the subatomic order. This is the most exciting development in the life of the mind in our civilisation, for here is the unique opportunity for describing a humanly meaningful view of the universe in terms common to science and the arts. For the first time since the Renaissance, art can be seen as an intrinsic aspect of a cosmology in which the human being features significantly. Much of this new evidence in physics is embodied in the quantum theory. Unfortunately this is a mathematical theory which even some mathematicians have difficulty in grasping in some of its consequences—nevertheless although the reasoning faculties are those generally required for understanding it, there are some aspects of quantum theory which defy ordinary understanding and can *only* be dealt with by the most abstract concepts which have a remarkable similarity to the kind of mental qualities which are made evident in the arts. For example the notion of 'substance' in the life of the mind which has a miraculous creative capacity not unlike the creative energetic entities of the subatomic realm, and the notion of time in the dream world and in art, which is so different from clock-time, can be compared with the fluctuating time of Relativity theory.

Does this mean that the aspects of mind involved in the arts share a common experience with the basic events of nature? I believe that it does, and the relevance of this belief is that it makes it possible for the central core and dynamic of such a theory to be caught and comprehended intuitively without recourse to the processes of mathematical thought.

Few mathematicians are concerned with this intuitive grasping of what the mathematics is about; most are content to use mathematics to account for events in nature which cannot be described in any other way. However, some of the greatest mathematicians and astronomers have themselves experienced an intuitive understanding of what the universe is about. There are also some notable mathematicians involved in physics who have recently made very important contributions to a meaningful vision of nature which substantiates the replicate model of reality. Readers requiring more information on the scientific background are referred to the appendix.

For the non-scientific reader it is hoped that sufficient will be found in the ensuing chapters to convince them that there is very much more to art as a natural phenomenon than the present culture of civilisation would have us believe. If this can in any way loosen the shackles of materialism on the sensitive mind, and so make more likely the individually experienced peak, in any of the arts, then the demands I have made on my readers' patience and perseverance will have been justified.

CHAPTER ONE

ART, SCIENCE AND REALITY

Since the end of the last Ice Age, some eight or ten thousand years ago, there have appeared less than a dozen distinguishable civilisations. Although each of these has had characteristics of its own, there have been some features common to all. One of these is a persistent preoccupation with the place of the human being in the universe, altogether more sophisticated and wide-ranging than the cosmic questionings of less developed cultures. The most distinctive feature of civilised life is the release from an otherwise smothering involvement in the bare business of living, which its elaborate social organisation allows; it thus provides the climate in which philosophy, cosmology and high religious undertakings can evolve. The historian, Arnold Toynbee demonstrated the close parallel development of these preoccupations with the rise of civilisation.[1]

Another mark common to all the great civilisations is an overriding concern with the arts. Most of the evidence which past civilisations have left us has come in the form of art works. In all civilisations art and religion have operated in close accord, framing the world view of a civilisation; the shared beliefs and attitudes, especially regarding nature and cosmos, have been generally accepted and have affected every thought and endeavour.

The partnership of religion and art has been a central theme in the rise of Western civilisation. One senses the mood of Greece in the Parthenon, and of the Gothic world in stained glass or a cathedral building; but following the Dark and Middle Ages, a development occurred in Western civilisation not found to such an extent in any other—the rise of technology and science, with its consequent impact on the environment and the whole of existence leading to the active, worldwide and in the long run destructive, exploitation of nature.

There are many reasons for this unique development; among them increased facilities of trade and commerce, in which the Mediterranean played an important role; the neighbourhood of the ancient practically minded desert civilisations of the Middle East and the bountiful natural resources and stimulating climate of the western end of Eurasia. The Greeks had already arrived at many of the key concepts essential to science, but they lacked some essential factor, which was supplied to the West by the monotheism of its religious background. The belief in an orderly universe, especially made for the benefit of mankind, provided that faith-in-order indispensable to science, and thereby licensed an assault on nature committed by no other civilisation.

At first the rise of commerce, technology and science was harmoniously tied to the religious world-view, but things began to go wrong in Europe with the turn of the fifteenth century. Violence and rapacity, inherited no doubt from the violent collapse of the anteceding civilisations in the Near East, and possibly even from the Ice Ages, found new expression in both religious and worldly rivalry, culminating in the great wars of recent history. The tensions and exploitations of the rising industrial age promoted a wave of violent revolution. The world-view of civilisation changed dramatically. Angered and disillusioned by the horrors of the wars of religion, people increasingly rejected the idea of a God-given world and progressively substituted a practical, opportunist attitude to life, purged of transcendental reference. As science increasingly explained the functioning of nature in exclusively material, mechanical terms, the religious world-view finally collapsed in the nineteenth century, unwittingly given its final blows by still religious men like Darwin. By the turn of the century many educated people took it for granted that the case for a self-consistent, exclusively materialist universe was proved, a new world-view which suited both the practical men of industry and the new political revolutionaries.

With the demise of religion, art as the means of revealing the profundities of life and nature, lost its authority and raison d'être. While it could depict the burgers and their families it now had nothing to say regarding the mystery of being; only a few rare artists were still in touch with the numinous, and they were ignored in their time. Cut from its religious inspiration, art eventually reacted against materialism in an explosion of new forms, which touched the heights and the depths, producing unparalleled music and painting and leading eventually to impressionism in painting. But, as science reached its apogee of confidence and the arts the full power of their reaction, an acute crisis developed. We are still in its midst today.

The crisis is the result of profound disillusion and a severe disturbance of the individual and social psyche. Only a few generations ago, the emancipatory movements which began in the eighteenth century, backed by science, promised a millennium of widely shared prosperity and justice. But progress to this promised condition has been attended by increasing violence and hatred, between classes and between nations. The psychosis is most advanced in rich industrial communities; violence and the suicide rate have followed closely on the curve of material advance.

Even more disquieting are recent reports of a creeping failure in education and a growing confusion of mind among the young. This is evident in the more extremist political confrontations in which students, the educational cream of modern society, have played a leading part, and in which dialogue, the mark of clear-mindedness since the Greeks, has been refused. In a wave of paranoid fury people, particularly the young, seem bent on destroying society and civilisation without reason. In such a situation art, in the full meaning of the term, is barely possible.

It should be quite evident that the world-view promoted by science is faulty, but many thinking people are either incapable of facing this fact, or are unwilling to because of the widely shared assumption that the scientific world-view, now with vast political involvements, is the only one possible if we are to avoid slipping back to an intolerable past.

The human mind does not appear able to accommodate itself to the meaninglessness of the exclusively materialistic and mechanical universe, proposed by science. It seems that the evolution of the human mind has only been biologically possible for so long because we continue to believe that existence has meaning and some sort of a cosmic reference. This is likely to be a profound genetic condition that has been instilled in the course of humanisation, and any disrespect of it is bound to lead to disaster. Possibly the violence and anger now proliferating throughout the world is a genetically in-built reprimand for such deviation. If this is so, then the dismissal of religion, myth and art, the channels through which all other civilisations have expressed and complied with this genetic need, is at the root of the present crisis.

There is some recent evidence still barely realised, of a corrective reaction in science.[2] There is in this the germ of a possible restoration of meaning, one which will be able to respect the key contribution of science to human thought regarding reality—the autonomy and self-sufficiency of the cosmos. One such possible world-view is that matter emerges from energy in a timeless universal continuum. As matter subsequently evolves, it develops the facility to organise the continuum in return, bringing into being a transcendental aspect of reality, made by matter but not material. Eventually it is in this parallel aspect of reality that mind appears, as the product of the material brain, simultaneously giving birth to a quite new universal transcendental level, the means whereby the universe can be said to gain awareness of itself.

What ever may be the world view that the new evidence eventually contributes to, it will be one of momentous importance for the arts. It is my aim in this book to substantiate this point, an aim which will require a weaving together of advanced concepts in both art and science, reconciling in its course an ancient split in the world-view of civilisation.

Every civilisation has been sustained by a body of belief formulated at its birth and rarely modified throughout its existence. Some societies have been controlled by a pantheon of gods who required to be placated regularly by sacrifice in order to keep a balance between human and divine forces. But the most persistent view of reality throughout the growth of Western civilisation, from its roots in the Middle East and Mediterranean, has been based on the belief that the hard material world was the most real.

Although some of the early Christians retained their interest in the practices of mystery cults, Christianity itself became increasingly preoccupied with tangible realities, and ultimately became a political force in its own right. Thomas Aquinas expressed this theological materialism when he pronounced that this visible and tangible world was the best of all possible worlds, especially made suitable for mankind. Christian art shows this progressive materialistic preoccupation, as art forms symbolising the underlying meaning of life—the ikon, mosaic, stained glass and religious music—gave way to banal pictorialism and the simple tonalities of hymns and psalms.

As Christian philosophers have shown it was the attitude of the Church to reality that paved the way for the rise of science.[3] Except for a small group of mystics outside the main cultural stream, the European mind has venerated substance, and this has become the common spur to commerce and conquest, as well as to science. In other civilisations, most people were prepared to accept the insubstantial and to express it symbolically which had evidently nothing to do with ordinary reality. But so strong has the substantial bias been that even today, when physics has revealed an insubstantial core in matter itself, many people simply cannot believe that there can be any kind of invisible or insubstantial reality.

There is nothing wrong with materialism, provided that the regard for matter includes all aspects of experience. Indeed, a consistent view of the universe demands some sort of materialism, as any alternative must imply a break in reality. Greek realism was so inspired. Even Plato and Socrates firmly believed in the gods. Matter was inherently magical. The sacred materialism of the early Renaissance can be sensed in Giotto, in Pierro della Francesca and many others. Something of it remains even in Leonardo. But the mechanistic bent of science, fostering the development of industry and maturing throughout its growth, soon obliterated the sacred in matter, so making the world easier to manipulate.

The power of mechanistic materialism was boosted by Newton, who explained the functioning of celestial bodies with the simplicity and precision of clockwork. By the dawn of the nineteenth century, it was firmly believed by the majority of educated people and by all scientists, that the mechanical laws they had applied to matter would in time explain all existing natural phenomena. What could not be explained was to be seen as the realm of illusion, or the non-existent. The mind, and all its creative fantasies, could be no more than some sort of material epiphenomenon. This matter-of-fact attitude to reality has been very successful. It has produced a rich harvest in the physical sciences, and the development of commerce and industry, and has freed most of humanity from fear of the supernatural. The impact of the age of science on society, on politics, on morality, and on religion has been decisive and irreversible. When Napoleon asked the astronomer Laplace if he thought there were any hidden directives behind the mechanical operations of the stars and planets, he answered with the solemnity and arrogance of the new age that he could find none.

Rising confidence in the powers of the reasoning mind enabled many to face an otherwise meaningless universe. But others, less idealistic, were consumed by the scramble for goods and power which this one and only existence could provide. A new kind of desperate brutality and callousness emerged in human affairs, in the race to bring about the materialistic millennium. It was only a short step for those holding the reins of political power to torture or kill, to ensure that the materialistic vision was fulfilled. The full, frightening truth about the impersonalness of the universe, dressed in various dramatic or religious guises in previous ages, could now be revealed. The 'age of liberation' rendered the world exploitable, not only by politicians and those in power, but by all who could share in its resources. In the advanced industrial countries a liberal capitalism, tempered by socialism, has alleviated want far beyond basic requirements. But in proportion to this success there has been an increase in dissatisfaction and violence.

Preoccupation with wealth and power has had a devastating effect on the arts. The struggle for material security has blunted artistic sensitivity and has largely reduced it to banal pictorialism or propaganda.

Anyone involved in artistic endeavour who has given thought to the processes involved, knows that all art worthy of the name must reveal the transcendental. It must, by its very nature, have recourse to the symbolic, and thereby becomes something different from any purely practical activity. The symbol is quite different from the sign. Numbers are signs; they stand for different quantities of things in the material world. But colours have such a profound emotional impact that they point to a quite different order of experience not easily defined in words. Art is distinctly different from ordinary experience. But there is some sort of important connection since art does not exist in a vacuum. It is difficult, however, to demonstrate this connection when science has shown that the universe has a particular order consistent with certain mechanical laws. Can any alternative be equally valid and real?

The established schools of psychology are of little help in this respect. Although their exploration of the human psyche reveals phenomena that do not conform to the mechanical principles on which they depend, they are still struggling for respectability. As for philosophy, it has more or less entirely sold its soul to science. If reality is exclusively materialistic, that is, entirely manifested in gross substance, then there is no way out for the arts. The Marxist insistence that only a socially related materialism and realism is to be tolerated would be justified and everything else could be dismissed as the ramblings of the insane.

At a meeting of the British Association in 1977, a leading scientist, Sir Andrew Huxley, drew attention to the clash between scientific freedom and bigoted political beliefs. Freedom of feeling and thought are equally indispensable to the arts. Although they fare well in certain periods when they happen to coincide with well established social norms, in times of challenge and change they can only perform their proper function when they are free to grope and experiment. There are many signs at present that this kind of politically motivated intervention, in both the sciences and the arts, is preventing new evidence regarding the nature of reality from receiving the attention it merits. The ferocity and viciousness of this opposition to new evidence indicates that psychologically sensitive territories are being invaded. Possibly it comes from the fear that there are no alternatives to a materialistic political solution, that any reaction opens the door to ancient confusions and oppressions. As we shall see, the new scientific view, although contrary to that of the nineteenth century on which materialism is based, in no way clashes with the rights of man. On the contrary, a far more sensitive and humanly rewarding vision of society emerges. Unfortunately one must conclude that some of the most violent political activities of the present day spring, not from rational or altruistic motives, but from the death of humanising sensitivities.

In nineteenth-century physics, there were still certain

phenomena that could not be explained by mechanical laws. Energy, the basis of life, which accounted for all the changes in nature, the birth and death of stars, as well as the actual evolution of life, remained an entirely inconceivable entity. In every manifestation of it which was examined, it proved absolutely insubstantial. Nor did physicists entertain any hope that some day the substantiality of energy would be demonstrated. They accepted that this fundamental insubstantiality was something they had to live with, and so they ignored it. But the universe only functions because energy can pass from one object to another. When material bodies are in contact, there would seem to be no problem. But when they are separated by the vast distances of astronomical space, the problem of the way in which energy is moved about becomes decisive. In the world-view of classical physics, on which materialism was based, space could not be empty, for if it was, energy could not be transmitted. It was hard enough to accept that energy was insubstantial, but to suppose that space itself was also insubstantial, challenged the very basis of materialism and the mechanical laws that had proved so useful.

The substantial medium which scientists assumed permeated space and all matter, providing energy with the means of its spatial display and interaction between objects, was called the aether. In order to accord with experimental evidence, this aether had to possess extraordinary and contradictory properties. It seemed that something was very wrong with the notion, and in the early years of the twentieth century, it was decided to put the aether hypothesis to the test. It was argued that, even if it was inconceivably thin and elusive, the passage of such a large body as the earth through it would be bound to cause some stir. Instruments were devised that could detect the very least disturbance, but alas, nothing was detected. To replace the discredited aether, physicists were obliged to postulate the existence of a 'field' or

Fig 1

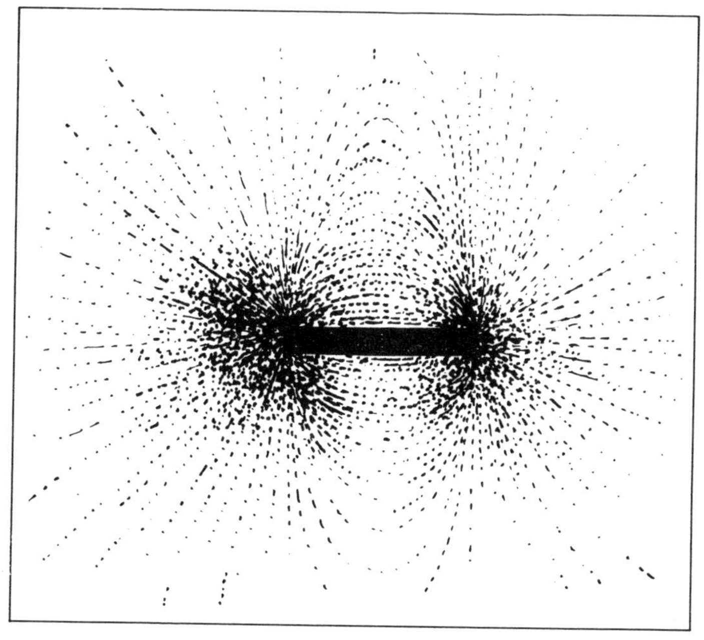

An electromagnetic field. If iron filings are scattered over a magnet they will arrange themselves like this. This force is equally effective in a vacuum, and clearly does not depend on any substantive agency

'continuum' (see Fig 1) universal and timeless, in which energy had its being.

Although the materialists insisted that such a postulate was nothing more than a mathematical convenience, and therefore no threat to materialism, all key mathematical concepts have had an uncanny way of becoming subsequently confirmed within the context of a previously unrealised aspect of reality. The concept of the continuum has been a part of physics for well over half a century, and yet its enormous philosophical implications are still ignored. To take it seriously means challenging the very foundations of traditional materialism and the political doctrines that have been founded on it. The game continues; many scientists believe that quantum mechanics, which is of the greatest importance in modern physics, supports the old mechanistic view of nature but, as we shall see, this is an illusion. In fact, since Einstein developed his theory equating mass with energy, the substantialist view of reality should have been rejected. (see appendix).

Ordinary awareness of the material world results from the way in which the senses and the brain interpret certain forms of energy. Human kind has always needed to be able to take this for granted, in order to know that things are what they seem, for had we been made aware of the ceaseless flux of energy itself, there would have been nothing but confusion. So it is that we interpret particular vibrations of energy as light and colour, others as heat or sound, and the organisation of countless billions of atoms and molecules as material objects, more or less hard or heavy, smooth or coarse. Because we live in a material world it has been necessary to us to believe implicitly that material objects and creatures not only exist as such, but are separated by an apparently empty space, in environments materially different from themselves, in spite of the fact that at the levels where energy exchanges occur, space is not empty, and the distinction between object and environment is abolished.

That the constituents of atoms are not solid micropellets, but consist of energy organised in different ways, is the most sensational conclusion of science, the key to the rejection of an exclusively mechanistic, substantial universe. The laws previously discovered governing the gross accumulations of organised energy-forming matter are still valid, but when it comes to dealing with the way in which energy is organised or transmitted these laws fail. Fortunately, nature has arranged for energy to express itself, not continuously, but in discrete packets, known as *quanta*. This makes it possible to deal with energy mathematically *as if* it did consist of pellet-like constituents, both in the formation of atoms, and in radiation, thus making it possible to apply to them the mechanical laws of traditional physics. Suitably modified, this is the concession that makes the quantum theory, and quantum mechanics, possible: without this concession on the part of nature, it would have been impossible to study these purely functional phenomena.

It is very convenient for the working scientist to deal with atomic events as if they were pellet-like, but in so doing, a price has to be paid. The insubstantial wave-like properties have to be ignored. Likewise, if the wave-properties are dealt with, then the pellet-like facility has to be abandoned—the gist of Heisenberg's famous Principle of Indeterminacy. The limitation, seldom stressed, is not in nature, but in the inability of the human intellect to halt, and examine the phenomena in order to be able to understand them; nature itself cannot be grasped by the intellect.

The irreducible insubstantiality in the very foundations of the material world opens a door to a non-material, purely functional account of phenomena. This has been ignored by science because any such account is bound to contest an exclusively substantial, mechanistic reality. But recently an increasing number of scientists, particularly in physics, have been exploring this functional interpretation of reality to account for phenomena such as telepathy, which fail to conform to mechanical principles. Resistance to the idea of such phenomena by the majority of scientists, and the emotional expression that this takes, is not based on rational thought but is motivated by resistance to the threat it implies to the scientific establishment, in which so much has been invested.

In the course of this book, we shall touch on some aspects of the current revolutionary view of matter, and the ideas and data in physics from which they have stemmed. Indeed, the underlying theme that matter exists at two distinct reciprocating levels, which seems indispensable if all the facts of art experience are to be accounted for, comes from this new view. But exciting as this whole subject is, we must confine ourselves to exploring only the facts relevant to this theme. Any reader who wishes to pursue the subject in greater depth should consult the works of M. Capec,[4] and E. E. Harris,[5] (see also *Nature Regained* and *Crystal and Cosmos*).[6]

The search for an alternative view of reality which is explored here, began with a very particular experience involving art and nature, which I could not explain by any of the conventional psychological or scientific theories available. In attempting to account for the indefinable qualities of such an experience, it seemed absolutely essential to postulate an entirely new level in nature, one which required a model making use of the new evidence now available.

The validity of this search depends entirely on the indefinable quality and very special nature of this experience.

CHAPTER TWO

VARIETIES OF AESTHETIC EXPERIENCE

Responses to art vary widely, both in kind and in intensity. They depend not only on the effectiveness of the work of art, but on the receptivity of the individual which is notoriously fickle. There are days when the most appealing art leaves one cold. Not only the state of mind, but bodily conditions affect the ability to respond. A tooth-ache or an overfull stomach can create distractions. Familiarity with a particular style or artist, prejudices, past experiences, the environment in which the art is displayed, are all potential influences. But one quality common to all art worthy of the name is an emotional experience of some kind.

This emotional response can be superficial or profound. An easily recognisable scene or tune can provoke a response that is so slight that it does not even interrupt ordinary conversation about the weather or politics. But the more profoundly moving and emotionally involving experience can absorb one to the extent that ordinary awareness is lost, and a new dimension is opened up.

However superficial the appeal, it is nevertheless the

emotional core which is the essence of the art experience. There is something about the emotional level which makes it distinct from ordinary material experience, and although one can pass from the ordinary to the aesthetic repeatedly, there is always this awareness that one is moving into a different dimension.

In conditions of what we call civilised life, art not only occupies an inferior position on the scale of priorities but may be vulgarised and superficial. It provides convenient gratification without making demands which might interfere with the day-to-day business of living. The unmistakable form of background music, the framed picture in the passage or the piece of sculpture in a corner, provide a pleasant temporary diversion or an association with particular memories, but are quickly forgotten. Most people probably obtain no more than this from the arts in the entire course of their lives. But there is another quite different type of art experience which is rare in modern conditions. This is a deeply moving experience which has repercussions long after the event, giving to the whole of existence an uplift and refreshment. It is always exhilarating, and at its most intense, rises into ecstasy. Those who have obtained this peak experience in any of the arts can testify that it amounts to life's highest gratification, which explains the supreme significance of art for all those who are sensitive to it.[1]

Critics, art historians and psychologists tend to ignore this heightened experience. It is not definable and readily examined, unlike those aesthetic experiences more closely related to the ordinary realm of existence. For the same reason, most people will tend to relegate it to the mystical, rather than to the legitimate sphere of the arts. Even the patrons of religious art in the Renaissance, repeatedly insisted that the artists avoid over-accentuating the numinous and stress the tangible. In asking anyone to consider seriously the reality and implications of a heightened or hyper-aesthetic experience, one is asking for a good deal, for it goes against the grain of cultural prejudice. Only the experience itself can fully convince one of its reality and power.

It is easier to say what the hyper-aesthetic experience is not, than to explain what it is. It is not related to sensual or sensorial conditions nor physical aspects of sexuality; although these are common in the subconsciously influenced arts of popular entertainment.

The subconscious is universally expressed in jagged, spikey, tortured forms, in clashing colours or in strong monochrome colours with the juxtaposition of black, in rough textures and crude organic shapes. When the subconscious influence predominates, colour cannot be used independently of form; form is literally coloured, so that any tendency towards the abstract remains figurative, no matter how deformed this may become. The high humanising uses of colour, on the other hand, are melodic and harmonic, with infinite subtleties of juxtaposition, and a quite remarkable transfiguration of form by colour occurs, so that in the move to abstraction, form becomes expressed by pure colour. Undoubtedly this marked difference between the subconsciously influenced and the influences of the high humanising aspects of the mind, has a genetic basis, and echoes the course of a humanising evolution, in which ordinary visual experience was literally transfigured by the harmonic, strongly humanising symbolism of colour with close musical affinities.

In such a situation, the subconscious influence must have been effectively silenced, otherwise this new humanising device could not have been picked out by natural selection. Therefore when one finds an active subconscious influence in art one can take it that this is an existential deviation. The influences in existence, and in the environment, that can revive the normally dormant subconscious, are legion, from shifts in bodily functioning, or an aesthetically impoverished environment, to social violence and insensitivity.

The fact that colour is, as it were *applied* to the object in subconsciously inspired imagery indicates the mind's way of reclaiming the human threat. Colour, one of the most potent humanising aids, literally reclaims the scenes and objects pulled out of the slumbering subconscious. The verve of the line, the holistic imperative of all art, is a further indication of such a reclamation.

The aesthetics of the high humanising mind, at its best in the hyper-aesthetic or peak experience, is thus in complete opposition to existentially aroused art, for although the latter does attempt to counteract human threats, there has to be a venting of the aroused devils of the subconscious world. While the peak is harmonic, beautiful and pure, sublime and uplifting, generally the subconsciously inspired cannot overtly appeal to beauty and is exciting or arousing rather than ecstatic.

When the subconscious intrusion is active, the strange and the bizarre may feature. Although lacking the high humanising aesthetics, this is felt as strongly appealing, fascinating, for it does strike a resonance with the subconsciously excited minds of the majority of people in existentially deviant circumstances.

In this sense, the arts can be seen to have an adaptive capacity, enabling a purging of the abnormally aroused primitive emotions of the subconscious, while reinstating the high human aesthetic appeals. It follows that the arts of any particular time and place, will largely depend on the prevailing existential conditions. In a particular circumstance, it would prove difficult, if not impossible, to force upon the public a psychologically unrelated art. For instance, in a strangely disturbed, dehumanised setting, the sublime and the beautiful become intolerable. However, the situation is never a matter of simple cause and effect. Strange currents get under way in the transcendental realms of the mind, and 'decisions' may be taken there which can dramatically reverse the usual psychological reactions to existence. One can find evidence of powerful healing or recuperative manifestations in the arts of the most depraved periods.

The distinction to be made between the magical and the high humanising aesthetic, is pertinant here. Those arts which may be described as magical are often crude, even hideous, whereas in the more ecstatic kind of art experience, harmony and beauty are paramount.

The hyper-aesthetic experience has evident connections with nature mysticism. The nature mystic, like the nature poet, obtains a peak experience in communion with nature. But there is an important difference. The nature mystic is usually so taken over by his experience that he has no urge to communicate it to others, whereas the artist feels an urgent need to do so, and this will not be denied—perhaps because the experience is less resolved, less intense in his case. But there can be no doubt that poets, artists and mystics, and indeed anyone moved by the beauty and harmony in things and creatures, all draw upon some common fount in the human psyche, quite different qualitatively from ordinary experience, yet linked with it. This association between a beautiful scene in nature or painting and the hyper-aesthetic experience, consists in a transfiguration of the scene or painting by events occurring in the mind. If these events do not occur, if the person is not moved or inspired, the same scene or painting appears quite ordinary. Evidently, for a scene or object to stimulate the mind and to bring about this highly emotionalised projection upon ordinary appearance, a certain fitness or compatibility between the external world and human sensitivities is necessary. The scene or object has to be aesthetically valid.

It is necessary to understand what is meant by emotion, and by the symbolic transfiguration of the visible world which follows an emotional intensification of the mind's inner world. Emotion appeared early in the evolution of life. It is an accompaniment of fear and pain. If such emotions were merely reflex, and incapable of being remembered, they would have little biological value. So one finds that the essential quality of emotion, even the most primitive, is a certain ability to persist beyond the stimulus and the reflex response to it. If one asks what it is that is remembered, one becomes involved in one of the greatest quandaries of psychology and philosophy. A purely materialistic account would insist that only chemical and physical entities are involved. These undoubtedly contribute but on their own they do not suffice to explain the phenomenon. In fact, to explain the 'memory' of an emotion, and especially its ability to transcend the purely material events involved, calls for a very elaborate model of nature and reality, which we have already mentioned—the replicating model whereby all material activity automatically engenders events in the continuum. As the continuum transcends space and time, 'memory' can be preserved as a purely functional, space and time defying event. Just as such events are fabricated by material systems, so they can be recalled by such systems.

This unorthodox view of mind, which the majority of scientists would probably contest, needs to be understood because there is really no other way of accounting for the totally different *qualitative* character of mind and emotion. As physics itself has been obliged to postulate the existence of a transcendental, universal continuum, it seems reasonable to call upon this concept to account for those biological phenomena that cannot be accounted for by any one-level, exclusively material view of reality.

The quality of emotion has been potentially available in all matter from the start. All that was needed was the appropriate organisation of matter, and the emergence of a nervous system, for the exploitation of the continuum to be possible. Once this evolutionary process was underway, it was certain that natural selection would eventually exploit it for many biological ends.

In the humanisation of the primate mind, it provided all thought and action with a humanising emotional aura qualitatively different from the reflex behaviour of animals. Humanisation required compassion, co-operation and altruism, emotional qualities that were essential ingredients in raising the human mind above the animal. Natural selection made a comparable use of emotion in the breeding partnership of birds, keeping the mates together by emotional ties so that parents would provide the rapidly developing young with the relatively enormous quantities of food they require. The humanising emotions were probably also developed initially for bonding human mates so as to provide the indispensable prolonged social and familial nurturing required by a large, slowly learning brain.

The emotionalisation of the mind was helped by emotionally evocative stimuli in the environment, in the beauty of the human face and form; the beauty and harmony of nature; the music of the voice; these are the biological springs from which all the arts have flowed. To become aware of these stimuli, nature had to make use of the senses of sight, hearing, and touch, as well as the poetry of language. As all these channels had been used for a very long time for practical purposes, survival would have been threatened if the humanising emotions had entirely superseded their practical use. The humanising emotions were therefore made extremely discreet, so much so that one is usually not aware of their influence. But, as the peak experience in art shows, human emotionalism is an extremely powerful, highly evolved faculty. We should not be misled by its discretion.

Although most people do not sense this quality in vision and perception, the artist is made aware of it by the intensity of his emotional life. William Blake expressed it in a poem, entitled 'With happiness stretched across the hills' which he sent to one, Thomas Butts:

> For double the vision my eyes do see
> And a double vision is always with me
> With my inward eye 'tis an Old Man gray,
> With my outward, a Thistle across the way.

The human mind must therefore be understood as primarily an emotionalising instrument which must have anteceded the rational, intellectual faculties, and has certainly closely attended and supervised their development, from which one can infer that the rational faculties are intended to be used in an appropriately emotionalised context, without which the mind becomes a dehumanising instrument. When this is understood it is not difficult to see where we have gone wrong as a civilisation. Because of the subtlety of the humanising aspects of mind, and the apparent autonomy of the intellect we have assumed that the intellect itself is the crowning human evolutionary achievement. Indeed, one recent school of philosophy, now fortunately in eclipse, deemed that the ideal use of the mind consisted in sifting away all emotional nuances from human communication, which amounts to a thorough dehumanisation of language.

The way in which the mind has been humanised is becoming evident through recent studies of brain function.

The cortex plays an important part in all experience, in culture and education; the conditioning to which it is subjected is also important in forming our attitudes to art. But the cortex itself is under the influence of the emotionalising regions of the brain, which are subject to precise genetic and hormonal control, so that the humanising influence over the cortex is incessant, and only interfered with in disease or in disturbingly inhuman conditions. Due to the integration of its functioning, the brain has been able to make use of primitive emotional centres that go back to the dawn of vertebrate life. Clearly these primitive emotions have undergone immense modifications from the animal context to one specifically human; the way in which this has come about is quite evident in the function of art—which has rendered man sensitive to beauty, harmony, and purity.

This transfiguration of emotion no doubt goes on to some extent in the cortex (see Fig 2); but the chief site is likely to be in the upper brain stem, in the medulla, in association with a very particular structure, the hypothalamus and the limbic system (see Fig 3). The neural wiring is so complex between these regions and the cortex, that they have barely begun to be unravelled, but specific regions are turning out to be particularly involved. The organ of Broca, the one part of the brain unique to man, has certainly a very important part to play, as has the encapsulation of the limbic system, which probably assures that humanly undesirable emotions do not reach the cortex.

Suggestions have been made that things have gone wrong in the evolution of the limbic system, allowing undesirable and dehumanising primitive emotions to pass through; these ideas have been popularised by Arthur Koestler, who has concluded that unless a drug can be found to remedy this natural blunder, mankind is

Fig 2

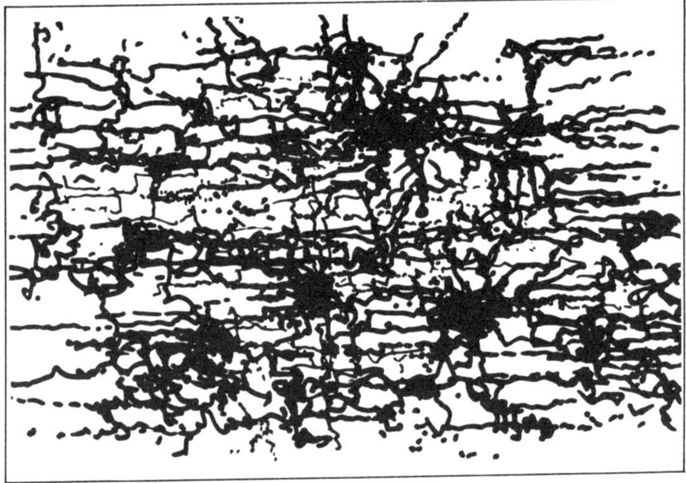

The human cerebral cortex. The most highly evolved and complex form of matter in the universe. It is here that matter has most effectively organised the universal continuum to form mind

doomed.[2] Because they have so recently been stilled, the primitive animal aspects of the brain are easily aroused; this is evident in the widespread intrusion of the subconscious into consciousness. But there are so many agencies in our deviant existence which can arouse the subconscious that there is really no need to suppose that humanisation has gone wrong. Possibly the most effective limbic check on such a dehumanising arousal is the achievement of love, a factor that has been particularly lacking in civilisation.

Quite recently, biochemicals which have similar properties to the most potent psychotropic drugs like LSD and morphine, have been discovered in certain regions of the

Fig 3

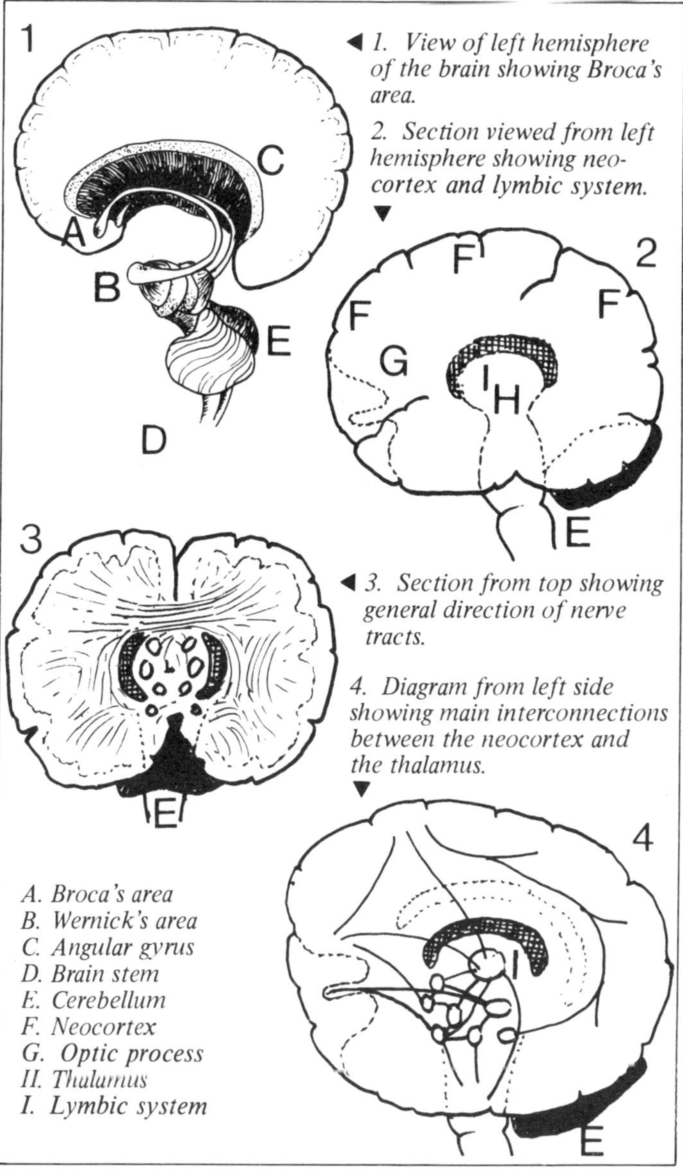

◀ *1. View of left hemisphere of the brain showing Broca's area.*

2. Section viewed from left hemisphere showing neo-cortex and lymbic system. ▼

◀ *3. Section from top showing general direction of nerve tracts.*

4. Diagram from left side showing main interconnections between the neocortex and the thalamus. ▼

A. Broca's area
B. Wernick's area
C. Angular gyrus
D. Brain stem
E. Cerebellum
F. Neocortex
G. Optic process
H. Thalamus
I. Lymbic system

brain. They are evidently connected with the peak experience since they seem to induce the ecstasy and rapture typical of the hyper-aesthetic level.

The opening up of these natural and biochemical processes in no way implies that the aesthetic experience can be reduced to the physico-chemical level, for it has certain qualities and an 'otherness', which cannot be explained as a physical phenomenon. But the biochemical processes do confirm that these experiences are not chimera or illusional fantasy. They do not exist in a vacuum, but are part of biological development. Complex processes of evolution must have taken place in order to develop in the human brain such an intensely powerful emotional potential.

The evolutionary transformation of the primate brain into a human mind has required tens of millions of years. This amazing story goes back to the earliest vertebrates. The evolution of bodies in different kinds of animals can be better understood as the means of evolving the nervous systems and brain. This is a reversal of the usual way of looking at it, but if nature has a sustaining creative theme, this way of seeing how its crowning achievement—the humanised primate brain—came about, makes good sense. If one could see this evolution of the nervous system and brain on a speeded-up film, the different kinds of animal bodies and organs along the way would fade into insignificance, as evolution pushed inexorably on towards the primate brain, and its unique capacity to become in time humanised, not so much by its size, which has chiefly to do with its computerising abilities, but by its exploitation of the continuum, in the humanising emotions and all that has gone with them; love, art and the strange worlds of the spirit.

As already mentioned, this process really got under way as the need arose for a large learning brain, requiring a prolonged juvenile period; this in turn called for parental and social protection and nurturing. The first crucial steps were taken when the mammals came on the scene.

With mother-love, came a new development in evolution. Unlike birds, in which both breeding partners co-operate, the female mammal took on the entire responsibility of rearing her young, so at first she alone developed an emotional faculty. There was no need for an emotional bond between the mates or for emotionalising stimuli in the environment, which explains why mammals do not share the bright plumage or compelling songs of birds, but are usually drab in appearance. However as the humanising process developed, co-operation between the mates became necessary in order to protect and nurture the young for increasingly long periods. Emotionalising stimuli were accordingly picked out by natural selection, and an emotionalised sensitivity developed, in the music of the human voice, in the beauty of face and body, in sexual and altruistic love. It also became evident in social communion and co-operation. This new faculty of sensitivity altered the mind itself, raising it above the animal level; this became the key biological feature of the human species.

Such an indispensable biological function had to be assured and exercising it therefore brought adequate reward in the form of the peak experience—the greatest possible gratification. As the function of this humanising emotion was to help man transcend the animal level of response, it had to have an entirely different type of appeal. The emotional level is indeed radically different from ordinary experience, with qualities and joys all of its own. Although in this book it is the peak or hyper-aesthetic experience in the arts with which we are concerned, it will be seen that all types of peak experience have common features. They all provoke intense joy amounting to ecstasy; they give the participant a sense of belonging and reassurance, and the impression of access to a reality greater and more important than that of the ordinary world. There is, therefore, much to learn from the peak experience through communion with nature, in the high dream, in the raptures of loving, in mysticism, and in drug-induced states, all of which point to a higher aspect of the human mind.

Despite the fact that the hyper-aesthetic experience is a uniquely human gift, its rare appearance in contemporary civilisation has enabled established psychology to ignore it. As a result, conventional theories of psychology are incapable of providing a satisfactory definition of the human condition, particularly of such phenomena as the appeal of the arts. This state of affairs exhibited by the various psychological schools suggests that man has, in truth, seldom been properly human. Although, as we shall see later, mankind is probably far older than has been supposed until quite recently, the planet has been generally hostile to the human condition for the last million years.

Existential standards have been imposed on biological reality throughout the rise of civilisation, fostering some developments and arresting others. We can suppose, from what we know of the conditions in which early man developed, that they were conducive to the growth of the humanising process and that this need persists in spite of the de-humanising conditions we predominantly find ourselves in.

This conclusion is supported by evidence gathered from the observation of the few remaining primitive communities, among whom the emotional mind is ceaselessly active, transfiguring all experience, insisting that when reason is applied, it works only to enhance humanising needs and never against them.

This is undoubtedly how the faculty of reason is intended to be used. Every thought, every motivation to action is subtly tested and intuitively accepted or rejected according to whether it is humanly compatible or a threat to the human condition. It is impossible to believe that reason could have evolved as an independent faculty. The impartiality of reason on which science has placed such stress, is a fallacy. Unguided reason is potentially an anti-human force. As the source of the humanising influence, the high-mind, sensitive to order and harmony provides the natural basis for a proper regard for nature, and for a humanly enhancing art. Its highest possible reward is an ecstatic, totally involving and reassuring peak experience—the hyper-aesthetic moment. In comparison with its intensity, the pleasures of the body, with their long animal lineage, are vapid and superficial. While the gratification of physical desires can be enjoyable they often leave an after effect of dissatisfaction, a feeling of deception and unfulfilment.

By thwarting the emotional life and accentuating the rational, a materialistic existence becomes synonymous with a subtle process of de-humanisation, providing the grounds for social dissatisfaction. In this context, the increasing fear and violence that has followed materialistic fulfilment can be understood. Herein also lies the reason why what is felt to be beautiful and whole is usually sound and that what is disintegrated and ugly, is bad. This is a principle which is true not only in art and living, but in the sciences as well.

This view of the mind, in harmony with the art-compatible humanising sensitivities, is in many respects contrary to that of present day psychology. The greatest fallacy, reinforced by education and philosophy, is that reason is the highest human attribute; an idea supported by the common belief that man's rise from a savage and violent state can only have come about through the application of reason. Admittedly much confusion in the past has given rise to human unreason which is mistakenly used to support the rationalist theory of progress. This view is not only supported by science, but by both Marxist and fascist politicians, who use it to justify their ruthless disregard for the individual and those unique characteristics of which human sensitivity is composed. Anything which opposes this view—as the arts do—is therefore seen as the enemy.

Time is desperately short to redeem this recognition of human sensitivity. We must learn that in order to be properly human our motivation, at all times and in all spheres, must be to seek order and beauty, integration and harmony through a transfiguring awareness. This means that while attending to the indispensable obligations of life—which includes a respect for science and logic—man must have a sense of unity strong enough to prohibit the desecration of nature in general, and his own nature in particular. The evidence that this is the *natural* and *normal* human condition has always been available, even thought it has been obscured, and at times obliterated.

Famous anthropologists like Sir Elliot Smith have supported this view and recently a refreshing new look at it has appeared in a book written by R. Clarke and G. Hindley.[3] But public ignorance persists. Any alternative to popular theories concerning the supposed brutalities of our early origins is greeted with prejudice or disdain.

This emotionally transfiguring view of reality means that aesthetic awareness is intended to be continuously present. Nothing—no creature, no human being—can be viewed as an isolated object. Everything that has meaning in human terms is related. The inherent cues to order, harmony and beauty in nature are intuitively perceived and expressed at every opportunity, through every action and act of social participation. The poetical rather than the rational is the basis of all human intercourse. In such conditions, there is probably little motivation to make elaborate works of art or to invent complicated musical instruments. The arts of nature and the music of the voice or reed pipe are adequate. But as the natural and social environment becomes less congenial the normally inactive subconscious is aroused, filling life with fears and anxieties, challenging altruism and compassion, and building tensions which are periodically released in anger, aggression or hostility.

Tolerance towards family, friends and strangers which is the norm among primitive people deteriorates into bickering and suspicion and ultimately leads to hostility, cruelty and destructiveness. The higher aspects of the mind react to threatening situations of this nature by attempting to restore normal conditions; and if the subhuman aspects which favour the magical, the uncouth and the ugly are aroused and expressed in the art form, they modify them. But there is a 'point of no return' where the mind sinks into a primitive state below ordinary awareness and expresses itself through the nightmare, the fiendish and the pathological. Dream life, the normal function of which is to reveal the higher aspects of the mind, can become distraught and terrifying. Art, if it can survive at all in these conditions, consequently reflects anguish and disturbance.

The 'fall from grace', from the maintenance of a receptive human state to one depraved and inhuman, is not simply a matter of environmental changes. Once aroused the subhuman aspects of the mind tend to persist, even when more congenial environmental conditions are restored. This has been the case with the rise of civilisation following the Ice Ages. Evidence of a full human recovery is scant, despite the powerful efforts of art and religion in every society to reinstate more humanising conditions. The state of the arts in a society is the best measure of its capacity for development, and its survival potential.

All the arts respond in their own ways to such conditions. The advantage of the visual arts—particularly painting—is that they make the process visible and tangible. Although the symbolic aspect is not easy to define, it is at least possible to discern the broad inferences present.

CHAPTER THREE

AIDS TO THE PEAK EXPERIENCE

Except in the most Arcadian circumstances the peak experience is limited by the complexity of social and cultural conditions. Most societies, however, have found their own ways of inducing the heightened experience through myth and ritual, through religion and the arts, and by the use of drugs. European culture has differed from others in this respect, in that it has condemned the use of mind-elevating substances. It has encouraged the reverse by permitting the use of only those drugs such as alcohol, tobacco, and caffein which stimulate the body and dull the more evolved parts of the mind. Although small amounts of alcohol, taken in the proper context, can have the effect of raising consciousness, it usually does the opposite; it paralyses the cortex. The latter effect has become the social norm, so that anything which stimulates the higher centres represents a criticism and condemnation of this materialistic civilisation. The attraction of mind enhancing drugs is part of a larger movement towards the esoteric and occult to which many, especially the young, have been attracted in reaction to the emotional sterilities of materialistic existence. The only alternative means of escape are violent protest or the reform of civilisation itself.

Throughout history, and no doubt way back into the Palaeolithic, when all natural roads to the peak experience have closed, existential devices have been resorted to, as they are still. These devices can be grouped as follows:

(i) **Meditation.** This is usually carried out in isolated groups or in monastic conditions. It does get results, but demands much more discipline than most people are prepared or able to accept. Furthermore, it may require the support of strong transcendental beliefs and predispositions, which only religious and sacramental doctrines can provide. And even these are only effective in their emergent, fervent stages.

(ii) **Group involvement.** This ranges from the meeting of small groups of people with sympathetic feelings to that of mass religious participation. Festivals, like revivalist meetings, can provide the right kind of atmosphere for peak experiences, and the aesthetic stimuli is produced by the people themselves through music and other aids.

(iii) **Bodily activity.** Carried to the point of frenzy and exhaustion, as, for example, in the Dervish dances, this can induce the peak experience. The intention being not so much to stimulate the high mind by aesthetic appeal, as to cut off physical sensation through exhaustion, so releasing the mind to make way for the high experience. This is not one of the more accessible ways, but there are a few stalwarts who push themselves to their physical limits in mountain climbing, or accomplish other feats, who do often catch a glimpse of the peak experience in their triumph.

(iv) **Self-denial.** This includes abstinence from food and sex, as well as mutilation and physically humiliating practices such as flagellation or exposure. Starvation is as conducive to peak experience as gluttony is an inhibitor. It is an observable fact that after a few days without food, the senses are heightened and more attuned; an obvious survival reaction. The sharpening of the senses is accompanied by a heightening of the emotions; aesthetic awareness is greatly increased; the beauty, harmony and purity of nature particularly amplified, and the resulting peak especially serene. This, no doubt, accounts for the worldwide prescription of fasting in high pursuits of every kind.

Because sex is more likely to be indulged for self-gratification than as an expression of love, abstinence from all sexual activity is one sure way of removing the somatic barrier to the peak experience. Indeed, such an experience seems to be the built-in reward for sexual control, which has always been a social necessity. Freud's condemnation of repression, which is unquestionably harmful, therefore applies only when sexual love is unobtainable or impossible. Unfortunately abstinence, while definitely favouring the heightened state, also denies the possibility of the fulfilling sexual response as a means of attaining the peak experience. As far as humiliating or sadistic practices are concerned, they are only likely to appeal to a small minority, and the resulting peak, if and when it comes, appears to lack serenity.

(v) **Over-indulgence.** This is what might be called counter-reaction, as in the longing for purity that follows brothel orgies, for restraint following debauchery and peace following slaughter. A kind of momentary peak experience may result, but it is invariably tainted with guilt and does not have the humanising effect of the genuine state. It seems that, contrary to Freud's contention, guilt is an inbuilt punishment for unbiological behaviour. There are only two ways of removing guilt: by higher resolve or by dulling sensitivity. The latter is the way of our present age.

(vi) **Sensory awareness.** Body sensitivity as a route to higher experience has long been neglected in our mechanistic society, but this is now being rediscovered through group therapy. Attempts to recover greater awareness through the sense of touch, seem more wishful than effective in these circumstances. Even though we live in a society without censure, an aesthetic sense is necessary if touch therapy is not to degenerate into sex gamesmanship. In the appropriate context, however, sensory awareness, bodily contact and caress, whether in massage or as a part of sexual love play, can be peak inducing. The difficulty lies in ensuring the right attitude, which can only come about through a strong aesthetic sense and a loving predisposition.

(vii) **Autosuggestive and hypnotic techniques.** It is probably true to say that normal human beings cannot be induced to indulge in inhuman activities through hypnosis. But if the subconscious is aroused and active, this becomes a good deal easier. The insidious influence of violence in entertainment works in this way. Given the existential conditions, it is much easier to plug into the demonic and magical by such means, than into the high experience. But there are cults, some of which are led by a guru or spiritual teacher, whose aim is to attain higher states. This is sometimes aided by particular aesthetic activities, such as the reading of poetry, music, movement, touching and even sex as in the Hindu Tantric practices.

(viii) **Dream experience.** These techniques which involve the remembering or re-living of dreams, are common in many societies. In the West, however, the analytical approach can prevent the dreamer from getting into real contact with the essential meaning. Dreams often reveal meaning on different levels simultaneously, and the technique consists of peeling away the inconsequential layers to reveal the essence. This often results in a peak experience when it is successful. Although it is possible for an individual to discover such techniques for himself, the sympathetic help of a trained guide together with aesthetic aids such as music, the coloured images used in Tantra, the poetry of the Sufis, and in some cases, soft drugs, makes success much more likely.

(ix) **Mental and physical illness.** Although most kinds of mental and physical illness arouse the subconscious and prevent access to higher states, there are one or two conditions which make it accessible. Unfortunately, they do tend to be unpredictable and difficult to control. Fevers, for instance, can induce a near peak experience, but they are likely to be followed by horrific experiences similar to the 'bad trips' common in the use of drugs like LSD. Although there is an effective barrier between the brain and the bloodstream which protects the brain tissues from fluctuations which may occur in the course of metabolism or disease, this only applies to natural disease to which the organism has been exposed in the course of its long evolution, and to which it has had an opportunity of reacting. It cannot protect the brain from the influence of artificially produced drugs.

(x) **Drugs.** Psychotropic drugs which, in at least one stage of their biochemical activity may induce the peak experience, have undesirable side effects. They produce a subconscious backlash in the form of terrifying experiences. This again is because of the brain's effective method of protection. Any foreign chemical substances which get through this defence are likely to have a disturbing effect, and are especially damaging if the mind of the individual is already over stimulated. Some drugs carry less risk, especially if the person taking them has evolved a certain level of awareness and the drug is taken in aesthetically conducive conditions. These drugs are probably more effective because they are similar in composition to the chemicals naturally produced by the brain itself.

Once an individual has had a peak experience through drugs, it should be unnecessary to rely on them to continue to induce it. Because its effect on the individual is so powerful it can be increasingly experienced through more natural means and, once achieved can be attained again and again. Until a more harmonious religious or cosmological context can be provided, the arts may be able to provide the necessary sacramental context, provided, of course, that the meaning of art has been previously established and accepted. Aldous Huxley pioneered such an approach, but his writings also make it evident that risks are involved.[1] The drug induced peak experience is never quite the same as the natural one. There is always something out of balance; a certain banality, a vague sense of disquiet; the colours are not quite right, the forms vaguely menacing, and the resulting ecstacy is adversely affected.

The genuinely inspired creative person avoids such drugs because he has no need of them. The less fortunate who drug themselves do so because of their desperate need to see the light and breathe the magic of inspiration. The fact is that our present conditions are not congenial to the peak experience so that consistent effort is necessary to obtain the remotest intimation of such an experience. Some of the aids described have been developed for religious, mystical or esoteric rather than aesthetic purposes, and may not be appropriate to the modern civilised condition. But one should be open-minded about them, in the hope that they may facilitate the peak experience for some whose lives would be enriched by their evidence of a hyperreality beyond the grey reality of day to day life.

What has long seemed to me sufficient evidence that the mind has remarkable powers of creation, and that such creations persist once adequately created, comes from my experience with 'mind paintings'. Since childhood, I have indulged in this game which is best practised in a hypnagogic condition when contact with the high aspects of mind are much easier. I set about this in the same way as I would an ordinary painting; I have my materials, admittedly more versatile and magical: I have my surfaces to work on, at times in fantastic situations. I get the same kind of kick in the initial preparations. As the work gets going, the painting acquires an increasing autonomy and reality of its own. I can put it away knowing it will be waiting for me to come back to and when the work is done I can obtain a peak experience by contemplating it. I can also dismiss it. Days and even years later, such mind paintings may suddenly and unexpectedly intrude into my awareness, sometimes in the midst of some rather boring occasion. I am then convinced that they truly exist in some other world.

I should mention that I do not make a habit of trying to translate such 'mind pictures' into actual paintings because there is a complete break between the source of inspiration and a painter's technique, a break which must come from the fact that the process of inspiration refers to mind and continuum, whereas technique is a problem of space, time and substance. One simply cannot 'see' the 'mind-painting' in one's mind's eye in a transposable form. The moment one tries to do so, the mind picture disappears. But the attempt is instructive, for it makes one aware of the proper relationship of inspiration and technique, and the extreme difficulty of allowing inspiration to come through, which is indeed the very purpose of technique. In our materialistic culture technique is seen as a teachable craft which will lead to the creation of art; but this is illusion. Technique provides the tools by means of which an artist attempts to express his intuitive ideas. Intuition may accept or reject them—most often it rejects them. The artist cannot know where his inspiration comes from. If he did he would no longer be an artist doomed, because of the enormous gulf between consciousness and the world beyond, to struggle and often to fail in his attempt to express his vision.

It follows from this, that an artist does not enjoy his work while he is creating it; he can only do so subsequently when he has no more special relationship to it than anyone else. He is obliged to contemplate his own work in exactly the same way as he would that of any other artist and the gratification he obtains will be completely unpredictable. Although the creative urge is strong and at times overwhelming, the actual business of creating is usually anxiety-laden and even distressing, because creativity and the temperament that goes with it come from a blockage and displacement in the emotional function. This subject is enlarged upon in Chapter 4.

The fact that the peak experience in the arts is rare under civilised conditions might suggest that it is an abnormal condition. But if this were the case one would expect it to be disruptive and attenuated, whereas the mark of this kind of experience is its intensification which is felt to be whole, absolute and reassuring, and to bring in elements which far transcend the ordinary resources of the individual, and leave him feeling physically healed and refreshed. This particular quality is absent in some of the artificially induced peak experiences, for instance, through drugs. The hyperintensity and some of the magic may be there, but the vision is flawed. No one has produced a great work of art under the influence of drugs. This suggests that although artificial means can induce a peak experience, it is not fully normal, which further suggests that whatever the peak experience is, it is extremely sensitive to artificiality and pathology. It is also intensely humanising; under its influence which may last for a very long time, it is simply not possible to entertain mean, ugly, violent or cruel thoughts. There is a feeling of sanctity in things, in people, which indicates that it has all the qualities of normality and plays a key role in the humanising process.

But undoubtedly, the peak experience in all its forms can become disordered. The test of normality is a simple one. Normal functions are always well integrated. Disease, in its widest sense, is disintegration. The normal mind is the most persistently integrated entity, but the least disintegration may cause severe neurosis. Characteristic of this condition, is a tendency for the 'complex' to challenge and temporarily usurp the holistic authority of the mind. Temporarily, the patient is possessed by fear, or what ever other subconscious emotion his complex happens to have embodied. The artist, always in some way or other neurotic, heals his neurosis, or at least temporarily alleviates it, by throwing himself into the intense totally integrated drive involved in creating a work of art. This absolute integration is the most indispensable quality in any creative work. Without it, whatever its appeal, there is no art, only arrangement or contrivance.

According to R. D. Laing, schizophrenia consists of an attempt to escape from an existence felt to be horrible and intolerable, into the hyper-realities and splendours of the mind's inner world—more correctly, surreality. This explains why schizophrenia is more frequent at puberty, when the sex hormones dramatically intensify the awareness of surreality as the key feature of a full humanisation of the individual. In the inhuman world, the adolescent naturally has an urge to retreat, which would justify Laing's contention that schizophrenia is less of a disease than an attempt at adaptation, and that it is society that is sick. Nonetheless, as schizophrenic art shows, there is a very severe disturbance of the emotionalising function of the sensibilities, no doubt accentuated by the mind itself, in its attempt to end its isolation.

In some cases of schizophrenia, there are phases when the patient is evidently subject to the most intense and ecstatic visions, which he is sometimes able to reveal with a vividness and power comparable to the revelatory element in all great art, no doubt it is why schizophrenics have been treated with awe in many societies. But if hyper-reality is touched upon, its revelation is too disturbed to pass as art.

Although probably all creative artists are neurotics no artist can be a schizophrenic because the sensitivities on which art depends are too precariously balanced. One can be reasonably sure that the truly integrated work of art, that which may give rise to the peak experience, is a genuine agent of revelation.

Integration is the most indispensable quality in any work of art. Even in a detail opposites are balanced as in the 'splash' and 'calm' shown here

The Freudian would be inclined to describe the peak experience as a superego sublimated orgasm, the result of repression. The fact that the peak experience in any form seems to occur less frequently or not at all in the course of a very active sexual existence appears to support this interpretation. But the kind of sexual activity in question is of the less emotionally involving variety, aimed at straightforward orgasm relief, which is in fact a male orientated pattern of sexual gratification. In direct opposition to this, sexual *love*, with a strong emotional involvement between lovers, is actively peak inducing and is in all probability the primordial peak experience.

Sexual love is more usual in some societies than in others. When the sexual pattern is little emotionalised, as it tends to be in a male-dominated society, peak-inducing procedures usually entail some sort of sexual restriction. In the West, the Christian attitude to sexual love has been complex and often contradictory, but in general it has considerably distorted all forms of peak experience, including that to be derived in communion with nature. This has been revived at certain times, notably in the Romantic Movement, but in general the peak experience has been related to the mystically inclined. Only music, and in certain periods poetry, have served as peak inducing arts, so that the European situation, now affecting others on a worldwide scale, is not ideal for a consideration of this subject. Nonetheless, one can pick out some interesting indications of the sexual role in the peak experience. Clearly women experience it more often through sexual love than men do; but both sexes experience it equally in communion with nature and in musical enjoyment. There may be differences in drug-induced peak experiences, but this needs further study. Women appear to respond more favourably to the colouristic arts, although such categorisation is complicated by the fact that every individual is psychologically bisexual. In both sexes, the peak experience is much more common around puberty, the rate falling subsequently, depending largely on the sexual pattern adopted by the individual.

Freudian theory is quite wrong in seeing a sublimated orgasm in the peak experience for although sudden, at times explosive, the peak experience has a sustained quality which is the very opposite of the spasmodic orgasm, at least in its male form. But there undoubtedly is a certain similarity between the peak experience and the protracted climax of the female, which is much more emotionally involving than the male orgasm which is essentially physiological. This suggests that it is the 'female' psychological component which is concerned with art sensitivity, irrespective of manifest sexuality, the 'male' element being chiefly concerned with the urge to execution and communication.

To this extent, one can conclude that the peak experience in the arts is the opposite of and opposed to a de-emotionalised sexual pattern, this makes sense when it is recalled that for the humanisation of the primate mind to have been at all possible, the opportunist, self-indulgent pattern of animal sex had to be reversed.

Creative people have an unusual psychological make-up, particularly in regard to sexual motivation. Everyone has a certain amount of creativity in his or her make-up, and owing to the selection of humanising qualities during our long evolution, this is likely to be more widespread than the disposition to violence; but in the artist this creative urge reaches a point of near paranoia so all-dominating that it suggests there may be a disarray of the X and Y chromosomes—this is a subject that requires further study. The diagnosis points to a degree of sexual immaturity and emotional blockage, evident in the male as an emotional sexual incapacity, and in the female as a reduced nurturing ability, a rather severe anomaly in a mammal! These conditions cause considerable frustration, which in turn leads to a desperate attempt to find compensation in an externalised, highly emotionalised way through the art object. The same process occurs in a more subdued form in the art-lover, and is probably not unusual. In Freudian terms frustration is entirely destructive, but the genetic sexual pattern has inbuilt reprimands for deviation, which present themselves as guilt, frustration and neurosis.

Nothing in life is free of sexual involvements. But in mankind this involvement takes a very particular form, unique to the human being, and not in any way derived from the usual animal manifestations of sexuality.

CHAPTER FOUR

THE HUMANISING PROCESS

The humanising appeals of nature—nature's way of making use of the environment to humanise the primate mind—are presented in a particularly subtle manner. The main features of the visible world—the shapes of trees and hills and animals and the general structure of natural phenomena, serve as a support for purely symbolic, abstract qualities, such as the integrative harmony of the components, the musical play of colour, light and shade, the frolic of lines and the diversities of texture. It is these which are the essential triggers of release to high aesthetic emotion, for a response to the harmonious in nature, the appeal of beauty and the sense of sanctity and purity.

These qualities are abstract because they can be ascribed to a wide variety of shapes and situations. In nature they are intimately associated with recognisable forms and scenes, so that it is easy to make the superficial assumption that it is the recognisable aspects that provide aesthetic feelings. But a more careful examination shows that the essential triggers can be abstracted from the structural and formal supports.

We shall deal with these abstract qualities later. Here we are concerned with the recognisable supports. These are the most convenient structures for the display of the abstract symbolic components, for it is on such recognisable supports that the symbolic process has evolved.

Not all the structures which nature presents to the senses are equally effective as supports for the symbolic display. It is only those which one feels intuitively to be themselves sufficiently orderly and integrated which are suitable: the forms, among many others, of landscape and flowers. With this in mind, one can trace back the scenery of the original humanising genesis. One can be certain that flowers featured abundantly; in no other way could the amazing colour sensitivities of the eye have evolved. Music, probably provided by bird song, must also have been present, to set the musical sensitivity of human ears and voice in the right direction. There are many things which one can be equally sure were *not* a part of this Earthly Paradise—ugly sights, predators, violent and cruel creatures.

As the symbolic process is intrinsically separable from its genetic supports in nature, it was inevitable that it would become increasingly free in the course of humanisation, for thereby the emotionalism involved was intensified. The justification for abstract art rests on such an ontological conclusion. The symbolic process performs a very important function for it can be applied to objects and scenes which are variously threatening to mankind. Such objects and scenes occur in nature, although one can suppose they were infrequent in the environment of the

Revelation of the 'substance' of surreality in the abstract marks of a painting

Earthly Paradise, otherwise the entire process would have come to a halt. It is the arousal of the subconscious aspects of the human mind which brings these humanly threatening forms into consciousness, not only in dreams of the nightmare variety, but also in a subtle distortion of the visible world.

This distortion is lavishly illustrated in worldwide myths of fiends and devils in great variety portrayed as evils lurking in the shadows everywhere; ghosts and goblins and menacing creatures. Primitive man, subject to aroused subconsciousness had no doubt at all that these things actually existed. In overwhelmingly troubled times even civilised man has come to believe in them. It is only a step further to the disturbing visions of mental disorder. In most civilisations the development of the critical intellect has tended to check this process and has obliged the individual to accept the notion that these menacing events only occur in the mind. But these aroused demons of the hinterworlds of the mind readily work their way through into art where they are to be found in the antimelodic throb of music and in many shapes in the visual arts.

The imagery and emotions of the subconscious refer to a period in evolution before the humanising sensitivities had come into being; they are therefore ugly, uncouth, awkward and potently anti-aesthetic. As such they are totally unacceptable to civilised man, except among the insane, or in outrageously inhuman circumstances. By superimposing the abstractable function upon these subconsciously inspired forms, they can be humanly reclaimed. Rendered orderly, integrated, harmonious in shape and impregnated with colour, they may be genuinely aesthetic, although this kind of art is not able to induce a peak experience. Subconsciously inspired art has in fact a quite opposite spectrum of appeal; it is exciting rather than sublime, sexy rather than love-related, agitated rather than vital and assumes endless organic anthropomorphic guises.

Unlike the high, humanising purely symbolic system, subconsciously influenced imagery is figurative. It thus has a superficial resemblance to the humanising, peak inducing aspects of nature and realistic art. But there is a fundamental difference. The sublime structure and figuration in nature and high humanising art, on which the abstract symbolic processes are displayed, is humanly acceptable. In a flower or a beautiful human face, there is no subconscious figuration at all. This is a point which is often not made clear when distinctions between figurative and abstract art are discussed. It stems from the common assumption that the subconscious influence is normally human. This is a psychological misinterpretation although it is true that such work may become humanised as we have already seen.

The archetype imagery evolved in the humanising genesis is steeped in the harmonious and beautiful; it is apollonian. The humanly reclaimed imageries of the subconscious, on the other hand, are dionysian. Whereas the apollonian refers to the genetic formulation of the human species, and dominates all art expression in fully humanising circumstances, the dionysian is existentially related, adaptive and therapeutic. It could be said that the story of world art is rooted in the dialectic between the apollonian and the dionysian. Some art forms are more suitable to one kind of expression and others to the alternative. For instance dance, ballet and mime appear to be particularly effective in reconciling the organic bodily involvement in this dialectic, from the apollonian direction of classical European ballet, to the more dionysian expression in Nijinsky. The orchestral and operatic forms were evidently particularly suitable to assert the apollonian, with varying admixtures of the dionysian—predominant in jazz—which coincided with the disturbances of the industrial age. Indeed, as subconscious pressures rose, so those arts most effective in resolving this expanding dialectic, because they possessed the more extensive apollonian resources, became dominant, which accounts for the phenomenal rise of European music in an age of increasing violence and materialism. Meanwhile the lesser arts were more dominated by the dionysian, as in popular entertainment. Painting, with the powerful apollonian appeals of colour, soared and flowered in Impressionism.

These compensatory processes between the arts, and in a particular art form, are extremely complicated and have been very little studied, because orthodox psychology has no grasp of the high humanising faculties and so can provide no explanation of the dialectic. Should there be a failure in this compensation, should there be, for instance, in a particular society a runaway dionysian tendency, it can legitimately be labelled decadent. In other words, it may not matter if certain art forms are handed over to the devil, as long as others remain to contest his supremacy.

Undoubtedly, a certain infusion of the dionysian gives to all the arts a stimulus typical of the most fertile art periods in all cultures. But the downward movement to the more disturbing end of the dionysian function is all too easy. Today one can observe a general decline in the high appeals in all the arts, probably related to the dehumanising influence of a materialistic civilisation. The mass media, a phenomenon unique to modern civilisation, has accentuated this movement, as we see particularly in the example of pop music. It is superficial and distracts from the more penetrative approach which civilisation requires at this juncture. Debasement and trivialisation monopolise the mass channels of communication and there is a demonstrable degree of decadence. In the past such a situation has usually brought about a profound reaction, so that the dialectic tended in time to resume its more usual oscillations. But the modern mass media are monolithic and worldwide; it is not possible to see where a reaction can come from, for vulgarity appears to be self-perpetuating. Channels originally committed to communications of a higher order have been swamped or taken over by those blindly pursuing popularity ratings. The dominance of the popular, however shoddy this may be, is one of the prices we pay for modern democracy.

By contrast the daily existence of benevolent primitive peoples is governed by decency and compassion. They experience peaks of rapture in sexual love and in social and familial living, enhanced by an intimate communion with nature, and by dance, song, ceremony and religious practices. Every aspect of their existence is ritualised, ascribed more than a common meaning, which gives all life a sacred and joyful connotation. The arts are elemental, for life itself is an art. It therefore includes the reed pipe and the gathering of flowers, to be worked into wreaths and necklaces. Attractive pebbles and minerals, the natural sculptures of wood and stone, are collected for decorative use. Utensils are largely those which nature provides: gourds and shells, woven straw and the intertwined stems of lianas.

The intermittent peaks of rapturous ecstacy that appear unexpectedly in the midst of everyday existence, necessitate temporary withdrawal from the common tasks of family and community life. It may take the form of daydreaming which is so typical of primitive existence, and which civilised employers find so exasperating in peasant labourers. In primitive societies these bouts of daydreaming—the means of a recurring peak experience—are encouraged rather than condemned. Many societies arrange for their communal inducement, often with the aid of drugs.

The usual occasion for a peak experience in communion with nature is love-making. In the Polynesian islands, for instance, lovers choose pleasant and beautiful boweries for love-making. They are not preoccupied, as modern western man is by the need to attain orgasm, and can go on for hours in a sustained rapture. The lovers' enjoyment of nature and of the human form is manifested in ceaseless caress and love play. Although the mutual attraction may begin with the sexual, the experience naturally evolves to a self-transcending, altruistic, socialised and compassionate level. This experience is, undoubtedly, the foundation from which all that is great and good in human beings springs. For Christianity to have missed this, is its greatest poverty. There can be no total experience of love when sexual love is ignored.

The influence of Christianity has meant that the peak experience has not been common in the West. At best it has been dismissed by society as belonging, like lovers and mystics, to those it considers mad. It has not been seen as a legitimate pursuit in the arts, which were required to remain materialistic, life-serving channels. The American psychologist, Abraham Maslow, is one of the very few to have taken the peak experience seriously—the term is his. But unfortunately, he was more concerned with its clinical than its aesthetic aspects.[1]

Most people can recall at least an intimation of the peak experience. It is certainly common around puberty, but sensitivity to such experiences is seldom developed, for the prevailing educational and cultural climate either ignores it or condemns it as irrelevant. The peculiar tragedy of this is that the ability to induce the peak experience weakens with maturity and usually disappears with age.

The frequency of this experience around puberty provides the clue to its biological intention. At puberty, the sex hormones are programmed for activity; they prepare the individual for a lifelong existence of love both sexual and compassionate in which the appreciation of beauty and harmony is the means of ensuring a humanised existence. Every society since the Ice Ages, no matter how far from the humanising ideal its conditions may have been, has ritualised this transition period between childhood and adulthood to teach the adolescent about his relationship to the cosmos. Every society, that is, except our own; we attempt to stifle this entry into the superconscious realm by overburdening adolescents with facts about the material world which encourage only a pragmatic outlook.

The peak experience also occurs in childhood, but in a simpler form, as an extremely vivid and detailed visualisation. As the late Sir Herbert Read and others have noted, the spontaneous drawings of young children reveal often intense visual symbolism rarely attained in adult art.[2] It may be that before the repressive measures of education take effect the child is in a state similar to the primitive which suggests that the peak experience is universally experienced.

It is interesting to note that stories, such as fairy tales, which are invented by adults, and enjoyed by children the world over, reiterate the same theme. Love and joy are always threatened by mythical beasts and dehumanised anthropomorphic creatures, but the good always triumph. These stories are the allegorical truths of what happens in the human subconscious which, when threatened by the monsters within, can only be rescued by love. Love and art are close genetic collaborators, and in a world where love is fouled and frustrated, the high experience becomes gradually less accessible as childhood and youth pass into corrupt maturity.

Communion with the more aesthetically endowed aspects of nature is the most direct means of obtaining a peak experience, provided a sufficiently pristine and pure aspect of nature can be found, and provided that the individual is sufficiently attuned to nature itself. A study of the evocative stimuli in nature shows how human art has come into being. The qualities in visible nature which have a particularly powerful symbolic appeal have to do with the wholeness and integration of the components in a scene; the wonderful relationship of hills; fields, vegetation and sky in a landscape; the harmonious integration of limb and bodily proportion. Other qualities in visible things have a strong symbolic resonance, the filligree of structure; the infinite varieties of texture; the verve and vitality of growing and moving things; the streamlining of functional shapes; the sparkling of dewdrop and crystal; the flux and flow of mist and water; the churnings of clouds and the fantastic varieties of natural forms everywhere.

It should be evident that the sensitivity of the mind to such wonders implies a fundamental accord between mind and nature or the forces in nature responsible for these aesthetically relevant expressions. Clearly at some profound level, the aesthetic expressiveness of mind and nature meet, so that nature offers the aesthetically tuned the perfect subject for gaining the peak experience.

Although the peak experience is not frequent in modern civilised conditions, it is intimated often enough to show its total difference from ordinary experience. There is a fairly common, if remote, sense of the invisible and transcendental order in things, that can be described as a partial peak experience. In communing with nature, or in contact with art, one may receive this intimation as a kind of intermittent dialectic; a rapid, repeated oscillation between two worlds, which, while it does have some of its characteristic features, yet falls far short of the totally involving, time-obliterating peak experience. Nevertheless a sense of uplift and refreshment, of hallowing and reassurance can result.

One may well ask how it is that such an easily distracted function as the peak experience has come about. The least malfunction in body or brain, the merest evidence of disharmony in the environment distracts it. If the human genesis had occurred in violence and depravity, as is now popularly believed, the peak experience would surely have been impossible, as it now so often is, in the dehumanising conditions of modern civilisation. One must therefore assume, on this evidence alone, that the process of humanisation through natural selection must have taken place under harmonious conditions, even if these were subsequently reversed.

But even in humanly congenial conditions, attention to daily problems of physical survival must often have been a distraction. Nature therefore devised an ingenious system which would be free from such distractions—the dream life. Through natural selection this strange and misunderstood function became the chief means of evolving and maintaining a humanising 'inner world' of the mind, in intimate contact with transcendental rescources through the very distinct peak inducing high dream.

Dreams are of many kinds. They range from those closely related to everyday experience, through the menacing and frightening experiences of nightmares to the indescribably ecstatic and beatific. The latter, the high dreams, are necessary for the regeneration, experienced in the act of waking from sleep.

The frustrations, tensions and cruelties of civilised living have reduced the dream life of most individuals to the level of reviewing ordinary events or to the nightmare. Even so, most people do still have the occasional high dream in which the peak experience occurs. They may experience the afterglow in their waking life, and notice changes in their moods and attitudes even when they cannot clearly remember what the dream was about.

The high dream is also related to the inspirations of art in its highest, most humanly meaningful forms, which is why such importance is ascribed to the high, revelatory dream among primitive people; and by artists and poets in civilised societies. The quality of the high dream is such that the participant senses the profound inner meaning of all things. The dream life seems to have been originally organised into a pattern in which disturbed, anguished dreams, evoked by a disturbed existence, occur at certain intervals during the night, leaving long periods in between during which the high dream may occur.

Recent dream researchers have congratulated themselves on having found the key to dreaming, in the changes of heartbeat and blood pressure, rapid eye movements and other body movements that take place at intervals during the night. But what they have discovered, in fact, is the kind of dreams that are least important in the humanising process. Their assumption that no dreaming occurs in the intervals between observable dreaming, suggests that they have ignored the true nature of the humanised mind. It is in those periods when they consider the mind to be inactive, that the miracle of regeneration takes place.

Although dreams cannot be ordered, there can be no doubt that the quality of waking life effects the quality of dream life. An inhuman and insensitive existence not only brings about a demonic art, but a haunted, terrifying dream life. A high humanising dream life requires a humanising environment similar to that required by high, humanising art. It is now possible to appreciate just how enormous was the punishment for having been chased from the Garden of Eden. In the same way as the arts reveal this sense of harassment and fear, so too do our dreams.

CHAPTER FIVE

INSPIRATION AND REVELATION

The materialist view of reality insists that all the resources that go into a work of art must come from inside the head of the artist. The feeling that the peak experience is much more intensely real than ordinary experience is impossible to explain, for in terms of materialistic dogma, the unconscious is regarded as less evolved than consciousness of the material world, and must, consequently, be less real. Psychologists have tried to overcome this contradiction by attempting to rationalise it as some sort of psychological energy which becomes intensified in the raw, primitive, unchecked channels of the mind, so creating the illusion of hyper-reality. Freud attributed such a power of intensification to his super-ego, the result of the blanket condition known as repression. But analytic philosophers have rightly concluded that such psychological explanations are not explanations at all, but sheer myth.

The point about the hyper-reality of the peak experience is that it is not felt as a simple intensification, but as an accentuation of the feeling of 'realness'. This is due to a complete transfiguration of ordinary reality. This 'more real than the real' quality of the peak experience in the arts or in nature, is an intimation of some quite different order of perception. To categorise it as mental is inadequate for even if it is accepted that the mental is distinct from the material, it is legitimate to ask how it manages to alter the appearance of ordinary reality to the extent that it appears *more real.* It is difficult to accept that the isolated mind of the individual with its limited resources and shadowy unconscious, can do better than nature in promoting the sense of reality.

Now that there is greater acceptance of telepathy as a natural phenomenon, it seems reasonable to claim that the artist, like everyone else, can have access to transpersonal resources. If these resources could become pooled in some way—in a transcendental aspect of nature independent of space and time—there would be available a well of data to provide inspiration in the arts; a resource far richer and more powerful than the available resources 'in the head' of the individual artist, writer or musician. The extraordinary intensity of the peak experience implies that a mechanism of this sort is the most likely explanation of the distinctive 'otherness' of all art experiences, from the subconsciously influenced to that of the hyper-aesthetic. But to be acceptable, such a proposition requires a completely new view of reality and matter and mind; for no amount of pooling can account for the distinctiveness of such experiences. In other words, if transmental or superconscious phenomena are involved, they must occur at a level of reality itself more effectively organised, more real than ordinary material reality.

The challenge has been to discover how such an aspect of nature, qualitatively so different from ordinary reality, has come into being, and what role it has played. Such an extraordinary faculty could not possibly have evolved without purpose. It must have developed to meet some very important biological need. But before we begin to look at a possible explanation of this phenomenon, let us look more closely at the distinctive qualities of the peak experience.

In the first instance, the shift from ordinary awareness into the peak experience comes quite suddenly, and then ordinary awareness is completely effaced. The slightest attempt to intellectualise or analyse the peak experience destroys it. One is either 'in' it or completely 'out' of it. This explains why it has been so neglected by the established schools of psychology which attempt to prove their scientific credibility through analytical procedures.

The conditions favouring such a shift, however, can be examined. The most pertinent requirement, either in nature or in human art, is a sufficiently resolved and assertive aesthetic situation that is orderly, harmonious and beautiful. The disorderly, the ugly, the repulsive and the impure are definite obstacles as far as the hyper-aesthetic experience is concerned. Although somatic involvement may be helpful to the subconsciously influenced art forms, it is hostile to the hyper-aesthetic. Except in particular cases, such as the physical feats mentioned in Chapter 3, the slightest pain or feeling of distress, anguish or fear prohibits the peak experience. Since it has evolved as part of the condition of a truly humanised state, it is annulled by the inhuman and antihuman. This permits a fundamental distinction between arts which are humanly related and those which are not, or in the difference which is to be found between essence and existence. This does not mean that the existential is not important—it evidently is in a world so far from essence—but it should be borne in mind that biologically, essence is indispensable in the pursuit of any worthwhile definition of the sources of a truly human art.

Regarding the approach to and appreciation of a work of art, the artist is no better placed than any ordinary person. The peak experience can only be pursued by the artist, poet, writer or musician, when the work is done. If the peak experience should appear in the course of the work, the practical application of the materials—paint, words, notes or whatever they happen to be—would be disturbed, and the creative endeavour sabotaged. Therefore, both artist and art lover must begin by finding the right conditions for a unitive experience which is invariably a recreative affair involving him or her in an active sense. Although the analytical faculty must be stilled, the procedure is outgoing not merely receptive. The only difference between the artist and the art lover, is that the artist literally expresses this creative involvement. The art lover has a similar sort of involvement, in that he empathises with the work of art and seeks an aesthetic experience through it; but usually has no motivation or wish to externalise it.

It is important to emphasise that the contemplation of a work of art is not aimed at discovering something fixed and concise that has been captured by the artist. For both artist and art lover, the work of art creates an opportunity for a unique experience, different at every exposure and totally unpredictable and indefinable. This makes nonsense of the usual inquiry as to what it is that the artist has tried to communicate; a conclusion which places considerable limitations on the role of the critic.

The leap into this other dimension which all aesthetic experience implies, also mitigates the importance of the artist's personality, the significance of which has been exaggerated in our materialistic culture. The only way in which the artist's personality can be made less dominant, is by bringing it into its proper perspective through the realisation of his function. As A. N. Whitehead has emphasised, basic reality is not composed of 'things', but of dynamic events which need have no concrete, separate definition. The concept of energy, as a universal and timeless force, is helpful, for as energy becomes organised into protons, electrons and atoms, so what we call matter arises.

Although consensus definition of personality refers to that aspect of the human being related to the ordinary world, and the face or image an individual presents to the world for psychological survival, it is merely a facet of reality which the more evolved or higher faculties transcend in actuality.

The most feasible explanation of what C. G. Jung termed the 'collective unconscious', is that it is a specialised, highly organised aspect of the purely functional basis of reality. This is why the totally involving, participative quality of the peak experience is absolutely different from common experience.

The peak experience can be understood as a genuine participative experience allied to the most significant aspects of reality, and art, like all forms of symbolism, is a penetrative act; so in its own way is science which goes beyond matter to encompass all natural processes. Although the rational mind will object strongly to this conclusion—its natural function is to object since it insists that the material realm is real—this is the only way in which human experience, at all levels, can be reconciled and unified; that is, in relationship to a consistent reality. As there are, as yet, no instruments available to tune us into this surreal or supermundane level, personal experience is the only evidence of its existence. There is no rational argument with which to convince the uninitiated of the supernal power and majesty of the peak experience.

The rational mind, which is highly competent at dealing with the material realm, must eventually come to accept that the universe has not been made in its limited image. It will have to realise that things are not basically what they appear to be in ordinary experience. Just as penetrative science has gone beyond this limitation, so also has penetrative art.

To grasp what is happening in both the sciences and the arts, one must realise the artificiality of the human intrusion in the universe. So strong is the intellect's genetic insistence that only what is visible and tangible is real, that even science has had a lot of trouble in this respect; scientists have remained fascinated by form, organs and structures for much longer than they should have. In fact, it is only today that physicists and biologists have become aware that the fundamental realities they have to deal with are dynamic, functional and beyond appearances.

But although scientists were bound to experience this difficulty—and still do—the ordinary person should have been spared it, for intuition is the means whereby we can overcome and surpass the limitation of our senses and ordinary understanding.

Unfortunately, in a materialistic culture, the relevance of intuition is minimised and people can too easily become imprisoned by prevailing attitudes. This means that they are excluded from the penetrations of both science and the arts. It is remarkable that when scientific language is beyond the reach of the uninitiated, the

The limits of penetration are set by the canvas or paper but the grain may itself be symbolic of basic events

A focus of penetration

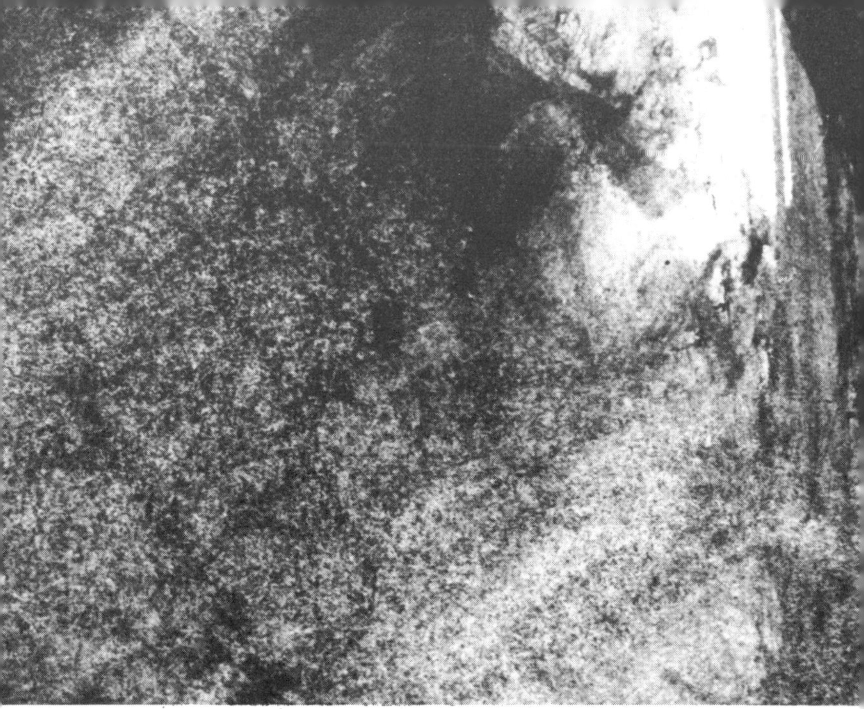

essential content can still at times be grasped intuitively even if an exact understanding is impossible.

This has a truly momentous significance, for it implies that the human mind, its intellect apart, is in communication with the ultimate levels of reality, far beyond the reach of the analytical senses and intellect. This is not surprising since the mind itself is an aspect of the continuum, organised by the most evolved matter in the universe—the brain cells; this intuitive grasp of science cannot be rationally analysed and any attempt to explain it destroys it. Although such intuitive understanding is naturally scorned by scientists they themselves have to rely on something like it, for they do not intellectually or fundamentally understand the penetrative reality they are dealing with. For instance, although the modern industrial world depends so much on electricity, and understands so well how to use it, the ultimate nature of electricity cannot be rationally explained; it has to do with the activity of electrons which defy conceptualisation. Scientists can deal with its penetrative qualities by applying a symbolic function—mathematics, but no mathematician can really explain intellectually the basic nature of this strange subject. Mathematics works because its equations symbolise the dynamic run of the intellectually inexplicable events of nature.

This means that for scientists, who delude themselves that they depend only on intellect and reason, success comes from a most fortunate fit between mind and the basic events in nature. This is so because both mind and these events are reflected in the continuum.

The same providential fit between the penetrative, all sustaining realities in nature, and the profound levels of the mind, can in fact be intuitively sensed, and thanks to the ability of brain and body to communicate this through the arts, in the use of pigments, words, sounds or movement, this penetration can be communicated to others, provided they are themselves open to such an intuitive revelation.

This subject touches one of the most controversial aspects of the arts, more especially in those which have a degree of symbolic freedom and can dispense with the structure and forms of ordinary experience. There is no difficulty in the case of music; its absolute symbolism is readily accepted by everyone. True music has no tangible references to the material life. But in the use of pigment difficulties do arise, for vision is a less specialised symbolically penetrative channel than hearing. There is probably a good biological reason for this. In the primates, the visual centres in the brain have been greatly expanded, while the centres of smell and sound have been reduced; vision is much more important for survival than hearing or smelling, which have the more easily become specialised as symbolic revelators without posing too great a threat to their function as alarm systems. Nor has the reduction of the sound and smell centres in the brain handicapped their use for symbolical, emotional purposes, because emotion, as we have seen, is primarily a continuum involvement and requires a modicum of neural tissues. Birds, the most intensely emotionalised of creatures, have a mere spoonful of brain tissue.

In Western civilisation, the analytical, rational faculties have been so hypertrophied, that the native difficulties of using the visual and olfactory routes symbolically have been accentuated, to the point where a majority of people can no longer use them in this way. In such a situation, effort and re-training is needed to recover their natural use. This is particularly the case with the abstract movement in the arts, which simply means the greater and freer use of symbols, less subservient to the supports of form and ordinary structure. Although language probably

The symbolic power of an abstract painting increases with magnification

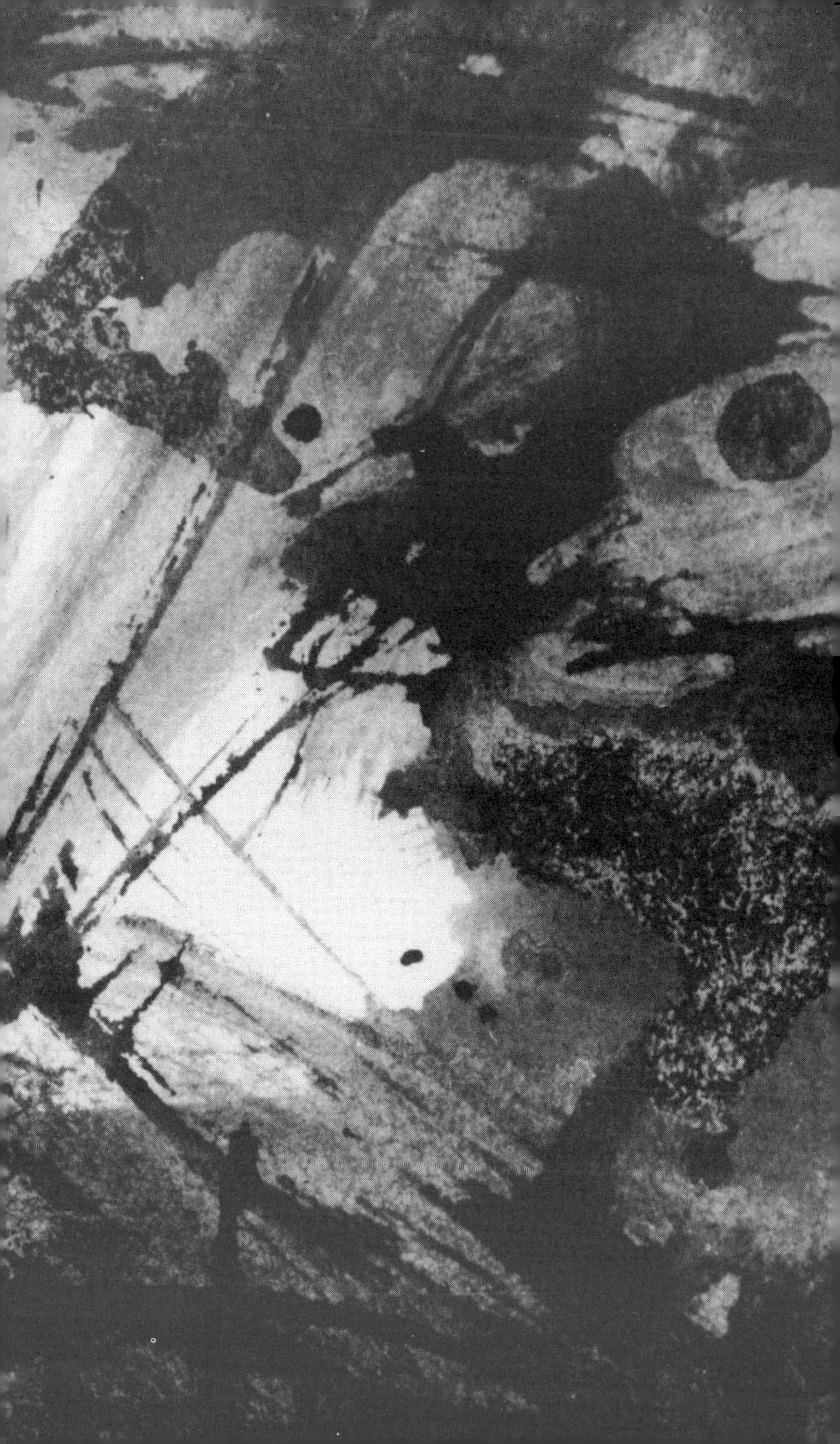

began as an emotional communication, its rational use only coming much later, the poetical expression which most closely reflects its primordial purpose, is now largely blocked by the materialistic values put on words. Classical music because it is purely symbolic is the one art that has escaped the worst effects of modern civilisation which accounts for its quite fantastic development in the Western hemisphere.

Provided the rational eye is fooled, it will accept the symbolic. This has been achieved in great realist paintings and sculptures, in great films and ballet; but the moment the symbolism is pushed too far the intellect objects. How violent this objection can be is shown in the opposition the Impressionists first encountered, and the objection to abstract art which persists today. In time Impressionism became acceptable, but cultural opposition to complete abstraction still persists, with waves of return to realism. It is strange that our culture, which is probably in the most need of an intensified symbolism in its arts is the least equipped to accept it.

If it is true that the intuitive faculties have access to the penetrative aspects of nature in the continuum, then it should follow that the arts are not only open to inspiration from the visible scenes of nature echoed in surreality, but also to whatever it is that engenders and supports these scenes. In other words, just as there are in the ordinary world organs, tissues, minerals, molecules and atoms which sustain the visible forms of experience, so in the transcendental aspects of nature, to which artistic intuition has access, there are insubstantial equivalents that can only be revealed, in art, in purely abstract ways, wherein the abstract captures the reflection of nature in the surreal world. Perhaps it is worth emphasising here that surreality is something quite different from surrealism. *Surrealism* is an art movement, and a very important one. That which has been described as the surreal is the replication of existence in terms of the continuum, pooled into a supreme universal and timeless entity by the contribution of humanised minds throughout the universe. Like all things in the universe surreality is an evolving state; there are aspects of it corresponding to the most primitive contribution of man on earth, just as there must be aspects transcending anything we can conceive or are aware of on our earthly planet.

Because of the natural handicap of the visual route, abstract painting is beset with difficulties and obstacles, and the aim of technique is likely to be to find the best ways of allowing intuition to work through opportunistically. The liberational techniques of modern movements such as action painting and tachism, and the techniques of surrealism in poetry and literature have made this possible in an entirely new way. But in more subtle ways the traditional technical approaches, the intuitively led verveful line; the impulsive touches of colour; the unpredictable emergence of texture in scumbles and unpremeditated dabbles, although necessarily subject to the forms and shapes of appearance, are identical to abstract expressiveness. The degree at which symbolic freedom must stop is arbitrary, and decided only by social and cultural circumstances; in principle, the creative resources in all the arts are as abstract as in fact they are in music, for all the arts depend on the same aspects of the high mind, with the exception of the subconsciously influenced arts already discussed, which do appear to require some sort of embodiment or concrete morphology.

As these penetrative abstract resources are unlimited and inexhaustible, virtually whatever the abstract artist does can be sensed to have some penetrative relevance. The rushes and leaps of the line, for instance, have evident analogies with the vibrations and trajectories of subatomic particles, which decide all the events in the visible world. Even in our visible surroundings every form we can imagine or invent, is likely to be discovered already existing in nature. What calls for much more in the genesis of an aesthetically satisfactory image, is the coherent assembly of such abstract ingredients, and that can only be implemented by the holistic guidance of intuition. It is this ultimate force that decides the effectiveness of an abstract image, and the artist is not likely to draw upon it unless strong feeling and developed sensitivity are present. The public is right in thinking that anyone can make up an abstract image, but to do so in a coherently artistic way, requires inspiration, and if the public then feels fooled, it is because it is insensitive to this most essential constituent of art.

I will mention briefly an examination of my own case which touches on this subject. As a student in biology I was fascinated by the immense vitality of sub-microscopic and intra-cellular structures. Unfortunately any attempt to catch this vitality in a minutely executed drawing or in a photograph failed, and it took me a long time to find an appropriate technique. This I found, shortly after the war, in an exhibition of the Cobra group in Paris. Here was an impulsive, opportunist technique which in its own gestures and materials symbolised an exuberant vitality, a conclusion subsequently confirmed by my first contacts with some post-war American paintings. So I developed my own brand of vitalist expressionism, not totally abstract, for some sort of embodiment seemed indispensable, but certainly related to nothing in the world of immediate appearances. When these intuitively, opportunistically grasped imageries succeeded, and that was rarely, they were truly hyper-vital, even more vital than those microscopic biological entities I had long admired. Of course this was symbolic vitality, but because all humanly meaningful things are at heart symbolic, this does not matter. Vitality, I now believe, is also one of these continuum qualities like mind, emotion and intuition, which are made symbolically visible in nature through organic evolution; all art has its own way of revealing this. There is symbolic vitality in music, in words, in forms and structures which is more meaningful than the ordinary vitality of living things.

There is a repetitive theme in my painting; this does not worry me, although it worries art dealers—because I am aware of the hyper-vitality that is in some way related to it. When I was painting in the early fifties, practically nothing was known about genes, those DNA concentrations along the chromosomes in every living cell, which initiate and control all vital activity and heredity. During the seventies the structure of the gene has been unravelled, and to my amazement, the resulting computerised forms seem to be closely analogous to the formal current in my paintings. I do not now believe that it is so preposterous to suppose that intuitively I should have been able to sense this kind of form, before it was worked out by science, for whatever is the equivalent of the gene in surreality, it must have the same decisive importance that it has in the life of space and time. Indeed, one might even suppose that the biological gene is an actualisation, in matter, space and time, of some such entity or potentiality in the transcendental aspects of nature. The inexplicable and remarkably sudden appearance of life on this planet, which must have required something like the gene from its inception can be understood as the playback, through the vital evolution of matter on earth, of a transcendental accumulation of living experience previously acquired elsewhere in the universe, but subsequently available anywhere.

The late Professor Waddington, the embryologist, was

struck by the similarities in the imagery of the new art and the new science.[1] His explanation of this is that artists were inspired by the revelations of science. But most painters suffer from the old animosity of the two cultures and are in fact hostile to possible scientific influence. Anyway, no serious abstract artist is likely to choose to copy the imageries of science, which would be no different in spirit from realism. Anyone who has worked in the abstract idiom will sooner or later realise that something very special happens which rules out any such mimicry.

What proves Waddington's explanation wrong is that the kind of imageries in question appeared in the visual arts long before their equivalents became known in science. For instance, in early Kandinsky paintings there are typical scenes of nuclear disintegration which only became known to science a generation later. Kandinsky's approach to art, which was deeply religious and metaphysical, confirms that no mimicry was involved.[2]

All the arts anticipate, in emotional and symbolic terms, changes in the life of a culture which only become evident later in ordinary existence. For instance, long before the degradation of the environment was generally recognised—through the publication of Rachel Carson's *Silent Spring* in 1962 and the work of other concerned writers which followed it, the Impressionists had reacted to the menace in their use of wonderful colouristic transfigurations, which drew attention to the threatened symbolic appeals in nature.

It needs to be emphasised that these transcendental extensions, revealed through the arts and by other means, do not minimise the importance of ordinary existence or the material realm, for the transcendental, it will be recalled, is the product of organisation and evolution. All material events are probably automatically recorded in terms of the continuum, for matter seems to be programmed in this way. All that happens with the advent of the humanised mind upon the scene, is that this process acquires a fantastic boosting. But obviously such a view of reality requires a very different understanding of what matter is about, and quite a different interpretation of the universe.

CHAPTER SIX

ART AND THE PUBLIC

For much of human time life has been precarious and the struggle for survival so crucial that there has been little energy to spare for the pursuit or accumulation of personal possessions. But with the coming of civilisation, with its sophisticated social structures, some of the population were released from the drudgery of day-to-day life, so that they had the time to develop a taste for art and to build up collections of art objects. The strange and wonderful things that different civilisations have amassed is truly staggering. In spite of periodical pillaging by vandals and dispossessed nomads, these hordes of treasure have been replenished time and again. This inherent accompaniment of the civilising process has been a fortunate one for its inheritors, for by their collections of art we are today able to judge the magnificence of the civilisations of the past. Is it not therefore strange that in modern times, when the means exist to produce more objects than ever before, to fulfil man's innate desire for possessions, there should have arisen philosophical objections to the concept of possession? As this rejection of the idea of individual rights of ownership is manifest especially among the idealistic young it must be symptomatic of a profound event in the transcendental mind group of our civilisation. The likely explanation is that it is a rejection of the materialism of modern society, which is anti-human. It does not mean that a humanising possessiveness should be rejected or that the great collections that have come down to us from past civilisations must cease to provide contemporary man with the source of much transcendental experience.

The extraordinary appeal of a metal like gold and of objects made from it, is probably due to its symbolic revelation of hyper-real qualities in surreality, much more than to its rarity, for there are other metals much rarer than gold. The appeal of light and colour; of beautiful minerals and jewels like that of exquisite scents and flowers, or brightly plumaged birds, all owe their fascination to the same thing. One might be justified in conjecturing that sensitivity to quality has been so important in human evolution, that particular genes have become involved. There may well be gold and diamond loving genes, just as there certainly are light and colour aspiring genes. Social history could be rewritten on the hypothesis that it is the pursuit of these correspondences in things, which motivates man's actions rather than the desire for power itself. This would explain the lure of beautiful clothes and personal adornments; of lavish gardens and treasure-filled palaces, for all of these carry with them the lights and delights of surreality.

This suggestion, that the collecting urge is a biologically motivated one, is not likely to please the drab egalitarians of today, because they equate it with acquisitive greed and selfishness. Unfortunately the urge to surround ourselves with beautiful objects for the enhancement of the human spirit, is a motivation that can easily go wrong. Collecting can assume a manic character, a pathological turn which wealth makes possible. This is nothing new; allowing for inflation, which has continued from Roman times and beyond, with only occasional respite the prices paid for art works today are not so much more than they were in the past.

The insensitive collector often cannot distinguish temporal art from transcendental art. So profound and little understood is the urge to possess some transcendental token that people of wealth or worldly power may delude themselves that the objects they seek have a monetary value and can therefore be purchased. This is the antithesis of the old alchemist's view, he knew full well that such a mystical talisman could not be bought 'Alchemical Gold is beyond all price'.[1] Those who truly seek the key to the transcendental experience are as likely to find it in nature or through their own artistic endeavours as they are in the most expensive painting they can buy. Nor is there any guarantee that the work of the established artist will provide revelation. Unfortunately worldly success is likely to blunt the revelatory powers of the creative artist, as financial reward and fame come between him and his inspiration.

Some of the greatest artists have produced exceedingly bad, uninspired work which, because of the general confusion that applies, often fetches much the same price as genuinely good work. The sad truth is that it is not usually a sensitivity to the revelatory power of a painting or sculpture which determines the choice of the collector, but vain glory, material possessiveness, convention, display or investment. The only reliable criterion as to what is good or bad in art is its ability to produce hyper-aesthetic experience. The one redeeming note in the whole sad tale is that occasionally the miracle does happen—the revelatory power of some piece of work breaks through to the observer, the eyes and the heart of the 'bank vault' collector are opened and a glimpse of the peak experience is vouchsafed, which may transform his view of life and art.

The vast public collections of the present, of which only a small proportion can be displayed, show some of these manic symptoms; their curators are only implementing the cultural belief that society has taken over, for the good of all, the collecting virtues once implemented by a privileged class. If such collections could be widely shown in such a way that people could truly commune with them, rather than merely gaping in distracting situations, they would indeed perform a social service, but this is rarely the case. These collections would be far better dispersed and decentralised into small collections to be specially displayed in small towns.

Although individuals throughout history have been subordinated to the service of a tyrant, a ruling class or political system, the individuality of each human being, apart from periods of mass dementia and possession, is evident and persistent. Even in the case of identical twins, with identical genes, there is an inbuilt degree of individual variation in the expression of these genes. For example, finger prints are never duplicated. Possibly brought about by slight differences in the environment to which each twin becomes exposed during development, the character and psychology of each are individualised. The human genome is quite unlikely ever to produce two identical individuals, even if humans occur on innumerable other planets throughout the universe, which suggests that this is of particular and specific significance in nature. The recent possibility of producing an individual from any cell in the body, by-passing the gene mixings of reproduction (cloning), will not overcome this innate individualism.

This astonishing attribute of nature is less surprising when it is realised that it applies to the inanimate as well as the animate. It is said that since the universe began, no two snow-flakes have ever formed in an identical manner. This must be due to the way in which the physical constants are set. These constants define the way in which the forces of attraction and repulsion, in relation to mass, are expressed. It is now recognised that if these constants varied in quite minor ways, the universe would be a very different place. Recently, several eminent physicists and cosmologists have commented on the fact that the physical constants are set exactly right for the evolution of life and mind in suitable planets throughout the universe.[2] Today few doubt that such planets exist in their thousands of millions. This means that the universe has a creative direction, in which the mind-producing creature, man, features. As I have already suggested the universal pooling of the mind's humanised experience produces the transcendental aspect of nature, surreality, a level in which the limitations of matter, space and time are overcome, and the universe can be said to fulfil itself. As a transcendental culmination of the entire pilgrimage of creation, surreality would be a dull affair if evolution had produced imitations rather than individuals.

This may seem a tortuous argument, but it makes an important point that needs to be widely proclaimed, because many of those who acquire power over human existence ignore it and assume that they have the right to limit human individuality for the good of society, whereas in fact society should be seen as existing to fulfil the needs of the individuals who compose it.

It might seem contradictory to insist on the value of the individual artist or indeed the work of art because the point we have been making in this book is that the transcendental aspect is far more important than the individual; nevertheless while the artist's name, that is to say the label by which he is known, is of no significance, his inspiration and the high revelatory value of his particular work can not be anonymous because a unique individual mind is involved in its creation. This does not in any way mean that the artist should be regarded as a celebrity or accorded the spurious attention that this gives rise to, but rather he should be seen as an identification of the divine streak in all humans; one able to reveal it and make it known.

In a materialistic society where everything is measured in terms of its market price the true value of revelatory art, which is beyond the market place, cannot be explained. For the Oriental all approaches to the high mind, and its natural overlap into the surreal, mean an expansion of the individual, whereas because most people in the West are only concerned with the outward-facing personality, this other world is regarded with suspicion or as a threat to the individual. But it is only through the higher aspects of his being that the individual can make a cosmically significant contribution to the work of creation, in boosting and enriching the resources of surreality. It is this process that makes it impossible to copy any work of art the creation of which has grown from inspiration, and why it is that a perfect mechanical copy is never art at all.

CHAPTER SEVEN

A TWO LEVEL MODEL OF REALITY

The model of reality that I have already outlined—a two level reciprocating universe—is very much in the scientific and philosophical air at present. The time may not be far off when surreality is accepted as a legitimate aspect of nature, the product of natural forces, without any appeal to supernatural agencies. As I have mentioned already, physics itself has provided the basis for such speculation in the universal field or continuum.

The limitations of a one-level universe have been sensed by several cosmologists recently, among them Dicks, Carter and Stannard.[1] In 1962 R. W. Fuller and J. A. Wheeler,[2] proposed the existence of superspace, not as idle fantasy, but as an indispensable concept in order to explain certain natural phenomena. One such phenomenon is the slowing down of the expansion of the universe with the passage of time. Energy, organised as matter, is the only way of accounting for this slowing down, but there is not nearly enough matter as we commonly understand it, to bring this about. Therefore there must be some other kind of 'matter' not existing in terms of space and time. Hence the suggestion of superspace which accommodates a transcendental form of matter.

Wheeler has since enlarged his ideas to include a 'pre-geometry', referable to superspace, which would account for the very particular way energy has emerged as matter in space and time. A different 'pre-geometry' would have resulted in a quite different kind of universe. In the reciprocating model of reality I have proposed, this 'pre-geometry' is what I have interpreted as the organising potential in the continuum which ensures that energy is made manifest in matter in a very particular way, the key characteristic of which is its discontinuity. The ceaseless exchange between material existence and non-existence at the subatomic level takes place in the quantum gap. The phase of non-existence refers only to matter, for the continuum is timeless and limitless. The existence of the quantum gap means that every change in every atom establishes a recording of itself in terms of the continuum, and that as a result of this continuing process, the entire universe, and all that has happened since the Big Bang, has been timelessly registered.

It would be misleading to draw an analogy between this pre-geometry or organising potential and mind, for mind does not in any sense pre-exist the evolution of matter. It only makes its appearance, and so brings into being surreality, when material evolution is well advanced, and has passed over into life, nervous system and brain, and a very special humanised brain at that.

A few scientists have gone much further than a two-level universe. Boltzman, for instance postulates an infinity of worlds, 'stretching out in infinite time directions from every moment in a person's life.'[3] It is only the strong conditioning of our birth into this one particular universe that prevents us from travelling in any other direction. Some quantum theoreticians have come to much the same conclusion. Given the discontinuity of existence at the subatomic level, accounting for the quantum gap, plurality of worlds becomes a virtual certainty. Anyone interested in feeling the pulse of advanced speculation in physics at the present time is recommended to read some of the exciting science writing now appearing in, for example, the *Scientific American*.[4,5]

Before dismissing the continuum theory it is worth reflecting that the vast electron-dependent industries of today, including computers, themselves exploit it. Thus electricity is continuum involving; the only difference between this man-made technology and the brain, is that the brain has not only mastered ways of exploiting the continuum—very early forms of life achieved that—but of ensuring that such exploitation persists. The form of matter which has evolved into the human brain impresses parallel events in the continuum, so that by the functioning of mind on a universal scale, in endless and innumerable planets, the continuum itself is organised in the image of the material world. This must be understood as a purely functional organisation, one nonetheless totally real and efficient. This is the distinction between material object and process, made by the great philosopher of science, A. N. Whitehead.[6]

Quantum theory is based on the fact that at the atomic level, nature does not exist continuously, but is ceaselessly recreated at the rate of 10^{23} per second, it is this pulsating hiatus that we call the quantum gap. This is both a shattering and a most convenient conclusion. On the one hand it enables the physicist to treat the pulse of creativity, the so-called quanta *as if* they were concrete entities, thereby applying well-established mechanical principles to them, while on the other, it completely demolishes a substantial materialistic explanation of the universe.

The quantum gap provides an explanation of how matter can affect the continuum, and vice versa. A

Fig 4

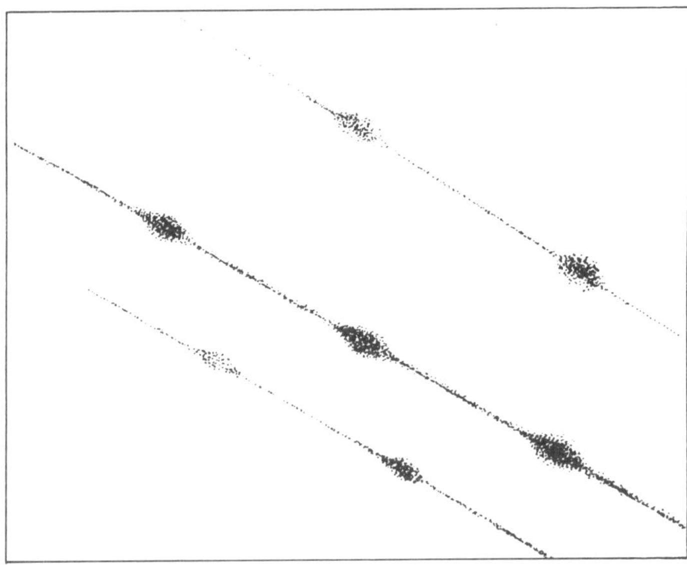

Pulses in laser beams, each about three tenths of a millimetre long and lasting for a millionth of a millionth of a second. These are the quantas referred to in the text

material change in an elementary particle like the electron, during the 'in' phase, will automatically replicate whatever state it happens to be in, in the continuum, as it passes to the 'out' phase. In reverse, such continuum replicates affect events in space and time. In this way every single material event becomes duplicated in a purely functional sense in the continuum, so that the universe possesses a complete universal and timeless 'memory' of its entire existence. As matter has evolved and become more organised and versatile, so has the replication in the continuum and, consequently, its possible influence over material phenomena. This is as good a model as can be found to account for such phenomena as mind, and the extraordinary correlations and directiveness of growth and evolution in general. As generations of stars have succeeded one another, so a 'memory' of star-making experience was acquired, enabling in time the remarkable efficiency of nuclear events in a star's thermo-nuclear cycle.

In nerve and brain, natural selection has been able to exploit the continuum connection, particularly in the storage of information and its transmission, not only in the electro-chemical events in nerve fibres, but by such means as telepathy. The information content of the brain of an adult human being has been calculated at a figure approaching the total number of atoms in the galaxy. If such a staggering accumulation of information took up measurable space, the human brain would be a most unwieldy organ.

Besides its exploitation in the evolution of the nervous system and the brain, this ability of organised matter to engender parallel events in the continuum in a purely functional sense, has been employed in other physical and organic phenomena. When sufficiently organised in this way, the continuum replications of space time experience have a freedom, beyond anything known in the material realm, to control, co-ordinate and direct. This is the most likely explanation of the 'onwardness' of evolution and of the still unexplained integrated development of the embryo.

While all matter has a replicative continuum ability, the advent of nerve and brain greatly enhanced the power and possibilities of the process. As far as mind is concerned, the high, humanising mind with its need for wholeness and its relationship with emotionalism, in particular, introduced a new dimension into the scheme of nature, for the continuum replication of the mind's experience was then incomparably more vivid, indeed, more 'real' than mere physical existence. Furthermore, as the process of evolution of the planet itself is now accepted as common to normal stars like the sun, and as the evolution of the high mind is likely to require much the same kind of humanising environment throughout the universe, it can be concluded that the experience of nature, in the widest sense, results in a transcendental pooling of information in the continuum.

In this way a complete transcendental replication of nature, created by the material brain, exists as pure process, not in space and time but in terms of the continuum. As the high humanising mind is programmed for order, harmony, beauty, perfection and purity, so these are the quintessential qualities of surreality.

As we have already seen, the universe is characteristically a functional enterprise. What we call matter constitutes no more than a tiny percentage of what exists. Most of this is radiative energy, which is by definition non-material. The replication of nature in surreality is the zenith of beauty and perfection which provides the fountain-head of inspiration for all that is truly great and fine in human creativity.

One can thus catch a glimpse of the theme underlying creation: the continuum, containing the cues to all creation and evolution, engenders matter, space and time, so that these can in return organise the continuum. Matter is an indispensable stage, but it is not the aim or end of creation; most people know this intuitively, in spite of the pessimism of materialistic science. Because the high, humanising mind and the high arts capable of inducing the peak experience, are involved with this surreality, the cosmic relevance of such arts is evident.

CHAPTER EIGHT

ART AS REVELATION

All true art proclaims the existence of worlds beyond space and time, and is involved in the revelation of splendours of freedom and perfection only hinted at in the ordinary world. This freedom and perfection refers to the transcendental worlds revealed in the hyper-aesthetic experience: the serene, beautiful, harmonious and pure, that which is able to elicit intense rapture; the most-profound experience available to human beings.

But as all activity has a continuum connection, it is to be expected that this humanising aspect does not exist alone, in a transcendental sense, in surreality, but that other levels of human experience also have their transcendental repercussions, which influence the arts in a particular social situation, and which the arts reveal in a symbolic manner.

Transcendental worlds are infinite in kind and quality; they provide an immeasurably rich spectrum from sublime paradise to hells unimaginable. When this has been understood the act of contemplating works of art, whether in a picture gallery or an ethnological museum, becomes a totally different and revelatory experience, one that confirms that true art refers not to imaginary worlds but to real worlds stranger and more powerful than the one we accept as normal. It is a common fallacy that art expresses nothing but fantasy—a damaging misinterpretation which prevents many people from opening themselves to the possibility of the peak experience.

Subconsciously influenced art may defuse existential pressures and provide its own dionysian, magical or exciting satisfaction, but it does not have the illuminative qualities of art inspired by surreality because wholeness and harmony, belong to the high, humanising mind. The transience of the subconscious influence is seen in art inspired by magical practices which depend for their continuing power on renewal through ritual. The power of the sublime, on the other hand, can be sustained. The recurring Faustian theme is ever-present in art and myth: the devil is given his due, but is eventually vanquished by love and beauty. Much of the power and universal appeal of literature and drama comes from the acting out of this opposition and its eventual resolution. The dramatic thread winds its trembling way through all great existentially preoccupied art. In a threatening existence the purity of the arcadian realm is beyond reach, so that atonement, sacrifice, and redemption offer the only way out. The work of art becomes a means of transfiguration through which the relationship with drama and myth is restored.

A glimpse of the peak experience may be achieved in such circumstances, when the full experience is no longer available. Given the conditions of modern life, this mitigated peak in the more existentially involved arts, should not be spurned, for it does carry the prospect of an eventual redemption, even if it is accompanied by a tinge of nostalgia. This is important for it can make one aware of the supernal realities of art. Furthermore, the process of becoming involved with such art increases awareness of its reality in a dimension far removed from ordinary existence. Even magical possession is better than no possession at all. In contemplating a painting with initially disturbing nuances, in listening to a discordant poem, or to violently eruptive music one does nonetheless become involved, as the eyes explore and the ears absorb, and quite suddenly a breakthrough into a totally distinct level of experience becomes possible.

As a way of revelation, art is entirely dependent on symbols for access into both the ordinary world—through paint, notes or words—and into transcendental resources whatever they may be. This means that the symbolic in both nature and art corresponds to equivalent existence in transcendental worlds, to definite entities, processes and functions in heaven, or hell. The power of revelation contained in a form, colour or sound, is possible only because material situations can be so altered and modified as to indicate the existence of their transcendental equivalents. However, this can only be done by that most elusive yet powerful faculty which all human beings possess—intuition.

In some cases these correspondences are more direct than others. The crystal is an example of a remarkably direct revelation of the formative cues to 'substance' from surreality. Hence its splendour and light, as the mystics have sensed, is as close as one can get in the world of time and space to the realities beyond; realities manifest in words such as light, colour, music, crystalline, sparkling and rapturous which are all intimations of surreality.

There are few things in nature which do not have some symbolic correspondence. This is also likely to be true of man-made artefacts. Metal, glass and plastics all manipulate light in unique ways which suggests that, in all probability, they are specific symbolic references to surreality. The uniqueness of the symbolic, which varies with every material through which it is expressed, is seen particularly well in the visual arts. Oil paint, for instance, possesses a creative expressiveness inherent in its oiliness. It has enormous evocative power, perhaps because it corresponds to the manner in which substance in surreality flows and churns creatively. Although acrylic and lacquer paints have symbolic powers of their own (see plate 7) and great technical advantages, they have less of this strange power. Watercolour, on the other hand, is more dependent on transparencies and translucencies of wash and runs of limpid colour and, therefore, has closer analogies to the transcendental references of light and illumination. The verve of the line in good drawing, in calligraphy or engraving, may correspond to some purely functional linear expression in surreality, to the ways in which creative energy disports itself, marking out and so creating entities and worlds in a way analogous to the elementary particles which make up the atomic world.

The two level model of nature that I have proposed conforms to the ancient concept of an invisible world corresponding to and reflecting the visible. This idea appears, in one form or another, in many different cultures. Thus the influence of surreality in the arts, and in ordinary existence, was anticipated in Plato's theory of forms. But whereas Plato envisaged these eternal prototypes as existing before the universe came into being, it is the evolution of matter in time and spacc which has engendered surreality.

Revelation through art is not a peep-show into another world, but the actual experience of that world, made possible by symbolic gift bestowed uniquely on the humanised mind in the course of its evolution. Once this experience has been gained, through communion with the higher reaches of visible nature, or through art, then the emotional basis of all human experience is permanently changed. Reality is no longer seen as something outside,

Acrylic and lacquer (shown here) have unique symbolic power

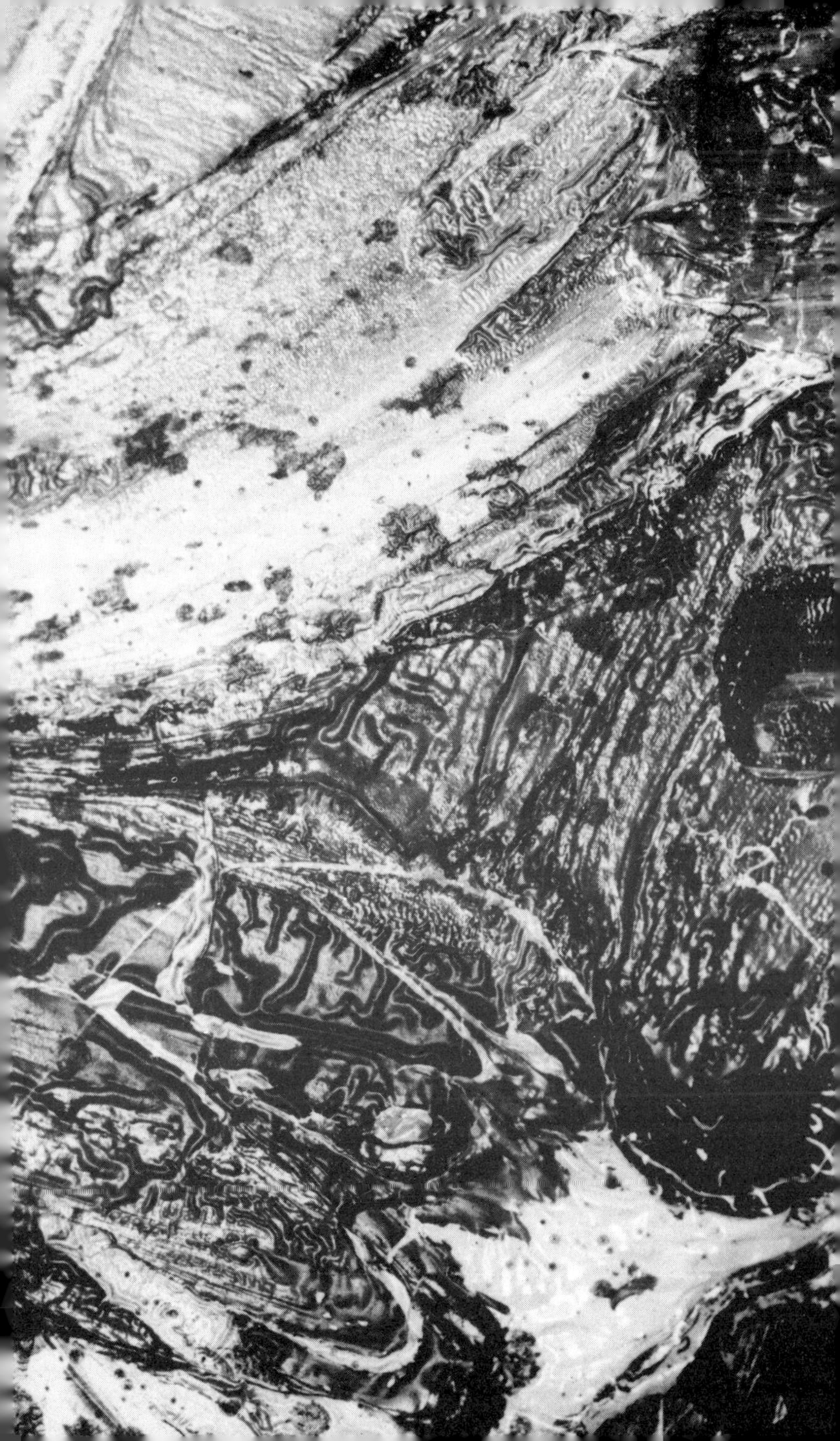

consisting of impersonal, separate objects which originate, change and die. It becomes hallowed, sacred, radiant, pregnant with supernal meaning. Such a revelation is the highest possible role of art. Art which serves the most evolved human and cosmic achievement, not only provides the highest joy available to the human being, but an absolute reassurance that life has meaning.

Although the inspiration on which art depends is transcendental, its social function is eminently adaptive. It reconciles an emotionalised mind to a world all too often deprived of emotional meaning, and aids in the transformation of that world to meet the human requirement. It is the inspiration which surreality can provide that gives the necessary guidance for the transformation of the anthropomorphic environment into a truly humanised place, as close to the surreal as it can be made. The original human environment was probably adequate in this respect, filled with natural beauty and harmony, otherwise we would not even have the underdeveloped sensitivities we possess in our better moments. But this arcadian earthly paradise—which vanished in the Ice Ages and was never fully recovered, is as nothing to the paradise which may be experienced through surreal inspiration, an order of inspiration which, we can imagine, has already been attained elsewhere in the universe.

The concept of surreality provides a useful basis against which the constituents of a work of art can be evaluated. The reason being that the aesthetically significant aspects of nature have been the means through which surreality has arisen in a universal pooling of the humanised mind.

Since energy is the prime creative force in the physical universe, it is to be expected that it has equivalents in the continuum, in the mind's ability to organise within the continuum an experience of surreality. It is just possible to perceive of some timeless and universal proto-energy that takes two forms; one accounts for the organisation of the 'elementary particles' of atoms; the other is utilised by suitably organised atoms of nerve and brain to engender events in the continuum. As the high aspect of mind has been presumed capable of participating in surreality, it is not impossible that some awareness of this outfolding of creative energies in mind and continuum can be remotely sensed. Sir Herbert Read, quoting Vico, has mentioned that in creative reverie and meditation the experience is one of being recollectively aware of a kind of formative, luminous flux. It churns and condenses into diverse shapes which lie behind the symbology of words in poetry, for example, or in light, colour and movement in the visual arts. The disappearing whisps of these energies can sometimes just be caught as one awakens from a high dream. Indeed Leary claims that the darting scintillating abstract images that appear in drug-induced trances are the actual revelation of neural events.[1]

The most elementary way in which this creative 'mist' can be visibly symbolised is by line. It may be tense or darting, firm or tremulous, and the manner in which intuition can guide the touch to impart verve and feeling to the line can be dimly grasped as a long and intricate neural involvement reaching into the continuum. The immense power which a simple brush-stroke can acquire comes thus from surreality. This also explains the symbolic power of texture and scumble; of the spot or splash of paint which may be detected with the aid of a lens in the paintwork of the great classical realist masters (see for example Rembrandt's self portrait) and, more immediately in the work of action painters and in tachism.

Form can also be conceived, and indeed experienced, as the particular condensation of this creative 'mist'. A tremulous, ethereal, luminous essence, akin to the plasma of the atomic physicist, able to engender scenes, objects

Fig 5

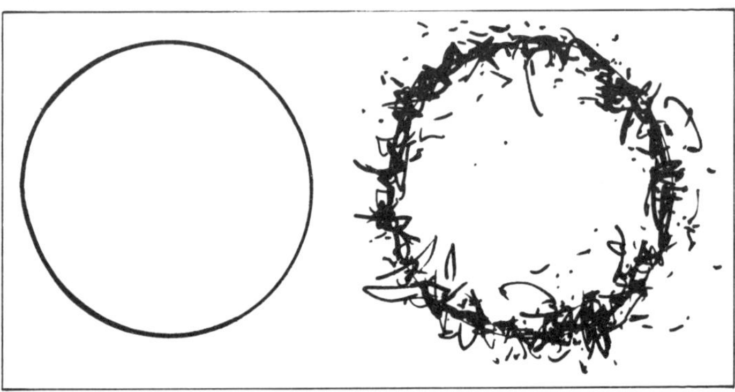

The vitalisation of line and form. The plain circle is not without symbolic power—it symbolises some sort of serene quiet, while the darting lines and runs of the second circle are felt to be vital. At the atomic level, and beyond, vitality is a throbbing agitating function

and creatures in the life of the psyche and in surreality. Such condensations of proto-energy are themselves necessarily immersed in an all-permeating energetic flux, so that no basic distinction can be made between the object and the space around it. Such a distinction only applies to the arbitrary material realm. The unity of the object and its environment in the dream, in the inner life and in surreality can be appreciated.

The aim of such a process is not the creation of scenes and objects in themselves, but rather their symbolic relevance to an emotionalised experience, one which is ceaselessly creative, changing and musical. Although the appearance of such images greatly assists the experience, they can be dispensed with, as the pure emotion of music shows. The creation of form out of this mist of proto-

The evocative power of line and texture

energy retains an essential quality of ethereality or luminosity that is vibrant and tremulous and quite distinct from the ordinary experience of form. This incandescent form that gives to the visible forms in painting and sculpture their superconscious dimension, is evidently created by the higher faculties. It also explains how the term *form* is felt to have a transcendental significance in all art. This applies just as much to poetry as it does to music, and underlies all valid order and structure.

Light and colour, and musical sound vibrations, are undoubtedly the most apt symbolisations of the creative potential of the proto-energy to which mind has access. Light is radiation, and radiation is the least material aspect of the physical universe. It is the most insubstantial aspect of matter involved in the continuum, the nearest to pure energy with its surreal portents both wonderous and sublime.

In its reference to surreality, light acquires its creative powers not only by its intensity—the 'light lighting the very light', as Walt Whitman puts it—but also in becoming spectrally segregated into colour. In the physical world this is achieved by the differential vibration of electrons, and in surreality the luminous forms, scenes and creatures. The transparent colour of a crystal provides a striking example of the superceding of form by colour and transparency. The crystalline descriptions of surreality by Plato, and by many poets and mystics, touch upon a most fundamental quality.[2] The visual arts attain their greatest moments when they aspire to this level.

Music is similarly a creative organisation of vibration, related to atomic and molecular resonances in materials,

Growth lines on a crystal of fluorite

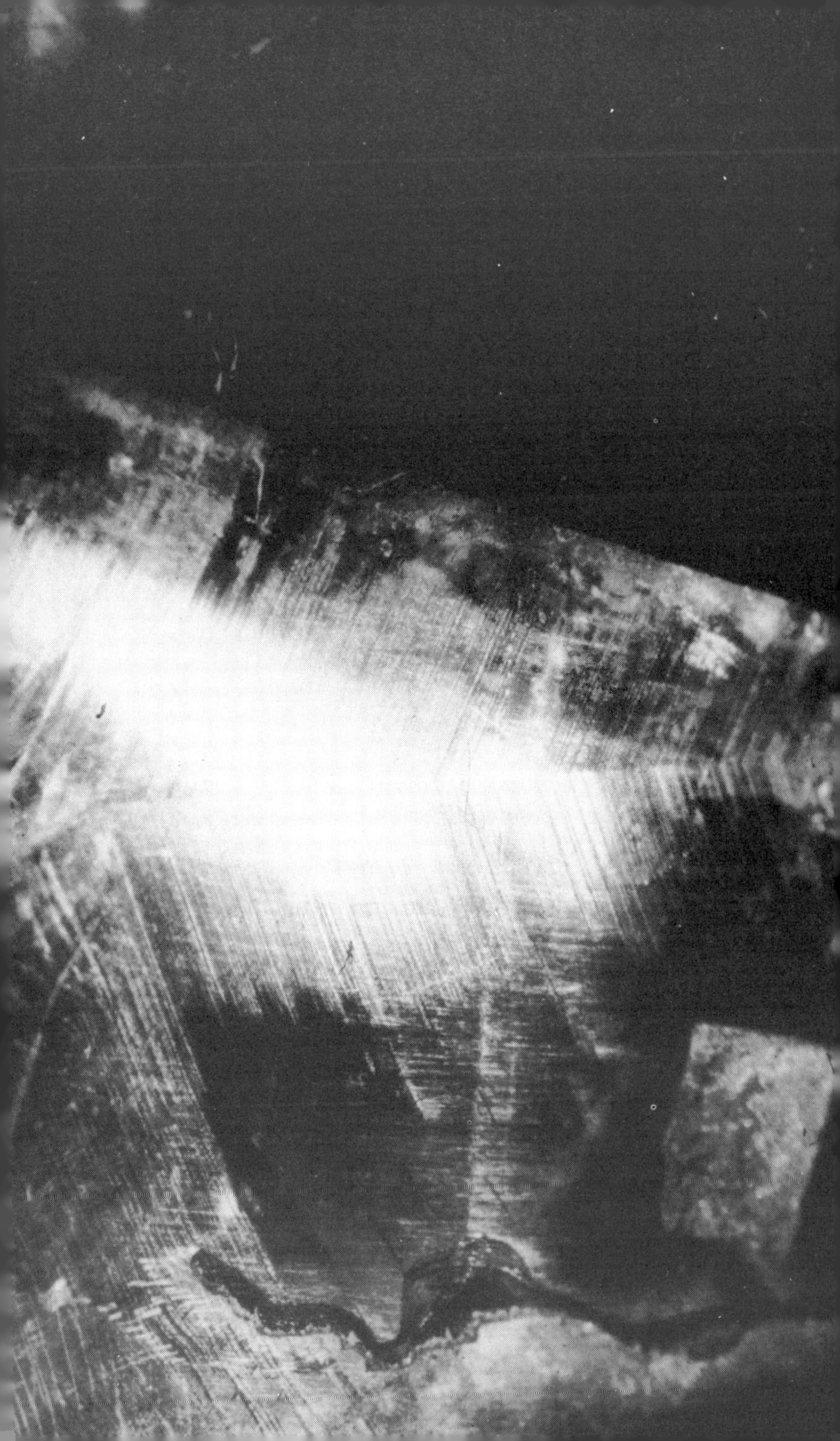

in correspondence to the musical content of surreality. When Goethe exclaimed that all the arts aspire to the sublime condition of music, he revealed a profound truth. Surreality is all light, all colour, all music, and all love, but this is only an approximation and fails to convey a condition that is beyond description. One can appreciate how appropriate and apt is this analogy of energy in the creative mind and in surreality by comparing them with the qualities of the atomic realm which are so different from the apparent reality of common material experience.

Just as visible nature is the actualisation in space and time of the organisational cues from the continuum, so these proto-energies, which engender the scenes of the mind's life and of surreality, call for an organising principle which gives them their particular twist and turn, their creative unrepeatable stamp. This is where the individualised mind comes in. With its singular and unique creative potential, it enables new worlds and universes not previously in existence to come into being. Every single mind, endowed with this kind of creative, expressive individuality, which has developed through the long march of evolution, is thus a godlike creative intervention in a potentially limitless creative flux of proto-energies in the continuum and, as such, is able to make a singular contribution to surreality. This power is not only evident in the individual work of art, but is especially obvious in the total output of a particular artist, and of a particular culture or civilisation.

Art is forced into being by the challenge and frustrations of existence, but it is nevertheless able, even under extreme challenge, to provide a glimpse of supernal realities. In truth, every individual life, lived in a truly human way with feeling and joy, is a supernal commitment to the enhancement of the life process. All life is intended to be art.

CHAPTER NINE

THE CREATIVE PROCESS

What kind of person is the creative artist? Evidently he or she has to be unusually sensitive and will have a more than average emotional inner life, and a more insistent and effective intuitive faculty. But this is obviously a matter of degree, for most people have something of the artist in them; poems and melodies have erupted in everyone's head at some time or other. After all, the aesthetic faculty is the most distinctive human mark, and if most people are not artistically creative or appreciative, it is likely to be due to restrictive forces rather than to special gifts bestowed exclusively upon artists or lovers of art.

The emphasis placed on the personality of the artist, and the importance of the name, the signature, or technical stamp—which is often no more than the result of some specialised repertoire—is fostered by a materialistic society as a means of promotion. This contrasts sharply with what happens among primitive peoples. Artists are not chosen because of precocious demonstrations of talent, but by quite arbitrary means. When art is related to ritual and religion, it is the high priest or sorcerer who chooses the image-maker and musician, the dancers and actors.

Alternatively, these skills may be handed on in families or other close-knit groups, as are the skills of metal working, plant lore and medicine. But, whatever the system of selection, the artist is invariably accorded a privileged place in society; for like the poet or interpreter of dreams, he is the revealer of another and more important world.

Technique in any art is decisively important, and usually takes a long time to master. This is because the aim of technique is both to allow intuition to work, and to ensure that the organisational faculty is exercised over the medium regardless of what the substance consists of. The vast body of technique can be taught, but each artist must find his own way of allowing his intuition to function effectively. It is this which takes time because technical gaps can only be filled intuitively through experience of the subtleties entailed in practice; this is probably true for every skill, from golf to surgery. It is easy to understand the reverence that artists and craftsmen have for their tools and materials. It is after all, in the act of handling these, that the miraculous intervention occurs in art-making and, indeed, in any constructive process. This is true in even the most realistic type of art; but the limitation of such a pursuit is that it can so preoccupy the artist that it hinders intuition. Nevertheless, the great realist masters made wonderful use of their material, going beyond technique and discovering the intuitive way of using appearance to reveal the divine.

The role which technique plays in any art depends on a number of things: questions of convention, contemporary feelings, tradition, the individual idiosyncracies of the artist and the demands and limits imposed by structure. Literature, for example, has an innate technical form subscribed by the dynamics of word use. So has music, but its formal precision is far less restrictive, for music is the most purely symbolic of all the arts. Painting and sculpture have a similar kind of symbolic latitude but have an added problem, the tendency to become so obsessed with the practical and material aspects of the visual, that access to the surreal is precluded.

Under settled conditions the techniques of art become stabilised, and evolve into a body of tradition which is perpetually challenged through environmental and cultural changes. If freedom prevails in any society—which it has rarely done in the course of human history—the arts immediately reflect this and offer the means of emotional adaptation to the changed circumstances. The arts even appear to be able to predict changes in feeling long before they become commonly realised. A striking example of this is seen in the move towards a penetrative abstraction in all the arts, in their own particular ways, well before science itself became penetrative.

The surreal is not a static photocopy of ordinary reality, but a dynamic flux. It may well possess evolutionary tendencies of its own and the ability to feel possible future developments to which the sensitive and attuned mind, particularly in times of impending change, could have access. In such times, the creative person is restless, and out of gear with prevailing attitudes. He is a rebel and an outsider, a condition provoked by these remote yet pressing presentiments.

Because of the inherent difficulty which the symbolic has in emerging through to the level of substance, not only is it indispensable for the artist to be in a very particular state of mind, but important for him not to be discouraged by the early stages of creation when progress is disjointed, regression frequent and stages of actual destruction unavoidable. These problems are particularly acute in the beginning of any creative process and the artist invariably experiences anxiety and restlessness mixed with a kind of pent-up desire which is not always pleasurable. Only in the most placid culture can the artist's approach be meditative and tranquil. More usually, it is his initial anxiety that drives him into action, oscillating between his materials, his subject—if indeed he is aware of one—and the unrealised intimations of the other world.

A Chinese poet of the thirteenth century compared the creative process in the arts to a blind bee approaching a closed flower. The common idea of how an artist works is that he begins with a vision in mind, perfects it by sketching and realises it progressively, until the process concludes with the meeting of reality and vision. Only the mediocre realist painter, the hack rhymer of words or the ding-dong tune maker proceeds in this way—that is, in a totally linear and uninspired matching of tacit vision to reality. This is not to suggest that such initial procedures are not useful, they undoubtedly are, and many artists believe that they do operate according to some sustained idea or vision; but even in the case of the writer, or the realist painter, any initial plan is subtly modified and at times completely transformed as the artist becomes progressively engrossed in the creative act. This may happen through one particular experience of total absorption or be staggered over years, but the subtle or overt modifications of any original plan are inevitable.

Take the case of the portait painter. As he diligently observes the model, marks out his canvas, and begins to paint, the interplay between mind and model proceeds; the portrait becomes much more than a photographic replica of the face. Strange, unpredictable qualities emerge. They bestow on the model hyper-real intimations that are not ordinarily apparent—a quality of transfiguration, an inner illumination of the 'other world' connotation of the subject. Of course the experienced painter achieves this by a most complicated repertoire of subtle touches and techniques acquired through years of practice, but these are the means of symbolic revelation, and watching such a painter at work, it is evident that the key contributions are purely impulsive and intuitive.

Here we are presented with an explanation of the strange fact that no copy or reproduction of a work of art can have the emotional, symbolic impact of the original. So sensitive is the creative co-operation of eye and hand, that minute touches are seen subsequently by the sensitive eye to have an enormous, unique and evocative impact. The ability of the attuned eye to sense the false, the wrongly modified or the merely copied is remarkable.

This is not to say that a copy of a work of art may not possess symbolic qualities of its own. Indeed, a copy may be symbolically more rich and versatile than the original. Artists themselves often work on the same subject, time and again striking upon some new, quite different symbolic experience on each new occasion. This makes the simplest of subjects virtually inexhaustible as the focus of inspiration in art. Some artists become possessed by a particular subject—Cézanne's recurring fascination, for example, with the Mont St Victoire. This is not surprising when it is borne in mind that what matters in a work of art, is not physically in it, but is what the physical realm evokes of surreality in the eye of the artist. The seer uses the same crystal ball for an infinity of visions.

When the symbolic works through and guides the creative finger, so fashioning a concrete revelation of the surreal, no one is more astounded than the artist. But it is a surprise which must necessarily await the completion of the creative act. No artist can ever exactly repeat a work of art; revelation is not merely being able to capture photographically a glimpse of another reality, but the symbolic transmission of its sheer functionalism, of its ceaseless flux. The most successful fakes are those which have been genuinely created, not copied.

The source of inspiration in a portrait is the intuitive seeing and sensing of the transfigured replication of the particular person in terms of surreality—what William Blake called the 'sensing of the angelic form'. Such an experience comes at some time or other to most people. When we are in love, the beloved is transfigured in this way, freed of blemish, utterly beautiful and pure. Good portraiture, like good landscape, is always genuinely revelatory. The writer is subject to this process even more than those in the visual arts. He or she may begin with a well worked-out plan, but as he gets under way, he finds himself being led to modify his original plan. As the organic develops, the theme gains momentum and the created personalities assert their individuality and unpredictable, indeed personal, sense of direction over and above any plan formulated.

In a one-dimensional view of reality, the story and the characters are purely artificial creations in the writer's mind. But when we look at it from the point of view of the model proposed—that is, with surreality the direct product of ordinary reality—any sustained creation by the mind is likely to engender a corresponding surreal existence. This, in turn, acquires a large proportion of life in its own right, the ability to exist independently of its creator. Although this may appear fantastic to the literal-minded person, it has a beautiful simplicity when once the idea of a surreal world is accepted. Moreover, it gives to the creative power of thought an awe inspiring dimension. When we can accept that it is owing to the creative power of the high, humanised mind that nature is able to continue its creative evolution beyond substance, time and space, then the individual mind's power to create can be seen as a truly human contribution to surreality. The characters in a novel, or the subjects captured in a painting are not only more than they appear, they are capable of continuing their surreal life within the continuum and as such are more than mere representative images. By contrast the subhuman and anti-human can only be transient. This is a reassuring state of affairs, for otherwise surreality would be encumbered by the deviant and the demonic.

Even in the search for appropriate theories in science, the metaphysical directive can take over, as theories gain momentum and order crystallises. Indeed, without this process there can be no genuinely creative hunches and inspiration, but only routine development of that which has already been creatively discovered. Throughout this mechanism, the extremely close collaboration of reason and intuition can be seen. It is so close, in fact, that the majority of scientists are able to delude themselves that only their reasoning faculties are involved. The exacting training of scientists insists on this illusion, for otherwise the scientist would be in danger of becoming an artist and failing to deal effectively with the mechanical aspects of reality to which he must confine himself. Although the scientist can profit from intuitive aesthetic guidance, he wishes it to remain hidden. Its full application must be left out of the routine experimental methods of science, being admitted only in the co-ordination of data which theory makes possible.

The resources from which intuition can draw are seen to be particularly consistent in their scientific and mathematical applications. This is sufficiently evident in mathematical discovery. As Poincaré put it, one gets the impression in framing what one knows to be entirely new principles, that one is walking into previously discovered territory—an uncanny and mystifying experience.[1] But the explanation is nonetheless evident. Mathematics must have correspondences with surreality, for it is constructed by mind in the image of the physical world. This explains why the great discoveries and systems of mathematics have come as bolts from the blue, already elaborately formulated and coherent. It also explains how it is that theoretical mathematicians, ignoring reality, can invent vast mathematical systems, even complete cosmologies which at the time may appear preposterous, but, if they are elegant and beautiful, invariably turn out in time to have practical relevance to reality.

This strange phenomenon is also frequently encountered in musical composition, an art that has discernible mathematical connections; the composer may be taken over by successions of elaborately resolved melodies and composition. Photography shows how, even with a dominant technique and an aim usually considered to be entirely mimetic, aesthetic quality can nevertheless intervene and inspiration play a part. The flatness of the image which necessarily transforms that key property of the material world—space and object separation—provides a particular symbolic quality. The eye can read no more than a realistic transcription of appearance. But at times the simplifications and enhancements of mass, colour and line controlled by the choice of lenses, and chemical techniques in development, have a high aesthetic implication (see Plate 10) and, at their best, photographs can undoubtedly induce a peak experience. As in all art, this increases with penetration. It conforms with the claim that the departure from the realm of ordinary appearance, and the closer approach to the more fundamental levels where forms and function have their being, brings a greater symbolic power and reality-feeling.

Photography may do no more than catch a passing scene, but at its best it can reveal the transcendental mystery of nature
Photograph: Ariane van der Elst

Few words have been more used than 'abstract' in art discussions and yet its definition remains elusive and unsatisfactory. The reason for this is that it was coined to describe a method of moving away from appearances which was assumed to be reasonable and analytical. To

Fig 6

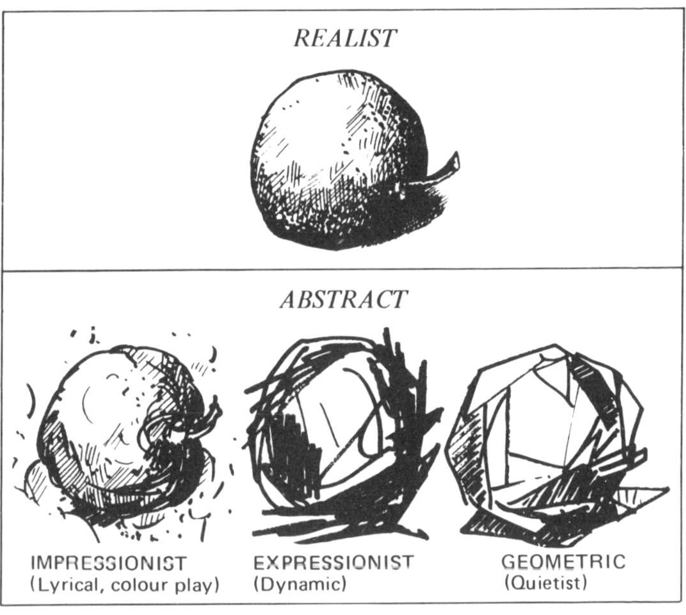

Ways of seeing and using recognisable forms to display intuitively grasped 'abstract' symbolic marks

'abstract' means to remove something from something else, to concentrate and isolate (see Fig 6). And this is what the early Impressionist painters were supposed to be doing when they made paintings of nature that varied from what was commonly expected of realism. If this is all that happens, then it is nothing at all. Clearly, even if the artist and critic agree that the abstract results from a diligent observation, followed by abstracting certain aspects of appearance to the exclusion of others, and believe that this is a rational, analysable act, intuition must still play a very important part in the process no matter to what degree the realist painters managed to fool themselves that they were doing no more than interpreting visible reality; they were in fact subject to intuitive forces. How far this self-deception can go is clearly demonstrated in the case of Cézanne. He firmly believed to his dying day that the cones and prisms from which he built up his images, were actually out there in nature, to be seen if carefully and persistently looked for. Perhaps he actually did 'see' them; yet what he saw was not in nature but was projected intuitively, and without his rational knowledge, upon the face of nature from the creative resources of his mind; a mind connected in its higher aspect to surreality.

Actually, the use of the word abstract is not as bad as it has been made out, for its techniques point to the way in which appearances can be surpassed. As this way was first knowingly taken by the Impressionists, it is usually termed Abstract Impressionism. It encompasses degrees of abstraction all the way to total abstraction in which there are no readily discernible cues of appearance left. The word impressionism is another one of those definitions from an age still hopeful that what the artist was doing was still rational and reasonable, for it means what it says. It is an artist's individual impression of some scene or object. It was accepted that artists were

(*See over*)

Impressionism–melodic, harmonious, lyrical and naturalistic

Expressionism—dissonant, tense, assertive and anti-nature

individuals, every artist being entitled to his particular impression, his view of the world—provided, of course, that this did not get out of hand and offend the public.

But art is basically a symbolic rather than a realistic phenomenon so the impressionist experiment was bound to get out of hand. Once the artist had begun to experiment with the symbolic, even if he didn't know quite what he was doing, the sheer power of the experience took him over. He found himself involved with much deeper, much more forceful symbols, until the entire process became visible and blatantly symbolic, the aspect of realism or rational control being obliterated. This is what Impressionism did, and it has been of invaluable service.

This move away from realism, and the world of ready-made appearances, was not merely an artistic whim, it was a profound psychological response to disruptive elements in the late eighteenth century. Everywhere nature was being devastated by the spread of industrialisation and the natural world was being visibly altered. Sensitive minds reacted against this outrage and impoverishment. The genetic satisfactions of beauty and harmony, the music of colour and the purity of form in painting, the lyrical, harmonic, tonal and rhapsodic in music, were as a result heightened and accentuated. The artist's impressions were in truth his aroused, reactive mental symbolism, inspired at its best from surreality, literally illuminating the sullied face of nature with the lights of paradise.

In painting this process can be traced to its roots. Colour in its musical harmonies played a decisive role in

Turner was the most celebrated forerunner of the Impressionist movement—in this painting the more primitive moulding of form by graded intensities of light and darkness melts into pure spectral organisation

Reproduced by courtesy of the Trustees of the Tate Gallery, London

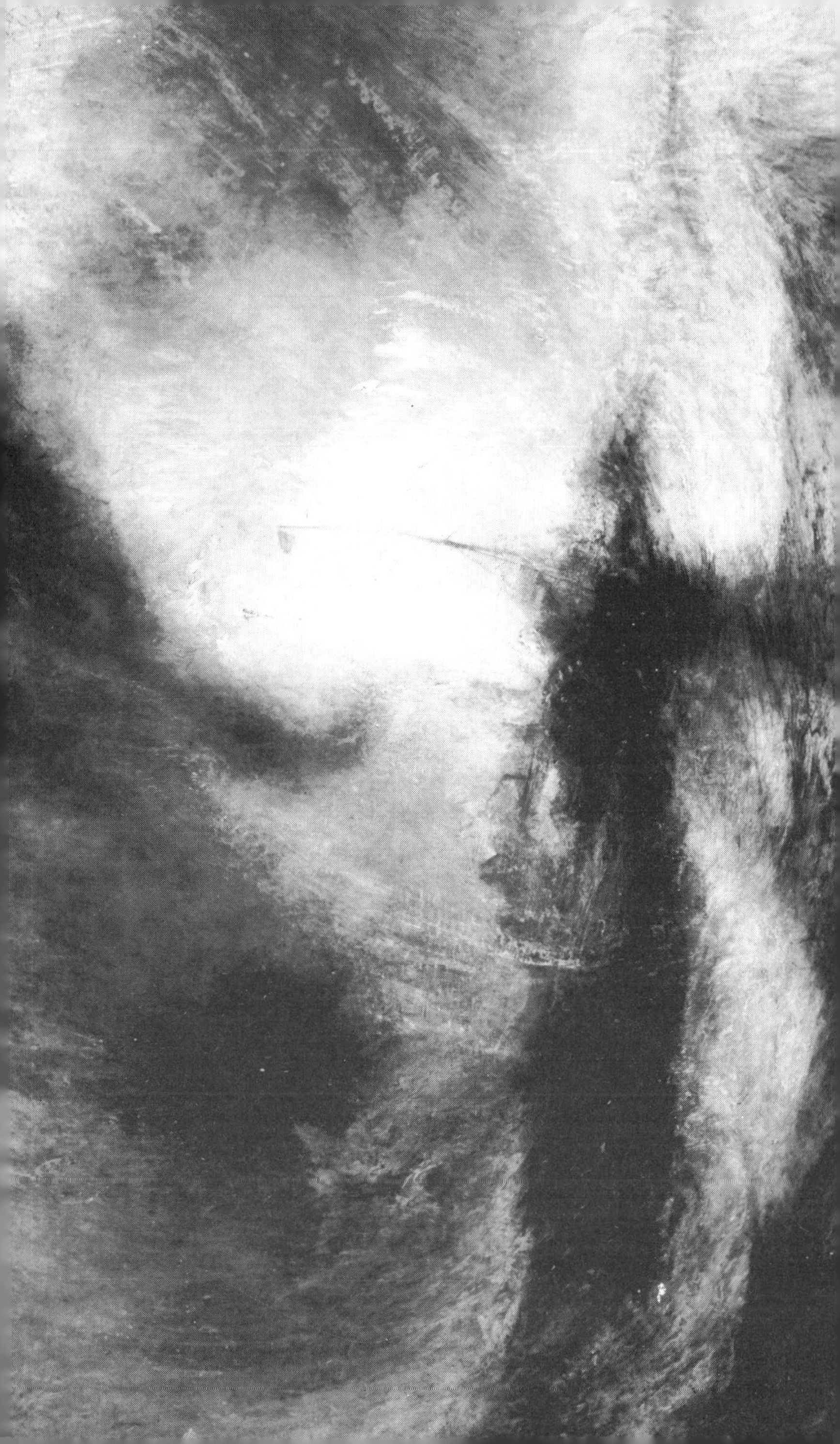

the process of humanisation, it was the music of colour that became intensified in the move away from realism. All was colour. Form itself, traditionally expressed by line and mass, by light and shadow, in carefully emphasised spatial relationships, was taken over by powerful edifices of colour. The use of black was the cardinal sin among Impressionists. Even shadows, which the eye usually perceives as darkness, had to be filled with vibrant, spectral colours. This revolution was not mere invention, but corresponded to an actual symbolic revelation of what takes place in surreality. It displayed how the purely physical demarcations of shape and substance are transfigured in what can only be called colour and light. Darkness, it was intuitively realised, belongs to the visible world, not to surreality.

The Impressionist image evolved in two different directions. In one, the image was visibly dynamic. It consisted of dashes of colour, darting lines, melting, churning, dynamic forms, all interfused in an orchestration of vibrant, spectral colour. There was vibration everywhere. Monet was the arch-master of this school, although it had been recognised and celebrated earlier by Turner. The other method, which I call the crystalline, consisted of planes, sheets, faces of vibrant colour, typified in its figurative expression by Cézanne's cones, prisms and cubes. In a later painter like Jacques Villon, nature became visible as a crystalline rhapsody. These two approaches can, of course, be blended, and they often were, in ways which are hinted at in the later classical colourists like Tintoretto. Clearly, a profound state of mind was involved; and if what has been said so far about transcendental resources in art is true, then Impressionism, and what followed it, was much more than a new school of painting technique; it was a psychic revolution.

Impressionist vision penetrated the appearance of

reality very much as an extremely powerful microscope penetrates beyond what is visible to the human eye. The massive, opaque forms of ordinary experience gave way to the transparencies and translucencies of tissue, cells and minerals, revealing the vibrant world of molecules and atoms. These methods—the 'crystalline' and the 'energetic'—were the salient revelations of surreal qualities touching upon the very heart of its own inherent structure and transcendental quality. The other arts had and still have their own symbolic ways of revealing these key qualities which can be discerned in for example, the rhythms of poetry and music.

Drawing his inspiration from surreality, the Impressionist, whether in painting or music, remains a naturalist. His methods are painterly and lyrical. Even in the totally Abstract Impressionist image, the lights and nuances of nature linger on. Indeed, they may become vernal and enhanced as the splendours of surreality come through, as for example, in the work of Sam Francis. The Impressionist's way of abstracting is not fundamentally different from the way of the scientist, for analysis and experiment are forms of abstraction. The difference is that whereas the scientist is restricted to picking out the mechanical symbols in nature, the artist penetrates through to the profound, surreal revelation. But the scientist in his own, somewhat limited way, also looks in that direction as he finds himself open to intuitive guidance in the building up of his theories, and in his resource to that most symbolic of systems, mathematics.

The Impressionist discernibly retains some of the style of the realist no matter how abstract he may become. His approach remains experimental, the materials he uses are judged emotionally and intuitively against a background of natural feeling. For those at the turn of the last century, who had become sensitive to the Impressionists' vision, this way of abstraction seemed the only legitimate one. In other great civilisations, especially in China, there have been remarkably similar impressionistic periods in the arts, provoked no doubt, by the same kinds of threat to nature; the threat of barbarian invasion; the spread of urbanism, and periodic climatic disasters to which the East has been exposed since the beginnings of human development. It can therefore be presumed that Impressionism is a valid response to very particular phases in civilisation. If humanisation and the environmental and cultural forces that promote it, are universal, occurring in endless variations on endless planets throughout the universe, then it can also be postulated that Impressionism has a cosmic resonance.

When the subconscious mind is affected by stress, disturbing cultural and environmental changes take place which are far from the humanising ideal; the 'magical' mind is aroused and possession becomes an alternative way into the other world. This use of the abstract is not natural but existential, and the techniques used by the artist are quite different. There is no longer the painterly, the tuneful and the harmonic approach, on the contrary, the mark of human assertion dominates. If recognisable shapes and scenes are retained they are deformed and assertive in a quite different symbolic manner; they express the symbolic images that have been aroused in the subconscious and its equivalent transcendental world.

Although Expressionism has usually favoured the figurative in world art, it can also be non-figurative, a point made especially evident in post-war Abstract Expressionism. But some sort of figurative transformation seems to be the more natural ally of Expressionism. This need not be derived from the subconscious. As earlier indicated, it can reveal existing protoforms in the transcendental realms. When the subconscious does provide the figurative matrix, it is so thoroughly transfigured that its primitive connotations can be annulled. It then deals with a truly human existentialist situation, sympathetic to the high elements of art expression, to order, harmony and wholeness, but also to man's awareness of his tragic alienation, a situation which has ties with existentialism. Even when the Expressionist paints the visible he is already in touch with an order which defies it; a fact starkly evident in the work of Edvard Munch, for example. He is only one step away from dispensing with nature altogether and striving for a complete independent, autonomous imagery. To make that step the artist's mind must have access not only to the expressionistic aspects of nature but to the symbolic equivalent in the continuum.

Those who contend that an aesthetically powerful image can be created without any reference to what already exists in nature—visible or invisible—fail to realise that beyond the visible there is a throbbing, dynamic, ceaseless creativity pregnant with infinite possibilities. Indeed, what is evident in our space-time dimension must be seen as an extreme limitation of what could potentially exist. What has made the universe the way it is, rather than any other way, is the rigid limitation of potentially infinite resources. This is evident even in the material world, for example in the case of carbon and hydrogen, from which billions of chemical combinations are possible. Many of these have been synthesised in the laboratory; but in nature, only a fraction of these possible combinations have been realised. There is evidently a strong discipline in nature's activity. Because the intuitive mind has access to the resources of the continuum, it is able to draw on these primordial creative potentialities, and images which are genuinely novel and autonomous can therefore emerge. Art may thus realise what nature has failed to do, just as science has created some new elements which have never formed in nature and are more complex than uranium. The enlivened and attuned mind achieves this through a dynamic involving approach well demonstrated in Chinese art where, following prolonged meditation upon his materials, a painter may make a few lines or brushstrokes, full of verve, which acquire tremendous symbolic power.

Fig 7

Examples of aesthetically organised energy i) in the track of a particle in a hydrogen bubble chamber and ii) in the mark of a Zen master

In the East, this lively approach has long been appreciated particularly by calligraphers. They have rightly insisted that provided there is sufficient vitality in the artist the line or touch acquires a vital hyper-real quality, for there is no doubt that the most profound springs of vitality, or energy, are to be found in the heart of nature. The European Expressionists discovered this in their own agitated, anguished manner which led to an Abstract Expressionism which first appeared in the United States, after World War II. Since it is without the meditative ingredient of the East, it has depended on a kind of 'dervish dancing' with the medium and material, which has become well known for its apparent buffoonery, but which when successful, though this is seldom—undoubtedly gains access to extremely powerful, super-vital resources.

The form does not have to be only splash, drip, or squirt; coherently structured images can emerge. They symbolise strange, super-vital entities, born for the first and only time, dripping in the orgiastic energies beyond time and space—vibrant, palpitating and immensely provocative. No one is more surprised and fascinated than the artist himself when he succeeds in creating such an image, for he has then proof that he has drawn upon resources which transcend his own limited life source. It is a god-like power which has a strong resemblance to what science has managed to do through atomic fission and fusion, without its essentially destructive ingredient. What the creative mind draws upon is supernal power, the 'white hole' power that has made the universe itself. Both nature, in its myriad forms and creatures, and works of art, can express this Dance of Shiva. Both are symbolic, in their own way, of infinite and timeless resources.

The human ability to create a super vital image shows how far one must go to grasp the significance of art. Judged at the ordinary level of common awareness the work of art, like a living plant or animal, is an isolated object. But if it were possible to plunge into the springs of their intrinsic being, it would be found that both are different manifestations of the same universal drive that is impelled to grasp at every possible means of expressing itself. The creative human mind provides the best opportunity for this expression, indeed, one far superior to that provided by nature. And yet, the human mind is the product of nature, it is the supreme organ of nature's expression, so human arrogance is not justified. Although art is only one form of this creative expressiveness, it is certainly the most important one. The aesthetic cues in all things are what ensure their ontological validity; this is a law which applies to the physical universe, to life, to city, machine or art object alike.

Such super-vital images are evidently capable of inducing a very special kind of peak experience, for they accentuate the verve and vitality that play such a large part in bringing it about. In contrast to the Expressionist image, the super-vital image has more respect for beauty and harmony, for integration and colour play; but it is closer to Expressionist technique and feeling than it is to Impressionism. The tension and anguish that often go with the dark side of Expressionism, its frequent brutality and crudity, are not found in the super-vital image where the boldness is more ecstatic and uplifting; evidence of a profound surreal involvement. It is not surprising that such super-vital images are independent, autonomous and without any reference to the nature of time and space, yet felt to be profoundly meaningful in a human sense.

Since a harmonious togetherness in all things is the key aesthetic criterion, it is fair to propose that works of art should not only be available for private enjoyment, but should be incorporated into the overall environment in such a way as to provide radiative, all-enjoying foci of supernal appeal. Nature itself works in such a structural, nucleated manner. From atoms to cells and organisms, foci and concentrations of power reclaim and assimilate the less organised environments in which they find themselves. It is interesting to note that there are such foci in the mind itself. C. G. Jung called them 'archetypes', and they are of such enormous relevance to both the manufacture and appreciation of art as well as to a proper appreciation of nature, that when such foci are intuitively uncovered great things happen: surreality is drawn upon, and the miracle can come about.

This constitutes a working hypothesis of how the entire environment, natural and man-made, can be reclaimed. In such a state of unity, human beings, provided they are *genuinely* humanised—have a positive contribution to make. The human face and form, human movement, expression, language, voice, communication and love, are nature's highest achievements, its greatest works of art, but just as flowers lose their high aesthetic appeal when blighted and faded, so if the human masses are de-humanised, through violence and fear, they may become anti-aesthetic.

CHAPTER TEN

THE LIMITS OF COMMUNICATION

To resume a point already made, the art object, whether it be painting or poem, music or drama, does not provide a specific package of communication, or a universal message. Rather, it provides an opportunity for the *re-creation*, by the individual, of a state of mind receptive to a revelatory experience. All art experience in this sense is creative, and basically the differences between the artist and the art lover are minor ones. Each artistic experience, whether it be an act of creation or appreciation, is unique and unrepeatable, which implies that the truly effective work of art is unlimited in its ability to serve as a source of the peak experience.

This is a subject of extreme importance and complexity, to grasp which we must make an excursion into cosmology and subatomic physics. Nils Bohr, Pauli, Heisenberg and others have long contended that beyond a certain limit, the observer of a particular phenomenon in nature loses his individuality and merges with the phenomenon; observation gives way to participation. This has usually been seen as a vague theoretical conjecture of no practical relevance to everyday existence. But recently two well known cosmologists, J. A. Wheeler and C. M. Patton, have concluded that it is decisive in cosmology, for it is the appearance of a conscious, observing mind, in human form, which gives meaning to the entire cosmic enterprise: the 'observer' gives the world the power to come into being, through the very act of giving meaning to that world; in brief, 'no consciousness, no communicating community to establish meaning, then no world'. Such a self-reference cosmology is not new; it was implicit in the ideas of Parmenides of Elea circa 500 BC and in the writings of Bishop Berkeley in 1710.[1] What is particularly significant is that this kind of universe can be seen to tie in with other current ideas in physics, in particular with a reciprocating model of the universe and with the 'many worlds' conjectures of quantum theory. These are theories that are extremely difficult for the layman to grasp, but they are of truly great relevance to art, because they suggest that the common way of observing objects as distinct from ourselves, is deceptive. At some level beyond ordinary awareness, we are in dynamic empathy with all matter and in some very fundamental sense participate with it, actively and meaningfully. To account for how this is possible would require a definition of mind and matter well beyond the scope of this book. One simply has to accept the fact that the distinctness one feels in observing things is an illusion, that the universe is so organised as to ensure an interpretation and communality of all its constituents; a process which may well become intensified when the high mind is activated. I have suggested that the mind is in fact an aspect of the continuum organised by the brain, and that the high mind, that most involved in the creative process, and the intuition that goes with it, is the most closely dependent on the continuum. One can thus just manage to sense how this participation of observer and object comes about, for the continuum is all sustaining.

Until very recently these theories could be treated as speculation, but in 1978 experimental evidence was found to support the idea of an observer having direct influence on physical events at subatomic levels.[2] Certain particles do not 'know' which way to go, until in fact they are actually observed. Clearly, such evidence, if confirmed, is going to demand a complete revaluation of the meaning of time, space, matter and the human presence in the scheme of things. This is of such vital significance that the effort necessary to come to terms with this evidence will be totally justified.

Einstein never really reconciled himself to the evidence in atomic physics, and in quantum theory, that nature was fundamentally beyond the grasp of intellect. To him, the evident orderliness of things implied precision, a survival of the old 'geometric deism'. If this was true, Einstein argued, it should follow that when two protons are brought together to form what is known as a singlet state, and subsequently allowed to separate, the properties of each proton should be predictable before they are separated. In 1935 with the help of two other physicists Rosen and Podolsky, Einstein suggested the kind of experimental set up that could settle the question. The two protons would be monitored before they were brought together, and the angular momentum of their spin—a characteristic quality of all nuclear particles—ascertained. It should then have been possible to show that these properties, opposite in a singlet state, would be preserved while they were together and maintained in their eventual separation. Only quite recently has the degree of experimental control reached the point where this experiment could be carried out. It has been found that Einstein's hunch that nature was fundamentally determinate and unambiguous was wrong, for it was evident in the experiment that while they existed in the singlet state, the spin of the protons was not fixed. This feature was only fixed as the experimental observer made his observation. This does not imply that the observer determines the spin, in the mechanistic way that a billiard player determines the spin put on a ball; the situation is incomparably more complicated. The only feasible account possible is to suppose that the observer's mind is an aspect of the subatomic events which control such properties as spin, and that mind and proton are intimately interacting entities, a theory which demands a completely revolutionary viewing of reality.

Given the long antecedents of such ideas in physics and cosmology, their relevance to the arts needs no further confirmation. In ordinary language, the mysterious element in artistic expression and appreciation which artists and art-lovers have always felt, and which seemed completely out of place in an exclusively materialistic universe, is in the process of being reinstated in the dawn of meta-science. Of all the activities of the mind, the processes of art are among the most important.

The essence of a work of art, whether human or natural, cannot be reached through intellectual analysis; rather it must be approached with a sense of wonder and awe; a state of empathy and participation must be sought. It is only when this is achieved, in whatever circumstances, that a peak experience is obtained. It needs to be emphasised, in this context, that human beings need to be recognisable as nature's highest art expression; if this becomes impossible, something is very wrong with the world.

The rationalist view of art as no more than an ordinary phenomenon, accounts for its impoverishment and the fact that the majority of people, even those with a leaning towards the arts, are not prepared to make the effort necessary to break the common bounds and reach out for the experience that appreciation of high art can offer. The social role of the artist, even if it is achieved through a worldly sponsor, is not mundane, but transcendental. But in a culture which provides no accepted meaning to existence, only the inspired can fulfil this role. Great art has always flourished when the transcendental reference was strong, as it was in the Gothic world, and during the Renaissance, and as it continued to be well into modern times. Unfortunately the materialistic stranglehold of the present often forces the creative artist to become an outsider, and thus unable to achieve his proper value to society.

This cultural crippling is nowhere better seen than in the negligent education of creative people. Taking the visual arts as the most evident manifestation of this diminishment, the art schools can be seen, not as centres for producing culturally significant and integrated individuals —as the great artists of the Renaissance undoubtedly were—but on the contrary, as taking in those most incapable of meeting the demands of education in a competitive industrial society. Because modern education induces an emotional withering, the art school is likely to attract the more sensitive members of society, while at the same time, because the curriculum is so barren, the system has become the refuge of those least able to benefit from or contribute to their cultural heritage. The fault can be traced to industrial civilisation's lack of a philosophy of art, ethics or religion; in it there is no reconciliation of art and science. For what, then, do art schools exist? It is a question which many people called on to vote money for their maintenance have asked. The answer can only be found in the deeper levels of social psychology. There, presumably, lingers on the genetic motivation to art, combined with the more expedient measure of isolating the cripples and misfits of society into the art-school as asylum. For the teaching of crafts, the technical colleges, suitably extended would be more appropriate. Meanwhile, the genuinely gifted usually have to jettison much of the clutter acquired in art school before true creativity can even begin.

If it is true that art, like all human activity, has a transcendental replication in the continuum, then the artist should be seen as the means of interrelating the two worlds. As the antennae of the surreal world, projecting into the midst of ordinary existence, the artist's role is to re-emphasise interdependence through revelation, in such a way and with such power that the revelatory message cannot be denied and the ordinariness of living can, at least temporarily, be transfigured by the lights of surreality.

Were it not for the smothering power of materialistic prejudice, at its very worst at the present period in human history, it would be quite evident, when contemplating any work of art with sufficient empathy and sensitivity, that it referred to a completely different dimension in living. When these are great and inspired, they bring a totally different order to every common object, every face and every natural form. Viewed in this light, art experience acquires a truly staggering power over life, and a visit to a museum or contemplation of an appropriate scene in nature, can at best have something of the life-transforming power provided in earlier cultures by the sacred grove and the tabernacle.

Whereas the people of earlier civilisations readily accepted the revelatory power of art, in modern times long materialistic conditioning demands proof and evidence. Unfortunately there are no instruments at

A work of art refers to a completely different dimension . . . and brings a totally different order to every common object.

present available for tuning into the transcendental resources of art, we have to rely on the artist and the work of art. On the other hand it has been found, experimentally, that images can be transmitted with astounding success and irrespective of time and distance, by telepathic means, a subject that has fascinated the biologist Alister Hardy and others.[3] Science recurrently denies all evidence of telepathy but to those with an open mind and no axe to grind, the evidence of its existence and of related paranormal phenomena cannot be denied.

The existence of telepathy further demonstrates the theme of this book, that the universe is organised in parallel worlds, the one in space and time, the other transcendentally. Besides the essential function of high art, that of revealing the surreal either in common appearances—realism—or in more symbolic, abstract ways, the reciprocating model of reality can account for otherwise inexplicable phenomena in the arts. Inspiration, for instance, can be the result not only of participation in surreality, but of a functional overlap between two individual minds—the telepathic occasion. This particularly involves mind-groups, of the kind speculated upon by Hereward Carrington[4] in order to explain certain psychic-phenomena, which can originate from otherwise fragmented minds, long after the individuals concerned have ceased to exist. In the course of artistic creation one is often aware of such visitations, convincing and compelling. This can pose a problem for the individual artist who tunes into a transcendental source of inspiration, for he must always be wary of the possibility of parasitisation by such mind-groups and influences.

Many students show evidence of such periodical possession in their work, as they become fascinated by some master, dead or alive. A striking case is that of the otherwise mediocre painter Van Meegeren who became truly possessed by Vermeer. Critics and art historians never forgave him for making fools of them. One of his copies was acclaimed by them as the greatest Vermeer ever produced. Eventually they turned upon him, contending that all his copies were bad. Admittedly, the later paintings, done in order to prove his case in court, when he was sick and weary, are poor. But even the faker is an artist, and the forces involved can be powerful enough to 'take him over' producing inspired work.

This kind of experience is particularly well known to writers. Sometimes the influences are so strong that they have been aware of temporary possession. The very medium—rendering ideas into concrete form through words and phrases—seems to make them vulnerable to this kind of psychic parasitism. In the visual arts this generally happens only when a painter, sculptor or film-maker becomes over preoccupied with the work of another artist.

The magnetic power of the visual image has a wide application. Many who have become fascinated by particular interests such as history or archaeology, can attest to the occasional powerful invasion of feeling and vision. Such intimations can have enormous practical repercussions, guiding enquiry and research along the most fruitful lines that are inspiring and emotionally rewarding. To the passionately involved, no aesthetically-loaded subject can be dull when it has such transcendental connections. In every field the greatest contributions have come from those who were most passionately and psychically involved; the rewards have never come to the equivocal or superficial observer. It is fortunate that the human past has left such a rich harvest of arts, the foci of a possible recovery of lost feelings and moods which offer the chance of experiencing other worlds and ages in a genuine sense, not merely as imagination or illusion.

If the human phenomenon is universal and has many points in common wherever it occurs, we can be certain that space (and science-fiction, at its best and most inspired), may be something more than a frolic of the imagination. If the law of aesthetic validity applies—that what is beautiful is true—then as the writer pursues his craft intellectually, he can tune into extant or pre-existing space and science-fiction cues. This seems to be confirmed by the number of times that the inventions of science-fiction writers are later confirmed by science.

It follows that it should be possible to draw on cosmic art forms that may be alien to and different from those of earth. Could it not be that the strange images which periodically erupt from equally strange people—the paintings of Redon and Max Ernst, for example, and many others—are truly visionary in the sense that they are entirely different from anything on earth?

Great art, according to the revelatory definition adopted in this book, has only occurred in Western civilisation under direct religious patronage, or in the security which the religious view provided, a situation which persisted well into the nineteenth century when the new technological age came into being, and nature the primordial fount of all art, was assaulted. The reaction that followed resulted in the symbolic accentuation of Impressionism and Expressionism. Deeply, instinctively one might say, these artists knew that life and beauty had meaning, and the more threatened these became, the more they extolled them.

The violent protest against the new directions in painting indicates to what extent they ran contrary to the cultural current of technological, science-oriented materialism, supported on every front, by merchants as well as revolutionary politicians and by Church and State. Western culture has always been suspicious of art as a potential threat to its full exploitation of the materialistic faith. This was a suspicion shared by the Church. The monotheism of the semitic background has always been extremely suspicious of the graven image. At one time iconoclast movements in Christianity threatened to block out the visual arts, painting in particular, as it has done in much of the Mohammedan world.

This suspicion goes back to the ancient Greeks. Plato excluded the arts from his ideal republic, probably because the arts in his time, like the arts today, were mostly ribald and dionysian. This was certainly the case with sculpture, the once-austere marbles being repainted with gaudy colours more befitting a modern Pop festival. Painting was probably much the same, if one can judge from the frolics of pottery decoration, while popular music was used for venting the aroused subconscious in rhythm and movement, easily developing into the sensuous and the voluptuous. Such dionysian trends in the popular arts can easily render all art suspect to those who have sensed the true seriousness of existence, as Plato and the Church fathers did.

There are many examples in the art exhibitions and music festivals of the Western world today that demonstrate the difficulty of drawing the line between legitimate titillation and sensuality, and an overt indulgence in pornography or violence. If there were no genetic basis to the arts, any expression would be legitimate, so long as there were people able to express it, and enjoy it. But if there is such a basis, as I believe, then there is a very great difference between the high and the low, between the genuine and the spurious; between verve and violence; for the aesthetic sensitivities have come into being, in the course of humanisation, in order to surmount the animal precedent. Admittedly, the world being what it is, a pure, high art is often out of reach, and much art is therefore likely to take the form of humanly reclaiming the dionysian intrusians from an aroused subconscious. This is fine and necessary, but a point is reached, especially in times of relaxation and debauchery, when this process of reclaim is overrun, whereupon the term art is no longer applicable.

The combined repressive and sustaining influence of religion on the arts of the West has, on the whole, resulted in a credit balance, the periods of destructive repression being outweighed by those of glorious creativity. The greatest output coincided with the waning of the Church's hold and the rising libertarianism of the age. The most splendid realist painting and sculpture of all time, the greatest poetry and drama and by far the greatest music, is to be found in Europe from the rise of the Renaissance to the end of the nineteenth century. No one experiencing this fantastic art can fail to sense that it is in direct contrast to the increasingly brutal realities of existence. It could not last, for as the brutalities increased, in an age of soaring violence and revolution, so the sustaining vision of the human presence was increasingly challenged. It could but be a matter of time for the evil brew to diffuse out to the masses, so bringing about a universal dejection and, for artists, the outraging of their sensitivities.

It would be unfair to brand all the productions of our times as bankrupt and devoid of revelatory meaning. There have been unpredictable spurts of great revelatory vigour, particularly in the post-war American contribution to painting and writing. But in general, the moment is one of decline, evasions, lack of verve and vision, which takes many insidious forms, pseudo-abstraction, tepid realism, the crude, the vulgar, the violent and the pathological. The only kind of art expression that can stand up to the futilities of *Jesus Christ Super Star* is probably not to be found in the visual—one of the most easily corruptible channels of revelation, today cluttered possibly beyond redemption,—but in literature, in works like *Waiting for Godot* which, as the title suggests, touches on the desperate and probably hopeless waiting for an absconded deity, which even some theologians have found to be dead.[5]

The tragedy is that art and ethics, religion, sensitivity, goodness and greatness—not necessarily morality and theology—have been so closely programmed in the humanisation of the hominid, that none can exist without the others. One has to realise that creativity in itself is not a virtue. There is plentiful evidence of malevolent creativity in nature, and in human history. Creativity is only significant to the extent that it contributes to the pilgrimage of creation, from the continuum, through matter, and beyond matter, a pilgrimage in which the human being shares fully and most meaningfully. What does not so participate is either in limbo, like the snake or shark, or is against the great work of nature, and therefore necessarily against the human condition. This is a law which can be profitably applied to the arts. The folly and futility of the present situation in the arts is that almost every one, including the creative artist, has finally succumbed to meaninglessness.

For most people, from the primitive to the sophisticated, a high appealing revelatory art is part and parcel of existence. It is the materialistic bent of this particular civilisation which prevents a wide sharing of such art today. That this obstacle tends to follow class lines derives from the fact that certain sections of the population, in all industrial societies, have been more crippled by the materialistic onslaught than others. In the earlier phases of the industrial revolution, the struggle for existence in a rapaciously exploitative society left little or no opportunity for any artistic interest among the unprivileged. Hostility to art, which was seen as an activity with no relationship to basic breadwinning, is manifest. But the rising industrial classes were equally hostile to art, for opposite reasons—they were too preoccupied with the acquisition of wealth and worldly power. Art appreciation was therefore relegated to what survived of the former privileged classes. It is to them that we owe almost all the collections of great masters available to the public today. It took several generations for the new moneyed classes to develop a concern for the arts, and it still remains a minority interest, except in the United States, where the sheer mass of wealth produced a clamour for balancing interests. Art has always been a visible means of atoning for the hubris of power and wealth.

The selection of artworks for these robber barons of the new age was mostly left to connoisseurs, dealers with considerable refinement and culture, now alas a lost race, overtaken by quite a different kind of dealer-bandit, operating at a high financial level, with little or no concern for lasting worth or revelation, but rather with market creation and promotion. Common psychological traits can often be found in this type of person, apart from financial expertise and acumen, a certain arrogance and superficiality and, at deeper levels, a contempt for or envy of the creative person. One finds such people at times openly admitting that it is not so much any intrinsic worth in art or artist which matters but the investment value of the purchased object.

CHAPTER ELEVEN

ART AND EROS

Apart from breathing and eating, sex is the most important activity of all creatures, so much so that one is entitled to assume that in its motivating drive there is some ingredient of momentous cosmic importance. If the humanised mind is the indispensable agent of nature's continuity beyond space and time, then an innately programmed evolution, in a unified and unifying Universe, must necessarily include very special provisions in human sexuality. Its unique feature, as we have seen, is in the complete transformation of the sexual drive from its animal precedents into an intense emotionalised bonding to meet the prolonged nurturing needed by human infants. The gratification nature has provided in the performance of this service is the peak experience.

The extent to which changes have taken place in nature to bring about the reversal of ancient and successful sexual opportunism is demonstrated by the transition from the mammalian stage to the human. The internalisation of the egg, which was the mammalian achievement, was the first great step towards the large brain, requiring the constancy of a high body temperature and nutrition which only such a device could provide. The development of the placenta was closely connected to the emergence of mother-love and the emotional bonding of mother and child. Initially the mammalian male was left out of this bonding; all that was required of him was to be available as the supplier of sperm when the female signalled, by pheromones and special postures, that she had reached the crucial stage of the oestral cycle.

For the humanisation process it was necessary to reverse the ancient independence of the male and to develop in him the emotional ties of sexual love, compassion and altruism. Social bonding followed a diffusion of the same emotionalised predisposition, shorn of its sexual connection. This makes the socialisation of the human species quite different from the reflex conditioning of all other animals, except birds, in whom it is also emotionalised.

Evidence that the course of humanisation through natural selection has been successful is nowhere clearer than in the strength of this emotional bonding. Had this not been the case the humanising predisposition which, at its best, can lead to profound human love, self-sacrifice and compassion, would not have been possible. Inconstancy to the human ideal follows from external pressures not to any failure on the part of nature. It follows that the emotionalising process in general is only likely to be fully successful in humanising circumstances.

The fact that existential influences have become so paramount, makes it extremely difficult to rescue the underlying genetic patterning, the basics of human sexual activity. One can be certain that this is pre-eminently psychological, a subject that has been most effectively explored by Jung. Other interpretations of this subject, such as the Freudian, have relied on animalistic analogies, in accord with the general cultural reductive approaches to the human phenomenon. Jung alone has worked out specifically human concepts, based on his dream studies, in which the high, aesthetic features have been particularly important. By contrast, other schools of reductive psychology have been barely aware of the fundamental relevance of the aesthetic process in the function of the mind.

As one might expect Jung has been accused by the reductionists of being unscientific, although the classical ideal of reductionism gets nowhere at all in dealing with the world of man. To gain an understanding of Jung's theories, it is useful to trace the origins of sexuality in its primordial division of male and female. Long before this became an emotional or spiritual matter, it was simply physiological and typical of nature's way of dividing effort for greater diversity. Another example of this natural principle is found in the original separate evolution of the organelles—the mitochondria, the chloroplasts and the cilia—which originated as separate organisms and only later assembled into the cells of plants and animals.

Sexual reunion is primitively achieved through copulation. Through the evolutionary process—and especially in the development of the mind and emotions—this act of reunion was raised to a higher level. The sexual principles of male and female within each individual were emotionalised, so that *reunion and fulfilment could be accomplished by one individual in the act of union with another.*

This quite remarkable device, which provided the possibility of an ecstatic peak experience in the fulfilment of sexual love was already developing as a characteristic in mammals. All the males in this group parallel the female structure. They possess rudimentary nipples which are symbolic of the maternal love fundamental to the mammalian way of life. Every mammalian male inherits this feature from his mother, in the tiny X chromosome in every cell. All females have two X chromosomes; the male has one X, together with a specifically male Y chromosome. Here is the proof—made visible by the microscope—of nature's achievement in creating dual sexuality in the individual, quite apart from its particular manifested gender. This bisexuality is absolutely vital to the ultimate reunion of opposites in the process of life fulfilment.

The effect of this bisexuality in mammals was apparent in their behaviour long before humanisation. It can be seen, for example, when a dog in a fight rolls on to its back and displays its vestigial nipples to its opponent. The extraordinary effect of this primordial symbol of mother-love, is to stop the fight immediately. Similarly, when primitive humans fought naked, the action was largely symbolic. The human form was revealed in all its vulnerability, and killing consequently took place less often than at the present time, when aggression is expressed from behind masks and protective clothing.

Thus the development of the mammalian stage was indispensable to eventual humanisation. But sex requires a partner, and some means had to be found through which this reunion of male and female within the individual could take place. Although this was biological in origin, clearly it attains a transcendent level through sexual love and thus is the peak of human existence. The nature of this fulfilment, in relation to human destiny, is effectively expressed in alchemical symbols, the most important of which is the union of the King and Queen. This occurs when 'gold' is obtained by transmutation from the 'base metals' of the psyche. The resulting elixir is regarded as the peak experience of alchemical practice.[1] When this achievement is blocked in creative people, they are driven to find reunion in the world outside their own psyche, that is through the art object—hence the close parallels between art, love and alchemy.

Jung called the male psychological principle the *animus* and the female, the *anima.* Although they refer particularly to the realm of the human psyche, their evolutionary biological pattern means they are still governed by hormonal and other somatic variations. In themselves these variations create the rich diversity of the human species, but, at the same time, they create ambiguity in the expression of the personality of each individual. This ambiguity is particularly apparent in the artistic temperament. The male artist frequently has a stronger than average anima and the female artist a more active animus. The creative drive in all art is instigated by the artist's inability to achieve unification in his own being. This probably stems from the biological drive toward humanisation, but it sets up contradictions in the artist's personality: he may search for the sublime, but frequently backslide; he has a desperate need for love, yet most great artists have been singularly bad lovers.

There is no escape from this situation which, paradoxically, is fortunate, for without it there would be no art. If an artist manages to solve his sexual problems or cure his neuroses, the chances are that he will no longer be an artist. Among truly great artists, both animus and anima have to be overdeveloped to the point of torment, so ensuring that the artist is condemned to the life of an outsider. It seems to be the case that the anima has little urge to express itself creatively. Perhaps this is because it is creativity itself, expressed through the supreme feminine gift of procreation, so relegating to the animus a life of tormented searching for completion.

Depending on the extent to which the artist manages to achieve symbolic unification in the execution of a work of art, he can find some fulfilment, for a while at least. But there is always this feeling of incompleteness which keeps him working as an artist. The present conditions of society are responsible for frustration in the achievement of love, so the work of art has a special function in providing an externalised arena for this symbolic consummation. It also emphasises the creative undertaking in all art appreciation.

There is such great need for fulfilment through love that its deprivation has been expressed again and again in art and religion, but the real peaks of artistic achievement can only take place in a society where love as a basic human requirement is fully recognised, not only through sex or altruism, but through the loving awareness of all other life-forms, plants and animals and nature itself.

Clearly opportunistic, self-indulgent, emotionally sterile sexual behaviour, a frequent pattern throughout human history, especially when it has been male-dominated, is not reconcilable with the above process, which on the contrary demands a humanising, profoundly involving interchange in sexual union; one which is bound to contradict the popular thesis of natural opportunism and promiscuity.

The emotional attributes of male and female are both incorporated in every human being, regardless of sex, ensuring a sexual democracy and egalitarianism indispensable to co-operative nurturing. As Jung pointed out, the male fulfils himself in sexual love—indeed in all love, all art and religion—by discovering and participating in the female attributes of the beloved, just as the woman fulfils herself through the man.

This bisexuality has been accomplished by a hormonal overlap in the course of mammalian evolution evident as we have seen, in the rudimentary nipples of the male, and the anatomical similarities of the penis and clitoris. In humanisation it has played a key role in the aesthetisation of the body in both sexes, because of the powerful involvement of the sex hormones in morphology. But the fulfilment of this 'unisexual', hermaphroditic drive transcends sexuality in a loving union. In this context, it is interesting to note the importance of the hermaphrodite symbol in many esoteric doctrines, notably in alchemy, where it refers to the non-physiological significance and power of sex.

All this is very important to the problem of art. It is the feminine psychological component in every individual which is responsible for aesthetic sensitivity and intuition, while the masculine accounts for the drive to creative expression. In evolution, the emotionalisation of the female long preceded that of the male, to the extent that the emergence of the high mind and the peak experience, can be justly designated feminine. By comparison, the masculine drive towards artistic expression is a lesser achievement, requiring completion in the work of art. When one looks at it more closely, sex turns out to be the essential creative polarity in all nature. It reaches its culmination in sexual love, in the sexual influence in the arts and in all higher pursuits, passing on into the very constitution of surreality. The universal and timeless fascination felt in the work of art is that it actualises symbolically this ultimate reconciliation of the male and female, or the Yang and the Yin.

As we have seen, the motivation to art comes from the blockage of the animus, ruling out a union with the anima in the psychological interchanges of sexual love, thereby forcing the animus to create an artificial anima-situation, the art object—in terms of which a symbolic union in the act of high participation, can at least temporarily take place. In terms of such a transposed basis, one must expect to find various anomalies of motivation and satisfaction in the sexual involvement in the arts. A similar phenomenon can be seen in mysticism, which is essentially internalised, while in the creative person the process tends to be externalised, not only in reference to the work of art, but to living. But the most characteristic feature of this displacement is an oscillation between abandonment and containment in the lives of creative people, the most effective creative output occurs in the phases of containment.

The bisexual composition of every human being, the dependence of sensitivity in all the arts on the 'feminine' component and the urge to create on the 'masculine', provides a clue to a notable feature of the art world—its higher than average proportion of homosexuals. How much higher no one knows. According to different surveys the probable rate in the general male population is between six and twelve per cent, and it is likely that among artists it is at least double this, may be as high as thirty or forty per cent, which warrants serious investigation.

The problem is immensely complicated, and is made the more so since even the definition of the description *homosexual* is open to different interpretations. Some psychologists suggest that all friendship, altruism and compassion between members of the same sex have homosexual features. This stretching of the term leads to an absurd confusion and ends by including every genuinely human person, including Jesus Christ. I shall therefore confine the use of the term to describe a relationship in which some form of physical intercourse takes place between two members of the same sex.

In the present wave of emancipation from a past where condemnation and persecution drove them underground, there is an understandable tendency, often promoted by homosexuals, to discover the trait in almost every famous historical or contemporary figure. Michel Angelo, for example, is a favourite candidate. Most of these cases, when subjected to careful consideration of the evidence, turn out to be no more than the partners in a close friendship, that is to say the psychological homosexual with which we are not concerned. However there is no doubt about the active homosexuality of many well-known figures in the world of art today. One of the most striking and intriguing features of this phenomenon is that its incidence varies greatly throughout history and without relevance to public approval or censure. Indeed approval follows automatically when the incidence passes beyond a certain threshold.

It is easy to see how a shift in the dialectic between the masculine and the feminine—whatever may be the visible sex of an individual—will predispose the subject to a more affective psychological homosexuality. Such a shift is likely to make active homosexuality easier, for humans have been programmed by nature to blend the emotional with the physical and the physiological. Whether or not an individual becomes an active homosexual will then largely depend on the psychosocial environment. In the arts, where sensitivity is at a premium, a rise in the rate of active homosexuality is therefore to be expected. This cannot, however, account for the rise of homosexuality in general at a particular period or in a particular society.

It is well known that smothering a male child with mother love predisposes it towards homosexuality—the explanation is that the feminine component in the child is over accentuated and results in an intensified association of the female with pure non-sexual love that consequently rejects the usual antics and approaches of heterosexual love. It is surely revealing that such exaggerated mother love is much more frequent in societies in which women are unable to have a compassionate relationship with men, as is usually the case in stern anti-feminist patriarchal societies.

Another explanation of the current increase in homosexuality is the growing aversion of women, in a libidinal social phase, to breast feeding and child-nurture in general. The breast image, fixed on earliest infancy, undoubtedly produces strong heterosexual conditioning. The buttock preoccupations of sodomy being a deviation caused by denial of the breast in infancy.

The power of the social environment to induce a homosexual predisposition depends on the conditioning of the cortex (see Chapter 2). If the normal sexual urge is diverted or blocked, for whatever reason, other outlets will be sought. In successful homosexual unions the adaptation can be remarkably effective, but there will always be some psychological deprivations, chief among them the frustrating of the powerful breeding motivation. Greater understanding of the fundamental and organic causes of homosexuality does much to explain the present compassionate attitude to the problem, but this greater tolerance should not be allowed to obscure the impact of the phenomena on society in general, and on such an important sphere as the arts, in particular.

Most homosexuals in the arts are exceptionally sensitive, perceptive and agreeable people, displaying characteristics of an essentially feminine kind. They are usually gentle, considerate and helpful; often very receptive and easily influenced. In their work they display exquisite taste and sensitivity to colour and tonal delicacies—but they lack the dynamic inspiration of real art. For an assertive, forceful art form depends upon the male component. There are some few really successful women painters and musicians, but they are the exception rather than the rule, and however distasteful such a view may be to modern women, it will not be changed, for it is gene dependent. It follows, therefore, that with a rise in the incidence of homosexuality in a particular society, there will be an increase in sensitivity towards the arts and in the amount of artworks produced and an accompanying decrease in the power and virility of the work. Exceptionally gifted homosexuals may produce great art, but the majority will tend to create agreeable but vapid work, which the frequent flourish cannot conceal. Indeed this is so typical a ploy that homosexual art can usually be quite easily recognised.

The exceptionally gifted homosexual artist probably owes his power to a combined accentuation of the feminine and masculine principles. Because in nature one or the other is geared to dominate (if this were not the case we would all be unisexual) this situation sets up a considerable psychological tension. These individuals, perhaps fortunately, are rare, and usually acutely neurotic and often violently disturbed. So much so that it seems likely that they have some sort of chromosomal anomaly. The brutal and assertive power of their imagery betrays a streak of disturbing violence which prevents it from being genuinely inspiring and peak-inducing. Possibly the more contained homosexual temperament has a great contribution to make to the arts, but overt homosexuality is undoubtedly a negative influence both to the concept of art and its social relevance.

CHAPTER TWELVE

THE EVALUATION OF ART

Is it possible to judge a work of art through intellectual study of the subject? Creative people themselves have long answered this question with an emphatic 'no'. The more assertive the creative drive in an artist the greater is his contempt for the critic likely to be. This reaction is usually put down to fear of criticism or envy or false pride, for most people assume that if art is a valid, genetically based activity, indispensable to human existence, then the art process should be capable of being studied and appraised.

But some of the features of this process, notably its reliance on intuition, suggest that art is created in a radically different state of mind than that employed in ordinary understanding. As we have seen science itself is in the process of a revolutionary reappraisal of the role of the observer in the study of natural phenomena, and the idea that observers are quite distinct and separate from the objects observed may well be an illusion. The actual creation of a work of art is usually accompanied by anxiety and tension; although some satisfaction comes with its successful development, the full enjoyment is necessarily post-creative, at which stage the creator's relationship with his work becomes no different from that of any other appreciative observer. But for the observer, whether artist or art-lover, achieving the peak experience through contemplation of the work, has nothing at all to do with the analytical or intellectualised understanding usually adopted by the professional art critic. It is therefore true to say that the judgements made by such people are generally irrelevant, but that the opportunity to experience a work of art is open to those who contemplate it in search of revelation, through coming to terms with the symbolic order.

Some of the main qualities of this order have already been mentioned, notably integration or wholeness, its dependence on intuition, the importance of technique for seizing and communicating the symbolic. These involve tangible aspects that it should be possible to appraise, even if only in a statistical sense, which is the scientific way of fixing the unfixable. But this raises enormous difficulties as can be seen in the history of the Gestalt school of psychology. When the original testament was announced by Koehler, Koffka and Wertheimer—that the whole possesses qualities which cannot be derived from the parts—a new holistic approach to psychology was implied. But in trying to make the holistic reasonable and scientifically acceptable Gestalt psychologists resorted to narrow mechanistic experiments and concepts which were in fact incompatible with the holistic properties of life and mind. The fact is that this property, like all the important, mind-connected properties of existence, is not basically referable to space–time events, but to the continuum, so that any attempt to give it a space–time meaning is contradictory. This applies equally to the symbolic and the intuitive in art.

The only way to attempt art appraisal is to look at it as

the genuine nature lover looks at wildlife in its complex natural environments; he does not catch the animals, uproot the plants or stuff the birds; nor should the art critic seek to reduce the painting or other work of art, by a scrutiny of its parts; rather should he seek to absorb its essence, to the best of his ability, and hope that by doing so he may become one with the object he is contemplating.

In literature, while the mechanism of language is minutely studied, there is a general respect for form and for other intangibles which resist reduction. One can adduce reasonable arguments for what is good and bad, but the ultimate criterion remains a matter of feeling, of intuition. This is also true of poetry and music. The learnable and teachable aspects are actually found to aid intuition; catastrophe comes only when teachers arrogantly assume that it is only the learned techniques that matter. It is an assumption all too easily accepted in our intellectually biased culture.

But even when instruction is sensitively carried out, it is evident that what can be eventually learned or taught about the arts is subject to convention. What may seem enduring can change, as in the move from tonal to atonal music, from realism to abstract in the visual arts. Discounting the popular assumption that such changes are arbitrary and subject to fashion (the extremely complex causes are barely understood, but certainly involve both the profound psyche and society) one must see in this process an inbuilt challenge to the fixity and order that the intellect craves for. Although traditionalism in the arts may be a strong factor in the short term, over the whole period of human history and the lives of civilisations, the arts have to reflect the dynamism of the high mind and of its continuum involvement, which defies the fixities of space and time. Nonetheless, each art has its limits of variation, like any living organism. Reptiles learnt to fly, fishes to leap and crawl and a few mammals have returned to the oceans, but humans simply cannot breathe the oxygen in water. In the case of language, Chomsky has concluded that there are genetically set limits, in spite of the fact that there are thousands of languages and dialects.[1]

In painting, the limits have generally been thought to be narrow, as the stubborn objection to the abstract indicates. But here also, the narrowness is largely conventional. The modern art movement has gone successfully far beyond such restrictive concepts, so much so that some may feel there are no restrictions. And yet there must be a genetic barrier beyond which a visual situation is no longer art, and it should be possible to find out something about this.

Those who overstress the importance of intellectual understanding should meditate on the proposition that computers have outstripped the reasoning mind, which is itself analogous to a computer. If the creation of a work of art had to depend on reasoned decisions the simplest image would need years of deliberation at every step. To calculate the proper moves, taking into account all the existing factors, would strain even the most advanced computer. And no computer is available or likely to be available, which can execute that arch requirement of all art, integration. But intuition can achieve all this in the blink of an eye and with a degree of certitude quite closed to the fumbling intellect. Evidently while the peripheral intellectually approaching aspects should not be ignored, any form of art appraisal must in the end depend on intuition.

The key property of intuition is its immediacy—its decisions and choices can be virtually instantaneous—and the unswerving certainty it provides. Although technique in all the arts tends to be dithering, stumbling and groping, what is eventually selected by intuition is absolutely convincing, and very rarely found subsequently to be faulty. One can in fact look upon technique as no more than the means of realising the intuitive in an orderly way consistent with an orderly mind and an orderly world. If these criteria are not respected, the intuition is wrong.

Intuition is perhaps best explained by regarding it as a continuum quality exploited by brain and mind, just as the best available explanation of the mind is that it is a special organisation and exploitation of the continuum by the brain. The rapidity with which intuition works come from the continuum's transcendence of time and space. As for the spontaneity and conviction that intuition carries, these also come from the unlimited resources of surreality, and the immediacy of 'connections' between surreality and the individual mind. The reasoning intellect, on the other hand, is a mechanism and like all machines it takes time to function.

Today words like beauty and purity are simply not included in the vocabulary of the art critic. Although art, or what survives of it, can become impure in violent, anxious, emotionally corrupt circumstances, high art, inspired from surreality is distinguishable by its purity of feeling, even of technique. Impure colours, and forms are felt to be intolerable.

The importance ascribed to art criticism in some quarters is a survival of the rational approach to the arts of the late Renaissance, when the vision and verve of that remarkable age had already waned. It is an aspect of the materialistic society that it prefers to reduce art to an analytical function. Recently the former ideal of independent criticism has given way to a much worse state of affairs. While there are of course critics who are genuine lovers of art, anxious to promote the interests of artists, there are others whose job it is to advise big business or nationalised industries on what they should purchase with a view to long term benefit. Is there then no function that the proper study of art, as distinct from its making and appreciation, can play?

In the past and in other societies, from the most primitive to the most sophisticated, the significance and value of art was found in its metaphysical references to existence. Not only art but every item of existence was accorded some sort of place in this chain of being. Art, however, held a supreme position; it was felt universally to be sacred, hallowed, to refer to another world. As the other world with which people have most often been in contact has been the world of the aroused subconscious and its metaphysical extensions, it is such a world that the arts have mostly revealed. If there were guides they would have been the witch doctor or priest, for realism in art barely existed.

But there was little need for guides. The human mind, programmed to respond to the revelation of invisible worlds, had no difficulty in sensing the content of such art, whether in imageries, music, myth and pageantry or dance. The simplest utterances of bard or poet acquired a potent revelatory significance. 'Good' or 'bad' art did not come into it. Any object made with appropriate feeling, by anyone, was readily accepted as the vehicle of revelation, as it is still among many peoples. So avid is the mind for tokens of revelation that it will even accept the crude and fumbled, bestowing awe and reverence upon objects which the uninvolved human might deem repulsive.

The roles of critic, collector and dealer, only arose with the sophistications of civilisation. Among more simple peoples art objects, like musical instruments, are usually communally owned. Art as we know it, comes with leisure and wealth and the divisions of civilised society. This is not to disparage such art, for one can argue that civilisation is a natural and inevitable emergence from more primitive cultural stages, and the different kinds of art that arise within it can therefore be seen as the necessary accompaniments of social evolution. Those who see nothing but evil in civilisation would contest this, but they are a small minority, and almost certainly misguided.

Those who have acquired power have almost always surrounded themselves with works of art. Although this art often served to enhance and advertise the wealth and power of court or class, it also provided pleasure and uplift. Art dealers probably arose long before the age of criticism, which can be fairly certainly dated, in Europe, to the time of the Renaissance.

With the deeply emotional and essentially religious reliance on the reasonableness of the universe, which was brought about by the Renaissance, art became a criticisable commodity, dealing with visible, experienced reality. If the transcendental and metaphysical were encountered they were clothed in the aesthetic delights of appearance. The technique which was evolved for such an art, elaborate and requiring much apprenticeship, could be evaluated by experts, in musical notations, in language as a vehicle of thought, in mathematical proportions, in perspective and other attributes of the visible world. The manner in which stone was chiselled or paint applied could be discussed, and the content—harmony melody, rhyme or the subject of a painting or sculpture, were valid areas of discussion. Using those limited criteria it was not difficult to separate the good from the mediocre.

This assumption—that art deals with life as it is experienced by ordinary people—persisted with little opposition until well into the nineteenth century, which suggests that it is in accord with very strong cultural attitudes. Indeed, it is still very active today. Many people still feel that any kind of art that ignores the visible and knowable, is surreptitiously fooling them, although it has become less fashionable to say so.

Western civilisation has been preoccupied with materialism from its origins, and has become increasingly so with the passage of time. The rise of science provided the finishing touches to a very ancient world-view, but there have always been those who protested against this view. There are doubts in Michel Angelo and in many others, doubts which increased and were expressed with the passage of time; but the belief that the business of art was to deal with tangible reality laid the foundations of an analytical aesthetics, criticism and art history which are fundamentally contradicted by the majority of those involved in the arts today, particularly among the more creative.

However that may be, the truth is that the most indispensable ingredient in any art is the symbolic core which cannot be defined or analysed. Nevertheless the vast supporting structure and technique that goes into every kind of art work, should be able to stand fair examination and study and, to this extent, art criticism remains a feasible activity.

With practice and experience it is quite a simple matter to pick out a painting, a piece of writing or a musical composition which lacks form and the critic may make use of innumerable rational assessments—the quality of the technique, the correctness of the grammar and so on—but the actual quality of wholeness remains intuitive. This is also true for all those other attributes which may be discussed, but can only be intuitively judged—brushwork, good drawing, effective line, harmonious tones and so on. No computer could ever be programmed to judge a particular painting, for the moment one attempts to categorise these symbolic qualities one realises how inherently elusive they are.

The human mind appears to be programmed in such a way that what *is* rationally ascertainable in a work of art must be sought out first, and this rule cannot be ignored. Although the realm of reason is not exclusive, there is an obvious connection between the reasonable and the transcendental. Physical science has made this quite clear. Although energy is a transcendental quality the forms it takes, in the organisation of atom and molecules, produces material properties, subservient to mechanical laws. It is truly amazing how far one can penetrate, beyond ordinary appearances, to the functional core of reality. That dictum of the medieval scholar, William of Occam—that a simple explanation should always have precedence over a more complicated one—can be modified to show that although ultimate reality is beyond the grasp of reason and open only to intuition, all that is knowable on any subject should be thoroughly explored before handing over to an intuitive judgement. As the universe is a unity, in spite of its apparent split between the reasonable and whatever lies beyond reason, such an approach ensures that intuition will be on target. Intuition may be infallible in a state of high inspiration, but in a distracting world, wherein the mind is all too often confused, reason and learning can be stabilisers.

What often seems to happen is that those who take up these subjects come to assume that they are sufficient in themselves, that art historians can explain the entire phenomenon of art, that critics can appraise it. The danger is that such people may distrust and discount intuition. But the observations of the critic and the art historian go deeper and rest on the growing accusations of error in the world view of civilisation as a whole. A few decades ago, the evidence of such error was overlaid by massive apparent success. But today growing numbers of people believe that the official view of reality and nature, and of many other things from health and disease to progress, is seriously flawed. The desecration of the natural world, which comes from this official view is now widely evident for all to see.

CHAPTER THIRTEEN

CONFUSION AND DIRECTION

The way one views nature is likely to have a profound effect on ones attitude to all aspects of living, most of all to art. Free will is a concept that has been debated by generations of philosophers, many of them ignorant of the scientific approach. Those who defended free will were often those ardently supporting liberalism in the emancipatory movements which began in the seventeenth century, before that the subject of free will was relegated to theology, man's duty being to follow God's will. To deny free will, or to stress its limits, seemed to be a denial of man's right to be master of his own destiny, a subject fraught with passion. To this day many people, especially those with no scientific education, believe that humans are indeed very largely free to choose what they want to do and to act as they think fit. This freedom has quite recently been challenged by some geneticists, who contend that even in mental predisposition, human beings are very considerably limited and programmed by their genes; this view has strong political overtones, for it is a part of Marxist doctrine that man can mould his own destiny, in defiance of any biological conditioning.

This subject is discussed here because many people, supported by socio-political doctrine, believe that nature, and the attitude one has to nature, is of subsidiary importance. Intellectuals and political activists speak of belief in natural law as if it were a depraved aberration. Yet we are very much constrained by our biological past and by the very particular way nature has made us; and we are by no means free to choose the attitude to nature which happens to suit our sociological or other beliefs. We are in fact genetically programmed in close relationship to a particular viewing of nature. Any other viewing is likely to carry considerable survival risks.

In medicine and agriculture as in all environmentally involved activities, we are now becoming aware of the terrible price paid for a faulty viewing of nature. But in subjects less practically or scientifically connected, the realisation of offence is less evident. It is surprising how defective the scientific support in such subjects as sociology or aesthetics can be. One finds learned treatises which might just as well have been written in pre-Darwinian days, not to mention pre-DNA and quantum theory. Learning and study in such subjects is not likely to prepare the way for intuition. If intuition is used at all—and its use is usually condemned—it is likely to be faulty. This means that there is no possibility of effective art criticism from this quarter—it can only develop with a revaluation of the meaning of nature.

Such a re-evaluation is proceeding in physics and biology, the truly fundamental sciences, but the main body of scientists in these subjects are not as yet necessarily aware of the lines of such an evaluation. Science, like all human activity, has a traditionalist lobby, resistant to fundamental change. Working scientists, not concerned with original research or discovery, are probably better as traditionalists. Others are traditionalists because it pays them to be so. In the field of scientific popularisation, for example, it is the ideas of a former generation which are popular, ideas regarding the animal nature of man, natural aggressiveness, innate sexual promiscuity, ideas of 'nature red in tooth and claw' current in Darwin's time. The emergent ideas in physics and biology are much more difficult to popularise because they do not support most people's own notions of human nature or reality.

There is also among some scientists and scientific popularisers an unmistakable element of mischief. Dr Desmond Morris, of chimpanzee-painting fame, wrote a book on the biology of art which reduces the subject to animalistic analogies, which are not only misleading, but incomplete for the emotional nature of art, in the fantastic activity of birds, is barely mentioned. But the applause which this and his other books have received shows what kind of biology people want. In any social gathering one will meet a fair proportion of people who have heard of Desmond Morris, but not one who is remotely aware of Dr Thorpe's inspiring studies of bird song. The public will stubbornly favour what it finds gratifying, rather than what is true, for in spite of a general consensus of adverse criticism by reputable scientists, the popularity of writers like Morris and Ardrey continues.

For sensitivity to art to have evolved very special conditions have been necessary; so complex and so exacting are the range of environmental, bodily, neural and psychological needs that the entire evolution of nature must have been congenial to it. But nature works under great handicaps and often fails. In its failures mechanisms come into play which are the opposite of creative; this destructive face of evolution has been made use of. In the inorganic world it often takes a crude and extremely violent form. With the emergence of life the dramas of extinction and the necessity of death became inevitable as the means of eliminating the failures. There is a close analogy in the creation of a work of art; where destruction is a necessary way of eliminating the failures of intuition and the clutter of the less inspired.

Like everything in nature, this creative destruction can go wrong. There are some notable examples of it in the natural world, for example the periodical self-destruction of large numbers of animals, among them the lemmings. One must expect that this urge to destruction occurs also in the mind. Freud called it the *thanatic* urge, and rightly traced its cause to the denial of eros, which should be interpreted as love rather than merely sexual gratification. It also contributed to the process of natural selection by eliminating the psychologically unfit—in mental disintegration, not only in individual psychosis, but in mind-group sickness of whole societies illustrated in intra-specific struggle, violence and destructiveness.

The cycles of social revolution and psychosis are lethal to all the arts, as we see from a study of the Cromwellian outrage, the inhumanities of the French revolution, and the destruction of Monte Casino in the last war. The arts cannot cause social disruption, but they can, like the lemmings, destroy themselves. This is a symptom of a culture that has become so deviant that it is in constant conflict with its own humanising roots. There is a close parallel in man's onslaught on nature, a characteristic feature of Western civilisation.

What is called conceptual art today, better termed a display than an act, is an instance of this phenomenon. Inaesthetic anti-aesthetic situations and materials are especially selected; random situations or footling objects, such as crumpled newspaper, torn maps, mud, even excrement are used. A fascination with materials has long been a feature of the modern movement, as for example in collage, but as Schwitter's 'merzbilde' show, for example, the pre-occupation was still aesthetic. But now the intention is desecration. This self-destructive art, which appeared in the early sixties, as well as 'minimal art' and 'happenings', are all a part of the same assault against the art object as the focus of high, revelatory experience. A strong thread of this runs through Art Brut and Dada; it is present in Pop which is also much more banal. But it is extremely difficult for the human being, even when no longer properly humanised, to create anything which has not some emotional content. In philosophy, for example, positivism, which aimed at purging language of every trace of emotion, soon ended up in blatant sterilities. So in the visual arts, in the beginning of these movements of desecration there is a strong intellectual flourish, which gives the appearance of revolutionary fervour. But sooner or later as the activities are taken up by genuine artists, the strategies become art, great art in the case of some Dada and Art Brut and tepid art in Pop. The fact that these activities draw a considerable response and acclaim, shows how far advanced is the social pathology, the disturbance of the individual mind. In the present wave of political extremism and violence one finds the same destructiveness working against all social order and coherence, proof of intrasocial violence as an inbuilt mechanism of elimination, in all probability gene controlled. A noticeable feature of this phenomenon is the relish of the explosion. The bang—a common name for orgasm incidentally—appears to be an ideal cathartic agency, much loved by terrorists. The Chinese have long had their forms of auto-destructive art as elaborate structures made up of crackers, a popular feature in the Chinese New Year since the discovery of gunpowder, in the twelfth century. One can predict that comparable art forms will become a feature of Western civilisation if the need for this kind of catharsis persists.

The same desecrating urge is evident in all the arts, even in music, wherein the resulting cacophony is barely believable. Yet one finds people listening to it with apparent relish, and possibly benefit. For although this is not high art it has undoubted value in relieving deep feelings of anger and hostility against life and culture, which are much better relieved than denied. There is no intrinsic harm in this so long as what is involved is not confused with real art. The lesson to be learnt is that if the arts are allowed to go beyond a certain point, as a medium for catharsis, the terrible road to total desecration opens up. One cannot subject the arts to a dictatorship of feeling or function, but at least artists, if they are to keep this designation, should be aware of what they are doing.

A couple of decades ago, I attempted to sift the significant from the less significant and the insignificant in the arts. Relatively few amendments appear to be necessary to describe the situation today, except that the deterioration in realistic imagery and realism has gone further and there is even more antagonism towards art objects.

The deterioration in realism is both technical and a matter of fading vision. The appalling clumsiness of realist techniques in painting and sculpture can no doubt be traced to the uninspired teaching of these subjects, which shows that art and its teaching are under the influence of an internal necessity. Realism can only be felt to be meaningful when it is inspired, quickened. Although today the penetrative, 'abstract' kind of imagery probably most closely accords with the sensitivity-front of the times, an inspired realism remains always feasible and important. However high the mind may soar, the reality of the world of appearances remains and the fact that this is the primal fount of the high experience can never be dismissed. The presence of uninspired realism today is therefore symptomatic of a psychological condition, the using of banal uninspired appearance as the means of blocking the heights and depths. To meet this deviant need, technique is compulsively clumsy, paint is used to produce a toothpaste-like surface and dead application, and vision becomes enmeshed in futile subject and visual banalities. The same evasion is to be found in some modern poetry. In the great age of poetry, the age of belief in man, nature and cosmos, it was the supreme means of revealing the sense of grandeur and the dramatic, almost beyond the reach of literal language. Today, with all belief gone, poetry fiddles in the petty world of daily experience and impression, lacking fire and passion.

In painting the lack of inspiration is particularly apparent in the treatment of the human face and body. The degree to which technique can be affected by the state of the mind can be seen in the extraordinary clumsiness of medieval draughtsmen and painters who worked at a time of intense mental disturbance, compared to the bodily and facial resolutions of classical Greek and later Renaissance painting. Probably portraiture and the nude can only be effectively used in the arts when the 'angelic form' can be sensed. Today the complete insensitivity of this transcendental state, and the intrusion of deforming subconscious visions, leads to a particular deadness in image and technique, with a curious but striking 'rubbing out' taking the place of the violent primitive deformation of face and body.

The eclipse of the magnificent enhancements of the naturalistic in Impressionism, and in its abstract forms in post-Impressionism, has continued until it has now reached a state where its links with nature are increasingly tenuous. Much the same situation arose in the intensely disturbed conditions of the medieval world, following the millennial psychosis. What features as nature-art in the imagery of those times appears etiolated, withered, deprived of the spark of life.

This 'rubbing out' of the human face and form is not only found in painting, but in the living use of face and body in the curious phenomenon of punk. This movement arose among art school rejects in the early seventies and manifests itself in defacement of the human person by means of luridly dyed hair and make-up, in absurd clothing and posture and adornment, combined with a stilted and often abusive vocabulary. Typical of the gesture of protest by rejection, punks mock the conventional, and even our wilted ideals of beauty and sensitivity.

But although punk aims at ugliness and thus is part of the phenomenon of anti-art, it has an evident surrealist content from which we can learn. The potent dream content in all the arts, and indeed in everyday occurrences such as advertising, indicates that the surrealist art movement possesses a metaphysical gossamer-like and kinky deviation of what we have called surreality. Surrealism probably draws its near ecstatic visions and inspirations from a fringe surreal experience. The punk is in a way living a surrealist dream, in which the human person is the art object, a genuinely creative, if at times ludicrous, reaction to an existence too drab to be tolerated. Possibly punks can achieve something of a peak experience, triggered off by their own strange selves.

Another phenomenon, which many would deny has any art connection, is the current wave of decorative graffiti in the urban sprawls of industrial countries. Initially opposed by the authorities, in the United States it has now become tolerated, even encouraged. Graffiti goes back to the Palaeolithic caves, and in the urban situation has a long history often with a strong sexual symbolism. The new graffiti refers to quite another world, one rather childish, serene and innocent, ludinal rather than libidinal. Occasionally one comes upon an image which has enormous evocative powers and which, in the right context, can no doubt elicit a particular peak experience. Lacking any professionalism, such graffiti may well spring from a strong human genetic predisposition namely the motivation to encompass and transform the environment.

If there is a human future on this planet, then the transfiguration of the man-made environment through art is the supreme challenge; it follows that if the human species is indeed on nature's line of significant-evolution, some such in-built urge must be indispensable. One finds precedents of it in many animals, even in insects, although the aesthetic ingredient is largely missing. Graffiti may be a ludicrous and pathetic expression of this stifled motivation, but it is better than accepting a dehumanised and desecrated environment.

Another manifestation of the same process is the extravagant landscape involvement of a few artists, mainly in the United States, for no other community can afford the deployment of the necessary materials on the scale involved, for example the hundreds or thousands of yards of sheeting stretched across valleys and strange totemic structures reaching to the clouds. Human beings have always enjoyed such powerful demonstrations; there is an irresistable fascination in contemplating an enormous dam or a skyscraper or a giant pylon. Because they are utilitarian, the sensitivities of pragmatically conditioned civilised man are not offended. Humans have also at times created enormous objects for no practical purpose, from Stonehenge to the bas-reliefs on the tombs of Assyrian kings, arrogance in part no doubt, but also a defiant comment on the smallness of the human scale against the mighty universe.

Apart from possible megalomania, there is also in such gigantic gestures the proclamation that the art object, the focus of all art until the last decades, is being superseded. If this were truly the aim, ie: the overall aesthetic reclaim of the environment—a task quite beyond the art object—one could express nothing but praise; but there is also the possibility that this whole tendency is part of an unrealised conspiracy against penetrative, revelatory art.

This conspiracy takes many forms; auto-destructive art is an evident example, but it is more clearly revealed in much subtler forms. I suggest, with certain reservations, that the present wide advocacy and popularity of art prints is part of this conspiracy. I find it curious that while a good photograph has at times induced a near peak experience for me I have never obtained such an experience in contemplating a print. This seems strange, for I have contemplated many aesthetically skillful and attractive prints. A possible explanation is their more or less complete lack of texture, or evocative space. Texture is extremely important as a trigger, which in good part accounts for the revelatory power of oil paint. Glass, on the other hand, epitomises evocative space, the allowance which a material or technique provides for the eye to exercise its symbolic functions in depth. This can also be provided by gradation of pigment and line and in many other ways, all of which however are usually closed to the print-making process. Even when numerous overprints are made, the trained observer still senses that only the surface is involved.

The technique involved in making the print ensures that the appeal is superficial. This superficiality is in fact the mark of all decoration, and distinguishes decoration from art. It is true that a single line, drawn with verve, can have a profound revelatory significance; so can the more calligraphic prints. Where the print fails, is when it tries to replace or serve as a substitute for, a painter's painting. But in a culture superficial in its aesthetic requirements, the lack of true depth in the print is not apprehended as a loss. The same applies to 'Op' art and Kinetic art which satisfies its observer by visual titillation, pleasurable no doubt, but worlds away from the true revelatory art.

Evidently the present confusion in the arts would benefit from some sort of guidance as to what is significant and what is not, for this could at least obviate subservience to any constraint outside the arts, while respecting the freedom essential to all genuinely humanising activities. In the past this guidance was to a great extent supplied by religious collaboration, at its best revelatory and at its worst a limiting bondage. When it was intuitively felt to be genuine such guidance was accepted, for what the artist needs is reassurance that his work is done against a background of meaning. (There are some subjects which no sensitive person would wish to touch for they would know intuitively that they were wrong.) The genuine guiding influence must be in harmony with nature: only what is felt to be humanly congenial is right, the rest must be rejected without compromise for the basis of natural ethics is a very close accord with aesthetic feeling.

Sadly, the decline of this ethical component in the arts, has been attended by the dismantling of any meaningful viewing of the human presence in nature and cosmos; literally anything goes, even the anti-human, the ugly, the foul and the prurient. The open jungle condition now prevailing in the arts has made many creative people pine for some sort of directive. This no doubt partly explains the soul-selling of so many of the less gifted to the Marxist anti-aesthetic cause. The situation is desperate, for just as the art schools provide no sustaining philosophy or belief in the arts as a vital and indispensable process, so the critic and art historian are victims of a society which has lost an inspiring, ethical belief in the significance of human existence.

The futility of criticism or any attempt at an analytical appraisal of the art process, results from the lack of a naturalistic basis to art; the failure to see, in the arts, a function related to nature and cosmos, a situation which in turn can be traced to the general cultural meaninglessness of present day existence. Non-creative people involved in the arts, like critics and art historians, psychologists and art sociologists, traders and dealers tend to protect themselves from the anguish and obliteration of a force they know to be immensely important, by forming an hermetic confederacy, self-sufficient and able to defy the emotional dismantling of a materialistic, scientific take-over.

Yet the naturalistic basis is available. Many people, particularly scientists, scoff at the idea that human art has a biological basis, but over half a century ago the eminent American biologist, Professor Jennings, made a convincing case for the genetic bases of art.[1] He postulated a consolidating aid, in mind and nature, to an appropriate socialising predisposition indispensable for the prolonged nurturing of the human young. His case has been largely ignored, although it is repeated by other eminent scientists, from time to time, for it does not tally with the official view of an insensitive human genesis.

This is the kind of evidence that should have been pounced upon as should the suggestion that there are definite genes concerned with human motivation, recently made by the American entomologist E. O. Wilson.[2] In spite of the controversy that these ideas always arouse it is now virtually certain that there are genes concerned with the sense of beauty, with the appreciation of order and harmony, even with the craving for purity. As we have seen, the process of humanisation consisted in a complete transfiguration of the brain and the integrated transformation of lower brain centres in tune with the new acquisitions of the cortex, an evolutionary feat which probably involved hundreds of very special gene adaptations. Since centres of ecstasy have been detected in the primate brain it is reasonably certain that there are also specific genes concerned with the peak experience.

These genes are not dictatorial, for that other characteristic of humanisation—the ability to side-step biological evolution and adaption by cortical conditioning—means that, if anything, the cortex has priority over human behaviour. It is in this respect that E. O. Wilson has tended to overstate a legitimate case, for while the genes are autocratic in insects, they are not so in humans. The crux of the matter is statistical. If there is a cosmic destiny working itself out through mankind, then it is certain that this must be through the genetic foundation of the human species—unless earth humans have been deviant since their origins, which does not seem to be the case. Therefore, although cortex conditioning can overrule this naturalistic foundation, the underlying genetics retain their teleological importance. If this is not the case for whatever reason, and human beings on our planets are outside the cosmic pale, then nothing in art has meaning —nothing matters.

However, although it is an act of faith to assert that human kind do have a destiny, a survey of human history from the viewpoint of the arts, indicates a very strong genetic assertion, even if for much of the time a deviant, subconscious influence has dominated existence in a disturbed planet. The solid biological core to aesthetic motivation remains. No doubt the human condition can become so deviant that this core is obscured for millennia, but given the chance to assert itself, it will do so magnificently as it must have done in the human dawn. If we take a positive stand, and assume that science, sociology, philosophy and art can help in the attainment of a more humanised existence, then these biological roots of motivation must be taken into account. As in everything else, it is what these humanising genes permit which alone can play a positive humanising role through the media of the arts. Anything else is either deviant in an interfering sense, or merely treading water while humanity wallows in its historically crippling deviations.

It follows that there is a naturalistic basis to expression in every art, and this basis alone can serve human beings, as the specifically humanised creatures they undoubtedly are. This does not mean a straight-jacketing of the arts by the naturalistic imperative; not only the genetic background is highly modifiable, but the cortical conditioning provides a virtually infinite expressiveness. Indeed, it is only the actively anti-human cortical conditioning which requires censuring. Everything else is not only valid, but necessary in the sense that evolution and existence work on the principle of maximal diversity.

CHAPTER FOURTEEN

ART IN NATURE AND MATTER

Human aesthetic sensitivities are nature-related. The peak experience derived through communion with nature is akin to the peak which can be obtained from contemplation of great art. This is as it should be, for unless nature was art in some sense, it would be impossible to account for the origin of such a singular phenomenon in the course of evolution.

Unfortunately the establishment view of nature provides no explanation as to how nature could be art; indeed, as we have seen, it leaves very little room for human art. Yet the art-making of nature is everywhere evident, in the streamlining of forms, graceful and integrated structures, colour and shape. The streamlining effect is not the automatic result of functional efficiency; nature must be inherently congenial to the aesthetic process and the dominant aesthetic appeal of nature should therefore be seen as the expression of its capacity for art. It is surprising how strong resistance is to the idea that nature is art. The late Renaissance may be in part responsible, because of its insistence on the 'individual' creative stamp of the artist. But the real blockage comes from the belief that no substance can create art without a human agent. The concept that the Universe could be self-creative has never been a part of Western thought. The dismissal of a Creator has left the Universe without any means of teleological guidance.

The origin of all art in nature is utilitarian. The way in which the utilitarian passes over into aesthetics can be traced in the evolution of human artistic sensitivity. The delicacy of correlation between the hand and eye, from which all art and craft profit, comes from the primate fruit-picking facility. Like the extraordinary sensitivity of the skin to touch and caress—other mammals have no equivalent to the touch cells in the primate, which are even more numerous in the human skin and probably originated in grooming for parasites and tit-bits in the fur. It is a humbling thought that *feeling*, which Susanne Langer rightly traces as the basis of all aesthetic experience, had such mundane origins.[1] But that is nature's opportunist way of working; every means possible is tried, every aid made use of.

A coral reef is a good example of this. No doubt the patterns and colours originated as a form of protection to startle and confuse enemies or welcome friends; but the sheer flamboyance of it is pure art. One cannot resist the anthropomorphic inference that these supremely beautiful creatures actually enjoy this exuberance, that the art of nature was never quite wasted even when it was created long before human beings were there to appreciate it. The frolics and spurts and graceful activity of these creatures seem in league with the visible art nature has bestowed upon them.

This can be easily demonstrated. The markings known as nectar guides in flowers can be removed or covered over in large part without affecting the efficiency of the insect's visits and the pollination of the flowers. In a few flowers, such as some orchids, artistic exuberance has so taken over the forms that, like the antlers of certain deer, their natural function is interfered with.

How awkward the inherent artistic expressiveness of living matter can become is demonstrated in the feats of artificial selection in, for example, the beautiful but cumbersome trailings of Japanese goldfish and in the puffed up breasts of pigeons which visibly inhibit their movements. In many cases, nature on its own has done much the same thing—making art at the expense of efficiency.

A remarkable case of sheer artistic expression is found in bird song. Undoubtedly this originated as a means of avoiding struggle by advertising territorial limits and in the breeding calls which developed over a long period of time. It had its origins in the strident noises of reptiles, but in highly evolved birds like the thrush and nightingale, true music comes into being. Each bird has its own elaborate individual repertoire that is as inventive as any human music, as Professor Thorpe shows in the following extract:

> If one records the song of a particular Black Bird daily, throughout the singing season, changes of apparently aesthetic significance are detected. First, in the early part of the reproductive period, the song may appear highly functional, but later in the season, when the functional needs have been fulfilled, the song becomes organised more closely, and in a manner so nearly resembling our own ideas of musical form that it is difficult to deny that it is musically improved. So we appear to be moving towards the type which we call 'art music', when an experience of musical scores enables us to guess what kind of change is about to happen next. This sense of form seems to fit a number of bird songs in a most remarkable way.[2]

As evolution got underway, art became more and more assertive. In the first stages of evolution beauty was ignored; indeed, the primary creatures were ugly and awkward; lumbered with an unattractiveness which has persisted to this day in a few creatures like the coelacanth and some of the reptiles. Plants were also different in the beginning. There were for instance certain aesthetic appeals in the sheer symmetry of leaf and stem but colour appeared very much later, a thousand million years and more after the first green things.

Granted that there must be innate aesthetic potentialities in matter, nature as a whole has a remarkably efficient aesthetic way of working that can only be accounted for by the playback of the continuum experience of life as art. It is only in recent years that the complicated and integrated ways of nature have come to be appreciated. In such a gigantic creative exercise as the drifting apart of continents, which coincided with the appearance of flowers and mammals, there is a breathtaking instance of the earth's creativity, together with its strong aesthetic overtones. Considering that the beauty and harmony of a landscape is very much decided by the way the land alters and moves in the course of geological time, in the rise and erosion of mountains; in the threading of rivers and the cradling of lakes, the wide-ranging power of this aesthetic overtone can be appreciated. At the time the mammals first began to emerge there appears to have been a temporary halt in this artistic progression. As a group they have little aesthetic appeal apart from a certain gracefulness of bodily form, particularly in the young.

A possible explanation is that the mammals originated in troubled geological times, encouraging competition rather than grace. During such times, the struggle for survival tended to obscure aesthetics; a fact that is evident in human history.

Perhaps the emergence of mammals and their particular

breeding patterns also contributed to the diminished importance of the aesthetic element. This trend was completely reversed, however, by the aesthetic transformation of the human form, which has been judged the most beautiful and harmonious object in nature by a long succession of realist painters. This was accomplished not only through the noble gracefulness of limb and perfect proportioning, but by the removal of body hair. Hair is a potent animal attribute, and could not have been tolerated in a creature whose emotional nature aimed at a transcendence of the animal condition. What hair was left became itself aesthetised as an adornment around the head, and in the male, around the face and chest. It is probable that the function of the remaining pubic hair was to discourage chance opportunist attempts at coitus, thus prolonging emotionalised sexual selection and love play.

The aesthetic transformation of the human form, although erotic, is the very opposite of pornographic. Pornographic publications and films demonstrate how this high appeal of the body and face can be obliterated, by exposing the body and its various parts through certain movements and postures. When the aesthetic appeal is superceded, sexual gratification, a primitive force without emotional connotations comes into play. It was more than conventional prudery that led the great painters of the nude to avoid sexually enticing postures, for through them Creation's greatest aesthetic achievement is annulled.

In the greater moments of humanisation in ancient Greece, in the Gupta civilisation of India, in the Renaissance—the beauty of the body was extolled. It is a mark of the times that today the human body has largely become an object of lust, and not of adoration. It is no coincidence that when emotionalised sexuality has been reduced to a level of self-indulgence pornography becomes associated with violence, since both share neural pathways linked to primitive reaction.

The human face and human expression in particular, reach an apogee of aesthetic transfiguration. The eyes are its main focal point, and heightened sensitivity of the lips its means of elevating animal-type coitus (mounting) to the adorative face-to-face embrace. But little attention is paid to these factors today. The beauty of the human form is as unlikely to be pointed out in a life-class at art school, as it is in a course of medical anatomy or physiology. And yet the development of the senses is necessary for the appreciation of beauty; without the ability to smell flowers for example, which evolved through much diligent natural selection, one means of attaining the peak experience would not have been possible. Neither would the eye have been able to appreciate the hue and radiance of colours without the exceptional sensitivity of the cone cells in the retina to extremely small changes in the wave motion of light.

There are many other aspects of nature apart from flowers that have resources to which the olfactory organs can respond: rain-soaked earth, fresh growing vegetation, ripe fruit and the healthy human skin.

Until such time as the ravages of chronic disease and other abuses of a dehumanised existence such as poor diet and excesses of all kinds take their toll, human body movement can embrace the divine. The human form is capable of perfectly correlated and profoundly expressive movements, which contain grace and harmony in every gesture, as is evident in the highly evocative arts of mime and ballet.

When we talk about the erotic sensitivity of the lips we are not referring to a transposed coital satisfaction; to believe this is to miss the entire point of humanisation. The extraordinary aura of beauty that radiates from the human countenance could not have emerged without aesthetic intervention from the surreal. Considering the inaesthetic appearance of the other primates compared with the beauty of the healthy human face—the extensive artistic work and the amazingly short span of time in which it was effected can be appreciated. It is not going too far to suggest that the aesthetic skills which nature had long aggregated in the continuum, were called upon, in the transfiguration of the human face and form, as if by a magic wand.

To gain some insight into how nature managed to create such great art, one can do no better than draw from the analogies of artistic creation. The creation of an image, particularly an abstract one, is much like the preliminary stages of evolution in that it contains a great deal of searching, experiment and rejection. But as the work gets underway there is an unmistakable sense of being guided towards completion, in spite of the fact that no conclusion can be seen at the onset. The same process can be seen at work in nature so that, regardless of waste and failure along the way, the end result is redeemed in glory and illumination.

This also accounts for the virtual absence of art in the initial steps of natural creation: the whirling nebulae and stars, the sprawling hydrogen clouds and exploding supernovae. Like the painter's initial dabblings, there seems to be nothing but chaos. Yet, as one looks with wonder at the churning masses of paint, or at the spiralling incandescences in space, the promise of eventual splendour can be sensed. The apparent disorder of the far-flung stars in a cold night sky—which so alarmed Immanuel Kant and others—is much like a tachist painting. But when the creation is looked at as a work of art in progress, bound by the nature of things to work towards ever-increasing order and magnificence, then the tachist image, like the star-filled heavens, provides the means of creative contemplation with in-built reassurance. Art was promised in the first luminous whisps of hydrogen gas that formed over twelve thousand million years ago, during that unimaginably gigantic outpouring of creative energy known as the Big Bang. The parallels between the Creation and creativity can be found in the painter's sudden and hectic grappling with the empty canvas. Out of the first marks and splashes new worlds arise. An initial onslaught, which is both demanding and exhausting, is common to all original creation in all the arts.

We must not allow the debased condition of earth in general to obscure the splendour of the whole creation, for it contains the possibility of a glorious participation, to which we can have access through the heightened moments of the peak experience.

Nature is art, and in time a humanised, creative primate had to emerge because of an inherent aesthetic potential in matter. No more than a few decades ago to propose the hypothesis of enlightened materialism, which included the aesthetic faculty, would have been thought preposterous. But recent discoveries in physics, the science most equipped to deal with matter, has made such conjecture legitimate.

This revolutionary view of matter hinges on the discovery of the astounding correlation of events in nature, which provided the right conditions for the evolution of life and mind, a subject which I have discussed elsewhere.[3] Quite recent evidence has also appeared in a letter by J. Silk, in *Nature*[4] and in an article by W. Reese, in *New Scientist.*[5]

To sum up, differences of a few per cent in the fundamental physical constants—such as the difference between the weak and strong nuclear forces—would have prevented matter from evolving in a life-making way. The remarkable precision required in nature to make possible the eventual emergence of life and of human mind is powerfully evident in the creative sequences of star-making in nebulae, and in nuclear processes in stars. Indeed, it can be found in virtually every aspect of nature when it is deeply and comprehensively examined. In the onward evolution of life, a quite fantastic collaboration of divergent resources has been achieved.

One can sympathise with the astonishment of scientists when confronted with the 'changed world' recent discoveries have brought about. Only a short while ago they were convinced that all matter arose as a result of random agitation and blind chance. The following extract from professor Melvin Calvin, a well known biochemist who was involved with NASA space projects, shows the kind of theological impact these changes are having on some scientists:

> The fundamental conviction that the universe is ordered is the first and strongest tenet. As I try to discover the origin of that conviction, I seem to find it in a basic notion discovered 2000 or 3000 years ago . . . namely, that the universe is governed by a single God, and is not the product of the whims of many gods. . . . This monotheistic view seems to be the historical foundation of modern science.[6]

I do not believe that such a theological involvement is necessary. It is a purely personal choice, for the providential aspects of nature, favouring life and mind, appear as a part of its self-consistency. But the implications are clear: a growing number of scientists are preoccupied with the metaphysical realm as an inbuilt natural feature.

The orderly existence of electrons in 'shells' around the nucleus is subject to Pauli's *exclusivity principle.* Pauli announced this principle from an observation of electron behaviour long before physical evidence was available. Now it is known that electrons have different quantum numbers, such as 'spin' and 'angular momentum' and that no two electrons possessing the same quantum numbers can cohabit a particular shell. Furthermore, the number of electrons in each shell is typical of each element, a set pattern which decides the chemical properties of each element. This arrangement forms a periodic succession of similar properties, so that ninety-two naturally occurring elements fall into groups with properties in common; a striking indication of the particular creative directive given to the universe by the basic atomic order in nature. Since the changes in the energy of electrons account for all material change under planetary conditions—other energy events take over in stars—Pauli's principle can be said to get to the heart of why matter is as it is. In a profound way this principle also decides how matter forms and evolves into particular kinds of nebulae, stars, rocks and living creatures.

How very exacting this basic organisation is can be seen in the absolutely precise amounts of energy that a particular atom can emit or receive. A little more, or a little less energy, and there is no effect on an atom whatsoever. This inherent limitation and directive in the

Although atoms cannot be photographed the beams of electrons can be converted into an image with the aid of a computer to show the locality of the atoms and their radiative characteristics. Here they are shown arranged on the surface of the rare metal, platinum

Electrons organised in shells around the atomic nucleus—this orderly arrangement largely determines the form of a particular atom. Here the bottom left and right are hydrogen atoms, the remainder are carbon atoms

Section through the protein disc of a virus—another example of the astonishing order and intricacy of natural designs

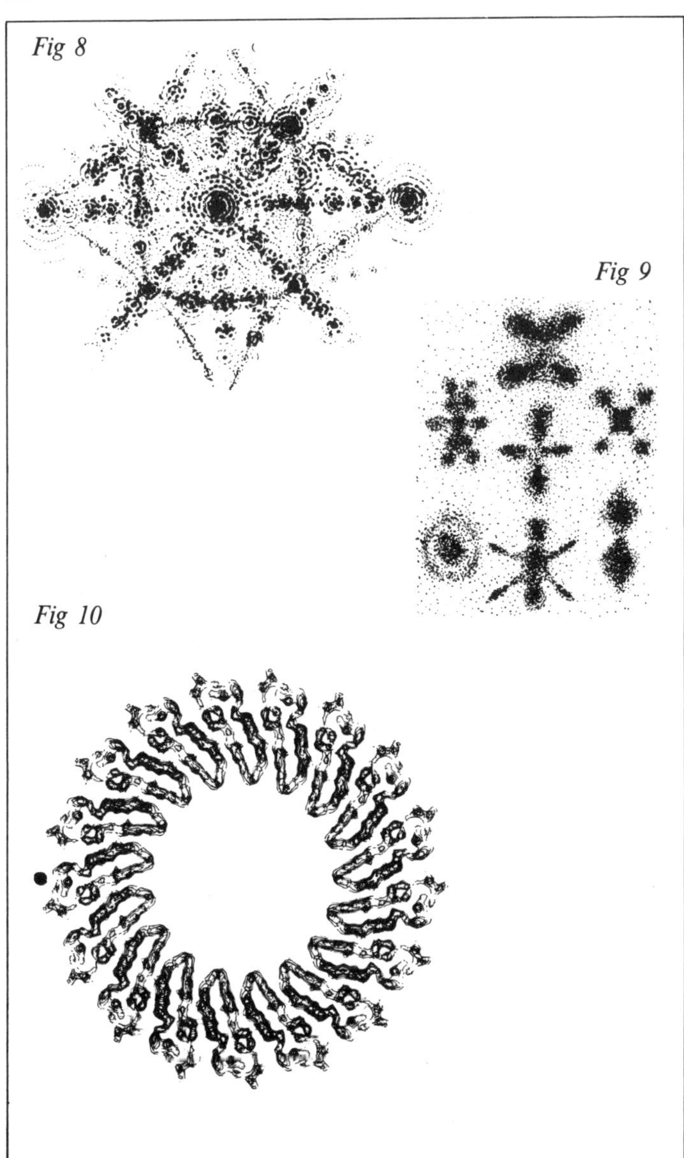
Fig 8
Fig 9
Fig 10

atomic organisation of all matter is under the control of the atomic nucleus. The nature of this control is still a mystery, for the shells in which the electrons have their being are absolutely insubstantial. They can only be conceived of as being organised by the continuum, in the way energy is organised in an electron, and controlled by the atomic nucleus. The atomic nucleus, still virtually a complete mystery in spite of assaults upon it by ever more powerful particle accelerators, is probably best conceived of as the executor of the organisational cues of the continuum. These cannot be thought of as existing until they are actualised by the atom into space and time.

What concerns us here is that this implementation of the cues from the continuum not only set the universe on its particular creative course following the Big Bang, but ensures that this course is aesthetically charged. The very first expression of this art-making Creation is to be seen in the symmetry of atoms.

Atoms are not static in their symmetry, like crystals, but are ceaselessly palpitating. They vibrate billions of times per second, and the shape of the resulting vibrations and the atom's spacial involvement, depend on its energy level. At the lowest energy level, most atoms contract to their minimum, assuming circular forms. As energy is added in precise amounts, various symmetrical forms arise: some have two, others four, six or eight arms; there are also double crescents, dumb-bells and other symmetrical shapes and patterns which can be calculated from the electromagnetic fields they generate.

Although this throbbing world cannot be seen, its reflection in more static forms in the ascending levels of material objects and creatures can be sensed in the exquisite symmetry of crystals, in many of the lower animals, and in plants. Crystals are remarkable. They are responsible for all that is known about atoms, and the orderly structure of matter. They also meet all the criteria of visual aesthetics, so providing the primordial evidence of nature's artistic intentions.[7] In organic forms, the simple symmetry of inorganic crystals is superseded by sculptural forms of enormous aesthetic impact.

The imperturbable symmetry which characterises the integrated nature of atomic organisation must go a long way to accounting for the build-up of beautiful and aesthetically powerful shapes. Atoms come together to form molecules and these in turn, build up into rocks and tissues. Although most crystals are simply symmetrical and owe their appeal to such simplicity, few things are more beautiful than a snow crystal (see Fig 11) or a fluorite cube. But even among crystals this simplicity is superceded by the complexity of shapes evident in the many variations in which common minerals like quartz and calcite can appear and in the way they grow together to form coherent groups.

It would seem, from the extraordinary diversity of nature's art, that artistic guidance is extremely complicated. As one cannot conceive how creative cues in the continuum exist until they are actualised by atomic matter, so one must suppose that, as matter evolves and combines in inherent and pre-set ways typical of this particular universe, there is a replication of both the physical and the aesthetic experience of existence in the continuum. It is, therefore, this accumulation of experience over the thousands of millions of years during which the universe has existed, that provides feedback of the continuously manifold and resplendent art expression of nature.

The method by which this guidance is implemented has already been suggested—that is via the quantum gap, the ceaseless 'in' and 'out' of all existence at the subatomic

Fig 11

The forms which snow crystals can assume are probably infinite— the individuality of every creature and human being is assured by the same principle

level in all matter. No doubt as matter evolves this facility is itself exploited. This explains the emergence of the nervous system, of sensitivity, of the emotional order on which human aesthetics and humanisation itself, have depended. But this aesthetic predisposition, at the very heart of nature, would probably not have been successful were not the universe as a whole congenial to the expression of nature's art during the course of its evolution. A very remarkable example of this concordance of emerging form with aesthetic expression, is seen in the way matter interacts with radiation. Visible light is a very small part of an enormous universal vibrational energy spectrum, yet it seems to be a region providentially favourable for a precise interaction of wave vibration and matter. The sun's radiation, and its conversion, by green chlorophyll in plants, into the sugars and starches on which life depends, is an astounding process. So is the attunement of the eye to the most minute variations of wave amplitude seen as colour. That matter is especially sensitive to such vibrations is borne out by the appearance of light-sensitive 'eye-spots' in the most primitive one-celled organisms that must have appeared on the stage of life at least three thousand million years ago. The sensitivity of the human eye to several thousand variations of hue and tone, all occurring within a very narrow waveband, demonstrates the precision involved; a precision stemming from atomic architectures, for colour is indeed largely determined by the spatial orientation of electron vibration. Although sound vibrations are much grosser than light vibrations, they do depend on a quite remarkable ability of very large groups of atoms and molecules to resonate together. A sheet of metal which cracks when it is bent, or hums when struck, does so because of its resonant properties, traceable to atomic structure. This same property is what makes sound communication possible between animals, from the strident leg rubbing sound of grasshoppers, to birds and human music.

The aesthetic compatibility of structure which is used for expressing orderly and harmonic signals in radiation and sound, extends to the harmonics of visible structures and shapes. One cannot avoid the conclusion that just as the different materials of art have been chosen because they possess inherent and unique symbolic possibilities, so the materials and structures that have come into being in the course of evolution show themselves to be especially fitted for an expression of art by nature. Judged from the level of physical form—the visible work—this may seem far-fetched and not altogether necessary. Yet recalling that the universe is primarily a functional enterprise, that reality is largely a display of energy, and that matter is probably there to execute this display, one should be able to accept, without too much effort, that the universe is indeed unified, and that it functions like a fantastic art-making project. The purely physical and massive, like an artist's materials, only exist to enable this to come about.

This all-reconciling and unifying drive in nature and in art can be traced to the holistic property of atoms, itself the most direct revelation in space and time of the pivotal property of the continuum. Atoms can be split, but, apart from the dissipated radiation, the products of such splitting are themselves integrated atomic entities. Atoms can also be fused together and built up by the orderly addition of appropriate elementary particles; once again, this process is exact and unitive. There are no 'interval elements', only those which the continuum cues allow to energy's organisation in space and time.

The holistic, integrative property of individual atoms applies also to the vast associations of atoms, forming the myriad substances of Creation. This unison is well demonstrated in the instantaneous correlated reaction of atoms, in a particular structure or neighbourhood, to energy changes, a phenomenon known in physics, as resonance. No time taking occurs so that it is not a material, mechanical phenomenon. It is a continuum-dependent property from which it follows that atoms cannot be considered as distinct entities. They are better appreciated as foci of an activity universal in its essence, and having a direct influence on all the legitimate characteristics of the mind, notably love and art, without this property, there is only meaningless assembly, or the disintegrated jumbles of the insane.

In a unified Creation, one in which all that exists is interconnected and interdependent, it is reasonable to suppose that the art-making abilities of matter, so evident in its crystalline expressions, are related in some way to the emergence of art forms in plants and animals, and in the ability of the human mind to create art. But when one considers the gulf between unformed matter and crystals, or the enormous aesthetic distance between crystal and flower, or nature and human art—it is difficult to sense the underlying continuity. It is worth stressing again that this gulf is due to the continuum involvement of aesthetics, as it is of evolution in general. A clue as to how the artistic message has been passed on from matter into life and mind, comes from a singular feature of cosmic creativity. Much of evolution consists of very slow change, giving the opportunity for natural selection to work. There is much evidence of such progressive change, as for instance in the succession of fossils in succeeding geological strata. But the genuinely new in organic evolution appears with startling suddenness. Examples are the first appearance of life itself; the creation of the cell; the discovery of key molecules such as DNA or chlorophyll or haemoglobin; the passage from ocean to land and many others, for which there is practically no succession of fossils, so sudden were they.

Another aspect of this creativity in jumps, rather than in a continuous succession, is seen in the emergent organisation of the universe in levels. For instance, as energy becomes organised into matter, quite new properties appear which are lost if matter is reduced to energy once again. (For further discussion of this subject see appendix).

Although this creativity in jumps and levels is recognised by biologists, there is no explanation of it in a single-level view of reality. The two-level model which has been proposed accounts for the phenomenon admirably. I have already suggested that the essence of evolution is to provide organised matter with the means of exploiting and organising the continuum itself. Although this exploitation began with the very first whisps of hydrogen in the beginning of the universe, the process was raised to quite a new level with the emergence of life and was further raised with the appearance of mind. Both the jumps and the quite distinctive qualities of levels in matter, life, mind and aesthetics, are accounted for. The jumps are due to the need for an accumulation of experience to be first established in the continuum, before new steps are taken. When this has occurred, the creative decisions are quite sudden. As for the distinctive qualities of the different levels, they are due to jumps in the revelation of the continuum connection in space and time. This is as striking between the living and the non-living, as it is between brain and mind. The distinctiveness of emotionalism is due to just such an exploitation of the continuum, discrete in most animals, but assertive in the human.

When this very distinctive way of creation in nature, as in art, is understood, it is no longer difficult to accept both the relevance of nature's art, and the irreducible distinctiveness of human art, both of which nonetheless are unitive manifestations of a universe.

CHAPTER FIFTEEN

THE AESTHETICS OF LIFE

I have suggested that the great art of nature—although originating from the need to fulfil purely practical purposes—transcends the process of natural selection in its exuberance and colourfulness which is typical of the great moments in human art. This artistic bravura can be seen when one gazes at a tray of tropical butterflies, a drawer of beautiful mineral specimens or a tropical lagoon.

Nature's art-making process appears to have reached a sudden and astounding peak in the Cretaceous era, some 170 million years ago, which means that on this particular planet nature had already had over three thousand million years to gather the necessary experience to achieve this peak. Not only the flowers but the colourful fishes, birds and even the few attractive reptiles, appeared in this great geological age, rather like players brought into concentrated activity by the stroke of a conductor's baton.

One example is a tropical lizard of breath-taking beauty which I observed on palm trees in the Mascarene islands. The body is a bright, scintillating emerald green with vertical purple stripes, and the head is adorned by the brightest reds, yellows and cerulean blue, producing an opaline irridescence. These creatures stand out like jewels, but their beauty must surely endanger rather than help them. Such extraordinary beauty in a group of animals not generally very attractive, indeed quite often hideous, must have been inspired by an extremely persistent transcendental process.

Besides a variety of biochemical pigments, colours in nature are produced by the microstructural interference of light vibration. Common physical examples of such an effect are found in droplets of atmospheric water in a rainbow, and in the monomolecular layer of oil on water in oil slicks. To make use of such an effect in the creation of definite patterns requires a micro-grid of extremely fine precision. To change apple-green to blue-green, for example, requires a microstructural change of a few thousandths of a millimeter.

These microstructures are often arranged in patterns of great complexity, forming mosaics of different colours as complicated as those in a tapestry or carpet. Remembering that genes are designed to mutate and, therefore, have inherent instability, the fact that these patterns are repeated generation after generation is quite amazing. This has struck one notable biologist, Sir Alister Hardy, who believes that some sort of transcendental guidance is indispensable to a satisfactory explanation.[1] He, in fact, postulates a two-level model of nature which is able to override the ever shifting gene background in natural selection by imposing a transcendental directive to biological organisation. This is also a wonderful explanation of many unexplained biological phenomena such as embryonic development and, for that matter, the apparently simple process of wound healing. Thus the organised continuum—organised by life itself—comes to act as the source of inspiration much as it does in the case of human art. Because of the existence of the surreal world, the universally pooled product of nature's experience provides the universe with what amounts to a supreme, all-encompassing and all-experiencing mind of its own, a mind, it will be appreciated, which is itself supremely humanised. From this one can better appreciate the analogies of nature and human art, and the key role of human creativity in the scheme of nature.

Molluscan shells provide a curious instance of the overflow of the innate aesthetics of living matter, for their varied and beautiful patterning and colour have no practical purpose. It is difficult to find even a practical origin for them, for they are often covered over by the flesh of the animal when it is alive. Only in death is its full splendour revealed. It is not impossible that the aesthetics of the spiralling forms, which do have a practical origin in the succession of growth chambers they provide, might have drawn upon other high aesthetic resources in surreality.

In the case of flowers, the spur to their evolution was the association of insects in their pollination, for wind- or water-pollinated flowers are not colourful. But the practical aims of this relationship are far transcended in the extraordinary forms and colours of plants and in their scent range. So strong has been the floral intention in nature that it is echoed in other forms of life. Many medusae, holothurians and echinoderms, are remarkably flower-like. There are sea-slugs with 'blooms' as lavish as the blossom-bedecked cars that are paraded in the Cannes 'battle of flowers'. The importance of the crystalline theme throughout nature no doubt accounts for such floralised outbursts, just as it must have given rise to certain archetypes in the unconscious with an obvious floral lineage, like the mandala, for example. In the landscape of the mind, as in surreality, such foci of enormous evocative power must constitute the most essential features, hence the peak-inducing power of contemplating such forms.

Examined through the simplest magnifying glass the patterns and colours of flowers seen in a single petal reveal demarcations, contrasts and enhancing devices that must make the painter envious. But nature's greatest achievement among flowering plants is to be seen in the ecological integration and intergrowing of different species. They are as complicated as a Persian carpet, providing a harmonic, musical, orchestral appeal in colour-play, which justifies the millions of different flower species. The human painter can never work with such a rich and diversified palette.

Striking orchestrations of 'flower music' occur in the Mediterranean, in Asia, on the West coast of North America and in a small part of South Africa. They provide natural gardens which no gardener can surpass, in the harmony and diversity of intergrowing species, the principal condition of the earthly paradise. This amazing creative ecology—of the highest aesthetic relevance since humanisation depended on it—cannot be accounted for in a one-level reality. Although it is known that particular plants repel or favour others by certain hormones they secrete, this creative integration is far too complex and magnificent to be elementally accounted for. Nature's mounting experience in surreality is the only possible explanation, playing back into the ordinary world at just the right time and so transforming a drab planet into one full of flowers.

The idealised landscapes which have attracted a long succession of painters originating in ancient Greece, Rome and the East, are the result of a vast concert of divergent creative forces. Well-watered and well-drained soils, themselves the product of very particular mountains containing specific types of minerals, are the end result of a gigantic cycling of earth materials with which continental drifting is related. Flowers first appeared in Eurasia, in what is now upper Malaysia and Burma, but the original floralised locus may have stretched from the Polynesias (connected with the mainland in Cretaceous times) to Asia Minor, with a particular concentration in what is now the Himalayas but was then a vast rolling plain. The kind of gentle sloping hills and verdant valleys with beautiful trees interspersed with grasses typically associated with such physical conditions, with metamorphic soils composed of the fossilised remains of billions of marine creatures.

The idealised landscape in question carries with it a host of subtle aesthetic appeals of a particulary humanising sensitivity. A land so interspersed by hills and broad valleys with moving waters, induces a particular kind of weather. The cumuli clouds sail by in great majesty, bringing gentle and regular showers, providing dew at dawn as well as mists. They have a highly poetic significance in that they are pure and uplifting; conditions which are also favourable to that strange glory of natural optical art—the rainbow. Varied and colourful sunsets are also a feature of such conditions, providing a magnificently colourful ending to the day and a prelude to dream-filled sleep, vitally necessary in the humanising process. The human skin does not only experience tactile response in human contact and caresses, but is also affected by gentle breezes which are highly evocative because they caress the body as a whole. It is interesting to observe that the body does respond *as a whole* to such stimuli, but that such sensitivity has been widely lost during the process of civilisation.

A landscape so essential for humanisation, cannot have been produced accidentally. It must be yet another example of the achievement of a long apprenticeship and information accumulated in surreality, playing back into the organisation of the world of space and time. This ancient drive to provide the humanised brain with a suitable environment is so strong that we can find in nature indications of some awareness of beauty before the emergence of Homo Sapiens. Is it too much to suppose that the butterfly enjoys some degree of its flutterings? Birds undoubtedly become emotionally involved, indeed perhaps even more intensely involved in their environment than humans. Lyre-birds and bower-birds, for example, elusive in normal circumstances, are easily caught in their courtship display. And to show how not only aesthetic appreciation, but art expression has been intended all along, there is even one species of bower-bird which selects special sticks with which to paint its bowery with plant juices! Can one doubt that the urge to artistic expression and appreciation runs throughout the fabric of nature?

Although mammals are not noticeably involved with art, the primate undeniably has a certain aesthetic relish in the handling of objects. This is especially so in the case of colourful fruit. And that, in fact, is how it all began, for the colourfulness of fruits is close to that of flowers, and they too have the added rapturising influence of scent. Although the apes have fewer cone-sensitive colour cells in their retinas than humans, they have enough to sustain quite an advanced colour vision. What is lacking however, is the motivation to express colour which as we shall see, has been a unique condition of humanisation; as has the ability to appreciate the scent of flowers.

The painting prowess of a few chimpanzees has been sensationalised in an attempt to make human abstract art look ridiculous, which always pleases the public. But it is possible that the higher primates do possess a very rudimentary aesthetic faculty. This is not surprising since they are remarkably similar to humans in many respects and even molluscs may show some rudimentary artistic urges—the octopus, for example, decorates its lair—nature has been waiting for the right opportunity to produce artistically creative creatures since the dawn of time.

To understand fully the role of art in human existence it is helpful to study the progress of humanisation and see what changes have taken place since the genesis of man. There are few facts and inevitably many biased opinions and, as is usually the case in such a situation, the meagre material that exists can be used to support two quite opposite concepts. On the one hand it is argued that the inescapable evidence of violence and brutality throughout the history of civilisation is the result of a loss of natural grace; on the other hand the view expressed is that what man has achieved in art and culture proves that throughout his time on earth he has progressed upwards from his savage animal origins.

There is no doubt that this latter, more violent way of seeing man is not only the more popular, but until quite recently was the one which appeared to fit in best with the anthropological evidence. As far as the popularity of the bestial picture of human origins is concerned, this is understandable for it seems to excuse the recurrent violence and beastliness of our history and even suggests that we are making progress in spite of the evidence that violence still largely rules the world. It is a comfort to be told that this is not really our fault because nature has made us this way. As a result the concept of a fall from grace, what I term the benevolent view, is usually written off as idealistic. Those who hold it are commonly accused of failing to consider the ruthlessness of nature in general.

Until the recent discoveries of even earlier hominid remains in Kenya and Ethiopia, the unchallenged view of the anthropologists was that the first humans appeared during the Ice Ages. If this had been the case the benevolent view would have been inaccurate, for no creature arising in such terrible times could possibly have been sensitive and benevolent. Until recently biologists had no reliable means of measuring the geological time scale, nor a knowledge of the time needed to effect evolutionary changes. However during the last hundred years the geological time scale has been extended several fold. An accurate system of geological dating, using the rate of decay of certain radioactive atoms which feature in living processes, has been perfected and it has been discovered that fundamental biological changes that drastically modify the way of life, through nutrition or the reproduction systems of a species, require very much more time to develop than was formerly supposed.

Coupled with the above, in the last few years there has been mounting evidence of the extreme antiquity of man. Far from being a mere hundred thousand years old, his origins are now put at around four million years ago. As the Ice Ages only began about a million years ago, and were originally interspersed with long inter-glacial periods favourable to a benevolent existence, the theory of the glacial origin of man has now been disproved. Although recently a growing number of scientists have become aware of the alternatives the majority of anthropologists and sociologists are still committed to the violent and predatory point of view.

It is currently assumed because of the large number of hominids and pre-hominids found in Africa, that the essential steps in the evolution of Homo Sapiens took place on that continent. If the picture of a beauty-loving, sensitive, benevolent hominid is an accurate one, then

Africa is not likely to have been the site of human genesis, because the African environment, at the presumed time of this genesis, was not humanly congenial. Not only were the conditions tropical and competitive, with an abundance of predators, but Africa was and still is, poor in flower species. Although flowers spread rapidly over most of the world in the Cretaceous era (170 million years ago) from their origins in Asia, their colonisation was halted by desert and dense tropical forests straddling tropical Africa. The rich flora of South Africa is presumed to have got there by way of a land-bridge across the Indian Ocean, which was subsequently destroyed. Without a highly floralised environment, the higher human faculties, nourished aesthetically by the beauty of the environment, could not have been properly evolved.

There is no doubt that hominids were common in Africa, but they were probably not sufficiently prepared to survive in a truly human way. They would have destroyed themselves through violence and disorder. This may in fact be the built-in assurance that only the properly humanised hominid will in time inherit the earth; in this theory it is accepted that war and revolution are a part of an inbuilt system of elimination.

One particular piece of evidence against the African genesis has come recently from virus studies done on primates, which suggests a much closer affinity between humans and the Eurasian monkeys and apes. The importance of this evidence rests on the highly specific manner in which certain viruses affect the genome of a primate, the genome being its entire inherited genetic baggage carried in the chromosomes in every cell. This specificity results from the way in which the virus substitutes its own nucleic acid in the gene chromosome sequence, a substitution which is subsequently inherited by the primate. Following these substitutions in different species of primate, including man, it is possible to determine their genetic relationship and to trace their probable evolutionary history. From such studies, it appears that the human species is closer to the Eurasian primates than to those of Africa. The evidence concludes: 'Most of man's evolution since his divergence from the apes must have occurred in Asia rather than Africa'.[2]

Another indication of a closer affinity between humans and the higher primates of Asia, comes from the similarities of their body parasites. There is yet further evidence, although it is less clear-cut, from the study of blood-groups in man and ape. It would seem that many man-like creatures found in Africa may well have originated there, but that they have nothing to do with the human line. The most recent findings—*Homo* fossils discovered in Ethiopia which are even older than those found in Kenya—would seem to support a migration of the genuinely humanised hominids into Africa from the direction of Asia. Whether Homo erectus moved into a sapient stage in Africa or Asia, or on both continents, is still unresolved but the likelihood is that this also occurred in Asia.

The fact that those humans who migrated to Africa have failed to develop any high form of civilisation indicates how uncongenial that continent is to the humanising process. It is perhaps significant in this connection that the floral glories common in Eurasia, are absent in Africa.[3] This is also reflected in the development of the love song and the love poem in Eurasia which has not appeared in African culture. While music has evolved to a highly sophisticated level through the use of complex instruments in India, China and Europe, it has failed to do so in Africa, where it has remained at a subconscious level of appeal resonating to the human heart beat in its basic rhythm. African visual art, apart from semitic infiltrations which came with the Arab slave-traders, has been largely sculptural and subconsciously dominated; an aspect which has fascinated certain Europeans who have clearly felt a certain kinship with the condition that has given rise to it.

The question as to whether humans have a tropical or subtropical origin is crucial. If they are tropical, a sensitive, beauty-loving disposition and a related art is unlikely. Tropical conditions, like those in Africa, were not conducive to humanisation at the time when the human genesis is thought to have taken place. Large areas in India and the Far East are more subtropical than tropical, and their large populations—both past and present—demonstrate how conducive they are to human development. The popularity of the African genesis is supported by the theory that the virtual absence of human body hair is evidence of a tropical origin. This is a curious supposition, when the hairiness of the other primates found in that region is considered. A much better explanation has already been put forward in the aesthetisation of the human body as it evolved from animal sex to sexual love. If, on the other hand, the first humans were subtropical, they must have had to resort to some form of body covering, however rudimentary, for the diurnal and seasonal changes of temperature, even in the semi-tropics, would have necessitated partial protection of the naked skin.

No primitive, not even one living in the tropics, goes absolutely naked. The sexual organs at least, are covered. Total nakedness is found only among civilised nudists. There is also confirmation that the original humans were not tropical from the relative inefficiency of the black-skinned races to thrive in tropical heat. The evidence suggests that such heavy pigmentation of the skin is a relatively recent adaptation. The reason why black-skinned people adapt poorly to heat is simply because black *retains* heat. Black pigment protects the delicate tissues from ultra-violet radiation, but requires profuse sweating to alleviate the over-heating caused by infra-red rays.

The myth of an earthly paradise, like that of the fall, is common to Eurasian peoples, and probably echoes the original condition of the human genesis. Quite recently a theory has been put forward that the first humanising steps were taken in Asia, this is based upon the discovery there of a singular hominoid—Ramapithecus. What is remarkable about these creatures is that, like all humans, they are flat-faced. They do not have pointed faces like those hominoids still extant: the chimpanzee, the gibbon and the gorilla. Ramapithecus lived between eighteen and twelve million years ago, so that humanisation may possibly have begun around that time. They were also found to have other human features: small canine teeth and a semi-circular dental arch with thickened enamel over the teeth in a strengthened lower jaw. This is an important feature of the human jaw which indicates the adaption to tougher food, food that went with living at ground-level.

In an article devoted to Ramapithecus, E. L. Simons writes:

> In the late Miocene, 10 to 12 million years ago, much of Eurasia was covered by forest, but not tropical, and as a result, it did not provide the yearlong fruit production and continuous vegetation that is typical of the relatively seasonless forests where apes now reside. Under these circumstances, it seems likely that the larger of the Miocene apes often found that the food available in the trees was inadequate to their needs. A tendency to pursue an alternative food-gathering strategy—foraging on the ground and along the edge of the forest for small, tough foods such as

> nuts and roots—could have provided natural selection pressures favouring the survival of individuals with more robust jaws and thicker teeth enamel.[4]

This question of changing dietary habits is important, for a predatory ancestor could hardly have given rise to the benevolent humanisation suggested here. The hunting hypothesis—popular with both scientists and the public for obvious reasons—does not stand up to close scrutiny although during the Ice Ages humans undoubtedly did take to hunting in order to survive. Professor Kay, the anatomist, in a letter to *Nature* concerning the diet of the African hominoids—including Ramapithecus—points out that the study of the molar suggests that these creatures '. . . probably had diets consisting largely of fruits'.[5] Another food plentifully available in the mid and later Miocene was grass seed; it is still gathered today and made into gruel by the Australian aborigines.

It is widely believed by anatomists and anthropologists that Ramapithecus was part of the human line, the ancestor of Australopithecus and Homo Erectus. With regard to the site of the decisive event, Professor Simons has this to say:

> Judging from the history of the finds of Homo Erectus, it would not be surprising if finds of Australopithecus were found on other continents (outside Eurasia). What would be surprising, biologically speaking, would be if only that part of the cosmopolitan Ramapithecus population living in Africa gave rise to Australopithecus.[5]

In other words, that first step in humanisation is as likely, or more likely, to have occurred in Eurasia as in Africa, some time between the last evidence of the existence of Ramapithecus, and the earliest evidence of Australopithecus and Homo, four to six million years ago. That Eurasia rather than Africa was the site of the first steps in humanisation is supported by Dr P. Andrews, of the British Museum.[6]

Recent studies of the mid-Miocene vegetation of Eurasia indicate changes from forest to more open woodland, with considerable local variation, offering a great variety of conditions. It is quite likely that the kind of ideal humanising landscape mentioned in the last chapter was in fact abundantly provided in Eurasia. Referring to the newest finds of Ramapithecus, Dr M. Pickford suggests that the delayed eruption of the molars—a hominid feature—implies an increased juvenile period.

> Prolonged childhood is one of the hallmarks of man, and it is possible that the Sivapithecines (the genus that includes Ramapithecus) had evolved on this path, with all the material and social connotations which would follow such a development.[7]

This suggests that aesthetic sensitivity is likely to go back to Ramapithecus. Professor Pickford raises this very question when considering the round human-like face of Ramapithecus: 'Was it possibly linked to a Sivapithecine ideal of beauty?' he asks.

It is possible that the round, human-like, flat face developed to accommodate adorative face-to-face, participative love making giving rise to the peak sexual union, the source of all ensuing heightened experiences. If this was so, Ramapithecus was even further on the way to humanisation than has so far seemed possible. Even if it is assumed that this emotionalised humanisation had only just begun with Ramapithecus, it means that somewhere between eight and four million years ago a fully humanised hominid had appeared on the scene. He was surely very different in overall appearance from modern man; probably as small as a pigmy and brown skinned, he must have had, nonetheless, most distinctive human features, and a fully developed emotional life capable of intense feeling and expression. Human art is probably as old as that, although the kinds of art expression practised must have employed perishable materials, particularly flowers. But it is probable that pebbles, selected for their aesthetic appeal, will be found close to Ramapithecus remains.

Assuming that the prehuman Ramapithecus was a benevolent creature, aware of beauty, and that his immediate successors—those Australopithecines that gave rise to an emotionalised hominid—were also of this kind, the question remains: was this primordial benevolence subsequently lost, and did human beings change into hunters and predators long before the Ice Ages? Many millions of years passed in which that change could have taken place, and as no fossil evidence is available yet, it is open to conjecture. Because the hominids depended for survival on the cortex, rather than on instinct—the cortex can be conditioned to almost any kind of behaviour—it is quite possible that hominids, once humanised, took up hunting and adopted the role of predators even towards their own kind. This would be quite different from a genuine biological change, which would necessitate morphological adaptations as well as changes in body biochemistry; especially in the long and complex enzyme chains dealing with protein metabolism and the efficient excretion of waste products. Even though cortical conditioning can take place within a lifetime, such a biological adaptation would be likely to take millions of years. To change from a fruit-eating to a largely predatory or carnivorous animal would require fundamental genetic changes.

At the close of the Miocene age, world climate changed, and inter-species competition increased, favouring the more aggressive. Recently evidence has come to light which gives some indication of the time required to bring about such genetic changes. This evidence concerns the rate of genetic mutation found to be remarkably constant from bacteria to man. As most gene mutations are ineffective or harmful, the time required to bring about any fundamental metabolic or functional change would run into tens of millions of years. Accordingly, there has not been enough time since the human genesis to change the human type from the typical primate fruit-eating pattern, to one dependent on a predatory existence. Man, undoubtedly, became a hunter during the Ice Ages, but he managed this through cortical conditioning and learning, rather than through biological and genetic adaptation. Learning hunting skills is as elaborate and complex a process today as it was during the Palaeolithic era.

In the interglacial periods, humans were probably much as they are now: they had reverted to more humanly compatible ways of life but the severity of the last Ice Age disrupted the cultures and civilisations that came after it. In spite of his existential deviations, man in all probability remains fundamentally unchanged as a food-gatherer, predominantly fruitarian, benevolent, beauty-loving and socially compassionate by nature.

New evidence, experimentally arrived at by Gorczinsky and Steele, research workers at the Ontario Cancer Institute, supports the proposition that evolution does not depend exclusively on the Darwinian theory of natural selection.[8] In the 1950s Sir George Medawar found that if mouse cells of a particular strain were injected into new-born mice with cells of a different strain, these mice were unable to destroy the foreign cells if they were re-introduced at maturity. This was the first evidence that the body's natural immunological defences, the bane of organ transplant surgery, could be circumvented. Gorczinsky and Steele now report that a majority of mice born of parents who have been de-immunised in this way, inherit this feature.

This recent work is the first that indicates that Lamarck, an ignored biologist of the eighteenth century, was at least partly right.[9] One reason for the popularity of the Darwinian theory of natural selection over Lamarck's contention that traits acquired in the lifetime of an animal could be passed on to future generations, was that Lamarck's theory was too vitalistic as opposed to the mechanistic ideas in Darwin.

Evidence already available from the study of bacteria proves that these minute creatures possess the means of passing genetic material from one generation to another, thus defeating attempts to eradicate them with bacteria-cides. The explanation lies in the presence of *transposons* through which bacteria able to resist bacteriacides can pass this characteristic on, through their genes, to other bacteria, so that they become absorbed in the genome and rapidly render the entire species immune to that particular pesticide.

This suggests that all cells in all living organisms may be able to transpose nucleic acid or genetic material from special cells, to the gonads and so ensure their translation to future generations.

The remarkable aesthetisation of the human body cannot be satisfactorily accounted for by natural selection alone, indeed it is difficult to imagine how a beautiful hominid could have emerged from an inaesthetic primate ancestry without some other means. These means are provided by the Lamarckian principle. Like all new features in evolution beauty must originally have occurred in a minority of pre-humans as rudimentary aesthetic traits in a small group. This minority would be drawn together through sexual and natural selection, and would breed, thus insuring that the genes of their unique beauty were passed on. Left to Darwinian theory these rare attributes would have been dissipated by subsequent random breeding.

Only a limited number of generations, in some more or

less secluded place, preventing the swamping of the process by outside invasion, would have been necessary for these acquired characteristics to become generalised in the group's genome. Such a group, and other groups evolving separately, would ensure the evolution of a human predisposition. Thus the sensitivities and the high mind which go with the processes of art, played a key role in the very early segregation of those pre-human groups which were in time to become properly human. Other pre-human primates, even those intimately connected genetically, would be excluded, and in the long run, would fail to become humanised.

CHAPTER SIXTEEN

ART, MIND AND NATURE MEET

The case for the genetic validity of art rests on a common sharing of mind and nature in the continuum, the universal energy-deploying substratum from which reality arises and with which all things maintain a connection. The extraordinary power of art comes from its organisation by countless minds pooled into universal surreality. Through art all that is imperfect in space and time can be transmuted so that it can give rise to an experience of perfection beyond ordinary experience.

The continuum in itself can be imagined as pure energy containing cues to organisation. The initial organisation of matter out of energy retains much of this purely functional quality, but as such a state cannot be intellectually conceptualised, science is faced with an irreducible core in nature; matter becomes organised in ever ascending levels in space and time, in molecules, crystals, cells and organs and in entire worlds, so what is imprecise is progressively obscured; at the gross level, where the human being comes into contact with the universe, there is the impression of a rigid, solid reality. If one could make structures of pure light and colour, which some recent art forms have tried to do, they would visibly symbolise the inherent transparency and tremulousness of all things.

People have always been fascinated by glass, gems, crystals, light and water, all entities capable of symbolising this transparency. Although realist art deals with the surface fixity of things, its perennial appeal comes from its symbolisation of this other quality in all things. I have already suggested that this quality is the result of continuum properties working through into the visible and tangible. Since this otherness is pure function it should follow that the symbolism in all the arts is dynamic rather than static. This can be appreciated in the intuitive criteria of good line, form and content, all imprecise, throbbing qualities with close analogies to what the physicist is now grappling with in the subatomic realm.

But there is also an apparently opposite fixity in the imageries of painting with equivalents in all the other arts. A possible explanation is to be found in what can be called the quality of 'dynamic stillness' encountered in the penetrative imageries of atomic physics. Plasma, the state of matter at some twenty-five million degrees centigrade, is such an example. Extremely difficult to contain by mechanical means—the technical quandary of atomic fusion—the 'dynamic stillness' of the plasma state, is nonetheless present in all matter. Atoms themselves should be conceived in an analogous way. Colour, as we have seen, demonstrates this power with particular versatility probably because the vibrations of light are so close to the continuum. The enormous appeals of crystallinity are related. A uniform sheet of light or colour can aptly symbolise this plasma-like quality or it can be constrained into geometric planes. But the rigidly geometric 'hard edge' image, without any power of inducing a peak experience, is something quite different, related intrinsically to the superficial world of static structure.

That some people are evidently moved by such imageries suggests that a special psychological situation exists. It is an observable fact that an eclipse in depth-meaning encourages miniaturisation of the image in art and a phobic insistence on detail. The emotional blockage due to puritanism had just such an impact on Dutch painting, and the superficialities of court life favoured the miniature in which the image is kept to the surface, as it is more actively in some forms of Kinetic and Op Art. An uninspired, contrived and purely technical realism serves the same end.

If the theory that mind and nature meet is true, then a close relationship should be found in the ways in which events and entities come into existence through the techniques of art and nature. This key subject has already been touched upon, but for its proper appreciation the singular position of the mind needs stressing. Whereas our physical beings, and all material objects, are earth-bound, our minds are free to soar away to commune with nature at higher levels in their shared continuum. Science, as we have seen, encounters enormous difficulties in its penetrations of appearance, requiring approaches capable of immense magnification, whereas the intuitive mind can grasp comparable events instantaneously, and reveal them symbolically.

In the dream, as in art experience, the sense of time is fluid—it leaps, runs or falters according to the emotional intensity of the experience, ranging from a virtual feeling of infinity to a stunning imminence. The old physics, dependent on clock time, ridiculed this kind of experiential time. But the new physics has been made aware that in subatomic events timing of happenings is also inseparably related to their dynamism or intensity. This makes their measure, in clock time, appear ridiculous, as does the existence of some of those 'particles' with a life time of a few billionths of a second. Protons, on the other hand, which form the atomic nucleus, are virtually eternal. In both the mind's experiencing, and in the heart of nature, time is therefore functional, the measure of the existence of energy in its fantasmagoric forms.

This close analogy of mind time—the experiential time of art and of the peak experience in particular—with subatomic or universal time can be comprehended once it is understood that the mind is an exploitation of the universal continuum by the material brain, and that the subatomic world merges into the continuum. The fact that the intuitively attuned mind can sense this fundamental time, and symbolically reveal it indicates that art experience is participative, a condition which completely obliterates the demarcation between observer and observed. During the instants of clock-time for which the peak experience persists, seldom more than a few moments, there is a thorough immersion in fundamental time, which brings with it a feeling of eternality surviving, even when the world of clock-time is returned to. It is of singular interest that in their own way physicists are coming to a similar conclusion about the relationship of physics to the objective world.

In physics, the object is in truth no longer conceivable as a separate entity, but rather as an especially organised phase in a universal potential. In the high mind, in the high dream, and in the surreal revaluation in art, space has a closely analogous character. The aim of intuitively guided technique is to merge in various symbolic ways the object and the environment, ending in a total non-figuration. The mind, because of the very particular evolution of matter in the brain, is able to by-pass the usual laboured methods of revelation to organise the continuum directly, hence the conviction, however difficult to grasp, that the products of the mind's activity, whether they are in fact symbolically revealed or not, actually exist and persist in a transcendental sense. In the universe's fundamental sense, they are indeed incomparably more real than the usual productions of nature. From this conclusion it is obvious that the way the mind is used is of crucial importance; more crucial perhaps than how we use nature. It is, no doubt, the intuitive awareness of this creative power of the mind which gives to its symbolic revelations in the arts their commonly accepted other-worldliness, even in their reference to the ordinary scenes of life.

When the power of the human mind is accepted all those other strange aspects of nature fall into place—the individualisation of things; the problems of transience and eternality felt in so many instances and the relevance of the humanised mind in a transcendentalising universe, programmed to become aware of itself. Although this programming is wide open, there are constraints, so that a theme of significance emerges in an orgiastic, profligate creative expressiveness. Awareness must mean an eventual acceptance of these qualitative aspects of the universe's creativity, of the meaning of creativity in art and nature, which leads to the conclusion that there is a cosmological reference to the problems of fitness and unfitness, good and evil, the sublime and the demonic, beauty and horror. Awareness, at the individual, social, planetary and cosmic level, must therefore imply an ethical obligation. It is in this reference that art, in its highest, humanised revelations, has a potent if not precisely definable content. It is sufficiently evident that the good, the pure and the beautiful are consistent with it, while the opposites are absolutely incompatible.

Biological specification is all-important in the human species as in all creatures, for if there is a theme in the creative work of nature, it is only in this way that it can be realised. In the evolution of the human cortex this dependence has become camouflaged by the unlimited existential variations and adaptations of time and place. This has led many to suppose that the human being is completely free from this biological bondage, the source of what might be called the intellectual fallacy. But while a very considerable freedom in choice and behaviour has been the pivot of humanisation, humans cannot diverge from their basic biological conditioning without thereby threatening their survival. We have seen that the way nature has met this risk is by the subtle humanisation of all predisposition, motivation and behaviour. But for this to be effective, the humanising conditions must be met, if they are not and if human beings fail to respect their biological nature, then inhuman or dehumanising behaviour ensues.

But it is evident that a quite opposite motivation has been built into the human psyche, in the form of a restless inadaptation, an urge to go beyond what has already been reached. This is not an animal characteristic. All other animals are perfectly content to remain where they are, and as they are, in spite of the creative restlessness of nature. They change, only because their environments change. In humans, on the contrary, the restless quest seems to be inbuilt. This urge towards progress, which is an essential component of the human psyche, is also an internal threat to the survival of the species, for survival depends on the ability to adapt to the environment. It is all too evident in human history that this powerful drive towards change and discovery has led man to impose grave threats on the environment on which his future depends.

This restlessness is very relevant to the problem of art, for although one finds the arts at times becoming static, generally art expression shows this restless streak at its most intensive. It is so strong that it dominates even practical activities. Man has never been content merely to fabricate objects useful to his existence; he has been strongly motivated to use such objects as the means of an aesthetic expression. This is evident, for example, in the fantastic artistry of flint-making, even in the harassing Palaeolithic age. One has the impression that even when constantly hungry and under stress human beings have still felt compelled to give these silica chips beauty and harmonious form; in a brutal world they were objects of love, of delicate attention. This urge to create aesthetically satisfying objects has sometimes led to their losing their utilitarian value, as frequently seen in carving, pottery and weaving.

This impulse to go beyond the merely useful is inherent in all the artistic expressions of nature. What begins as necessity tends to become aesthetically assimilated, and occasionally fantastically and orgiastically so. In techno-civilisation this urge has been fragmented, because it has so often been aimed at the practical without aesthetic sensitivity. If one can see in this urge a tendency to go beyond the naturalistic, it should also be evident that nature's inbuilt protection against a dehumanising runaway has been the very strong impulse for its aesthetisation. Without it, a materialistic, nature-defying civilisation would have ended in the creation of a demonic world.

Although the particular turn civilisation has taken can be condemned and every effort should be made to put it right, this should not lead to the confusion of thought, often witnessed today, wherein a technological civilisation is condemned in principle; a condemnation associated with a yearning for return to a more naturalistic lifestyle. The inbuilt restlessness in the human constitution and the impulse to ensure that it should take a humanly acceptable form by aesthetising it, is not as important for the human species, as it is for nature. As I have suggested, the build-up of a replicate experience of living in the continuum enables the life process not only to accumulate experience, but also to compute the best choices in terms of future development, for future potentialities are necessarily inherent in past and present. Unless the human being had been motivated in this way to go beyond nature, the work of nature—from the continuum, through matter and beyond matter by way of the mind—would have been blocked. The tragedy of techno-civilisation is its failure to realise that technological capacity and environmental imperative are not the result of isolated human ingenuity, but nature's own destiny in the human phenomenon.

CHAPTER SEVENTEEN

ART AS AN AID TO INTEGRATION

Man the world over suffers from deviancy and disintegration at all levels, physical, mental, social and ecological. The search for a new life-enhancing wholeness is urgent; it is a search in which the arts, because of their integrating powers, can play a leading role.

The psychosomatic powers of art have been well known from the earliest times, from the floralised sanatoria of Hippocrates, to the modern use of art-therapy in mental illness. Its effectiveness is mostly due to that decisive aesthetic criterion—wholeness. It has such powerful integrating forces that the sick mind or body is stimulated towards healing and reintegration.

It will be recalled that the appeal of this underlying wholeness in art reflects the supreme need of the human organism for the utmost functional efficiency. This is true for the body and the mind. Indeed, it is the case for all biological activity, for only by an efficient integration of the diverse activities of life, can a particular organism—and an entire species—be assured of survival. Disorganisation, which is the biological definition of disease, whatever its cause, is necessarily a threat to survival. But this primordial need for integration applies even more critically to the mind. The slightest disintegration results in a degree of neurosis and more severe dysfunction leading to the total disruption and dehumanising state of psychosis.

As evolution proceeds, producing increasingly more complex and manifold forms of life, qualities only remotely intimated in primitive stages, become overt in the higher forms. Wholeness is such a quality. It involves not only the individual animal but, increasingly, the spinning of the most intricate ecological web on which all higher life depends. In a fundamental sense, the concept of health and disease should extend to the entire integrating enterprise of nature. Disease as such can then be seen to be due to some disturbance in that holistic interaction of organism, environment and ecology, an ecology that may well extend to the stars and the universe as a whole, through the interaction of the surreal dimension.

Science has avoided looking at the holistic properties of nature because these properties defy mechanical explanatin. They are the proof that nature is *not* a machine. They have the same aura of strangeness, of 'otherness' as the arts, owing to the surreal involvement. In no textbook of biology is this most important attribute of living activity mentioned, nor is it touched upon in most books on astronomy and cosmology in spite of the fact that the interaction and unity of the universe is implicit in Einstein's theories. This is even true of psychology, always sensitive to the accusation of being unscientific. Yet an unbiased viewing of nature and man shows this striving towards wholeness everywhere: it is evident as much in the homeostatic models which the weather-men have worked out to explain world climate, as it is in the healing of a wound.

It is sad that human beings, doctors, psychiatrists and

scientists included, prefer to blame the inherent faults of nature for all our ills, rather than to seek the far more likely cause in human carelessness and folly. As a result of this insensitivity and of the general state of disintegration, the virtues of wholeness are overlooked, and its importance in nature's most evolved organ, the human brain and mind, ignored. It is to be expected that the penalties for such deviations should be heavy, but there are also enormous potentials for recovery. These are not only in living organisms themselves, but in the wholeness of nature's art, as well as in human art. This ability to recover from mutilation is strikingly demonstrated in the hydra and other animals low on the evolutionary scale. Entire organisms can even be regenerated from tiny bits of tissue. The embryo provides a particularly good instance of this property. So strong is the regenerating force, that one can only suppose it receives its directive from the transcendental aspect of nature, which guides it persistently towards integration, the most diverse parts being assembled into effective holistic structures. It can also be presumed that, during the evolution of surreality—due to the movement towards humanisation—such intrinsic foci were played back into existence, so aiding the quest for wholeness. If a relationship with such foci can be discovered by the individual, by society or civilisation through religion, ritual or art, then the result will be of enormous assistance in finding an integrated way of life. The relevance of the arts which appeal to the higher faculties is evident. Not only can individuals be healed, but entire societies. Healing, not only as a localised effect in organic and psychiatric conditions, but in the diseases of group and social relationships as a whole, will then take place. Survival of the human species on this planet is dependent to a great extent on these social relationships and art can make a positive contribution in this direction.

The way in which such surreal foci can manifest themselves in our lives was shown by C. G. Jung.[1] Indeed his archetype was this whole-seeking, all-reconciling motif, embodied in the endless forms of the mandala. Jung implied that such archetypes were not to be conceived of as being in the head of the individual, but as belonging to the psychological genome of the species as a whole.

Starting from the absolute unity of the continuum expressed in the atomic realm—temporarily obscured in the first steps of material evolution, but gradually recovered with higher processes of development—one can appreciate the importance of the holistic principle by the time nature had reached the humanising mind. It was the prelude to its onward evolution in surreality. If lack of wholeness could become a universal distraction at such a stage, then the entire work of Creation could be sabotaged.

All art, whether poetry, painting, music, mime or ballet, offers the participant a way into a relationship with such foci. The mandala happens to be a concise, simple expression of this process, regarded as useful in meditational practice. All great art should do as well, if not better, and the strongly vitalising kinds of autonomous images already described, should be the most effective. But the proper contemplation of nature's art can also provide such integrating foci, justifying the floralised sanatoria of the ancient Greeks, an echo of which is still maintained in the association of flowers and convalescence.

Jung explained the way in which these foci can be entered into. At their best they occur in high dreams. One may not be able to order one's dreaming, but by aspiring to wholeness, and by making life itself a whole enterprise, the chance of having such dreams undoubtedly increases. It is a chain reaction: steady persistence produces tremendous rewards. Jung also discovered the value of the creative process; he encouraged his patients to draw and paint, and noticed that when they intuitively hit upon mandalic forms, they received a boost of healing energy. All art production, even the most elementary, possesses this power.

If this concept could be enlarged to embrace the entire environment, the inescapable conclusion must be that living itself could become a holistic attainment. It could only happen if the whole of nature were treated as the supreme, all integrating work of art which it should be. The challenge of art is that it must inevitably take part in social involvement.

The conclusion that the human being is nature's greatest and most successful work of art implies that the proper contemplation of the human form should be the most effective way of inducing a peak experience. If surreality is the replica of earth's existence reflected in greater splendour, then just as there must be supernal naturalistic aspects in surreality, so there must be supernal equivalents of human beings. Contemplation of the great paintings of the West which have featured human beings, leaves little doubt that their forms and faces acquire a supernal illumination. This revelatory quality is so strong, in a Rembrandt portrait for instance, that it can be quite breathtaking, leading to an uplift which cleanses and heightens our subsequent view of our fellow beings, in whom we seem to detect something of the divine illumination in these paintings.

Although many mystics have been preoccupied with nature, sensing in it a supernal revelation of the lights of paradise, they have all been entranced by the human person. Traherne, in some famous lines[2] describes scenes featuring spectral human-like creatures which come as close as possible to a revelation of the human surreal dimension. This transfiguration of the person is a common feature of the great humanistic tradition in poetry. It is potent in the poetry of love, showing clearly a biological feature of the emotionalisation of sex, the key feature of human sexuality. As the poets describe it, the condition of being in love completely transforms the beloved. All meanness and any possible uncomeliness is removed, and an absolute perfection reigns, irrespective of possible blemishes observable by others.[3] Something of this kind happens also in portrait paintings. Many painters have said that to paint an effective portrait requires a loving predisposition and although it has sometimes taken a sexual turn it can also completely transcend sexuality.

In contemplating such paintings, one is enjoying the display of art through other members of one's species, in much the same way as occurs among birds. Here the primary function is reproductive, but every patient observer of display in birds has become aware that the emotional transfiguration can take over, so that the joyful display becomes an essentially emotional matter. What I want to suggest is that what the mystic and poet and artist see, should be a part of the common human vision, that we are intended to see our fellow human beings in this vernal, illuminating way and to derive therefrom an inspiring, uplifting purifying peak experience.

This was one of the early, fervent appeals of Christianity, the uplift in ecstatic togetherness; it is probably the main gratification in the passionate phases of all religion, for nothing is more powerful than people possessed and boosting one another in ecstasy. Such a state of ecstasy may also be achieved through soft drugs, or indeed by alcohol, but only when it is taken in a purely sacramental context. In any other situation alcohol promotes interpersonal awareness at lower levels, not peak-inducing but dionysian. Having lost the sense of wonder in things and creatures, we have become singularly unresponsive to this high, peak-inducing interpersonal awareness. Indeed, many of the strategies of civilised existence are aimed at avoiding this awareness, which is felt to be awkward and embarrassing.

Not only ugly, insensitive, thwarting and disturbing environments block it, but crowding makes it quite impossible by cheapening and vulgarising personal relationships. Sex as a self-indulgent pursuit of the orgasm, treating the partner as a sex object, is completely hostile to it.

Children are especially able to elicit the ecstasy derived from the contemplation of the face and body which, no doubt, is why angels have so often been pictured as children. It is curious to observe that something of this response can also be evoked by the young of most mammals and birds. Nature has evidently long been preparing itself for this kind of awareness. Grace and form and movement are significant, but in adult inter-person ecstasy, the eyes are important. Every portrait painter becomes aware that the eyes have a supreme relevance to the entire facial expression. Eyes are like crystals, related to light, and light as we have seen, is the closest analogy to the transcendental in the world of appearances. The expression in the eyes, so elusive, so mysterious, is probably a special kind of mandala connected with the 'angelic form' of a man's or woman's reference to surreality.

There is a noticeable synergy between high art experience and the ability to sense this inter-person ecstasy. Music in particular can put one in the right mood for it. One can appreciate the relevance of music in the ritual of those religions which have recognised the importance of the peak experience. Once a particular person has featured in such an experience, there is a permanent uplift in the relationship; such a person is never seen as ordinary again. Its value in the bondings of love and of society, is evident; in all probability, it consists of knowing another person in the most fundamental sense, perhaps the only genuine way of human knowing, absolutely convincing, silent and permanent, while all other levels of knowing are open to doubt and misunderstanding.

Sadly, civilised living and education have effectively stifled this fundamental means of human communication. It does still occur, but when it does, like the peak experience in art and dream, it seems so far from what is culturally admitted, that it is played down, dismissed. A curious rather pathetic form of it may be seen in the adoration of the symbolic personalities of pop stars and film stars in the world of entertainment.

CHAPTER EIGHTEEN

ART, SOCIETY AND POLITICS

We shall probably never know for certain whether there was any civilisation before the earliest Ice Age or during the long inter-glacial periods. Probably little evidence of our own civilisation would remain a few thousand years after its demise, had we not polluted the whole planet with radioactive waste.

But assuming that some steps had been taken in the development of civilisation, and that this phenomenon is a normal development theme in a humanising evolution, it is certain that nothing as complex and sophisticated as the great civilisations of Eurasia and the New World came into being until the end of the last Ice Age. What this means is that for an extremely long time human beings must have existed in relatively small groups; for the most essential step in the civilising process requires communities that are large enough to allow for a range of specialised activities, and a workforce available to do the chores which allow the gifted individual time for reflection and art. It is a disturbing thought that this freedom was initially won by a social system steeped in injustice and the exploitation of man by man—a system of slavery, in other words. Without this kind of society there would have been no Plato or Socrates. It could be that such a stage of development would not have been necessary in more ideal circumstances, but post Ice Age conditions were such that civilisation on this particular planet arose in that particular way, and could only be transcended when society found a way of superceding human energy by technological skills.

The dependence of social organisation on cortical conditioning rather than on animal instinct suggests that the forms taken by the earliest social groups, are likely to have been as varied as those which higher culture and civilisation subsequently assumed. But one feature is common to them all: the family group. This is the biological matrix from which the humanising process emanates. So strong are these emotional bonds that they are effective with very large numbers of people, although as social inconsistencies arise, so the natural impulse to altruism, co-operation and compassion have to be socially reinforced.

Even during the depraved conditions of the Palaeolithic era, human compassion was not obliterated. This is shown in the care with which the dead were buried, and by the attentions accorded to the aged and infirm. These remote ancestors, who lived in conditions that were far more stressful than those of our present-day world, may well have been more humane than we are. Disregard for human life in war and other forms of mass slaughter, and the sanctioning of violence in every aspect of living—particularly in entertainment—has brought about a degree of social insensitivity, in our modern world, under which no primitive community could have survived.

The complexities and specialisations of civilisation made possible the life of the mind on which social organisation, religion and art depended. Whatever the existential conditions in society as a whole, the higher function of the mind persisted, especially in art and religion. The large amount of art works left by the great civilisations is a permanent revelation of their higher aspirations. If it is true that humans may have been in existence for three million years, one may wonder why it took so long for civilisation to appear. Possibly the severe challenge of the Ice Ages was necessary to bring about the self-awareness on which civilisation depends; but the Ice Ages were also massively dehumanising. If cyclical catastrophe is part of nature's way of working, this was overdone in the Ice Ages, particularly the last, the most severe of them all.

This terrible trauma no doubt accounts for the strain of nature-defiance in mankind, particularly in the antecedents of Western civilisation. This strain was intensified by desert conditions in which survival depended on meticulous attention to the practical problems of existence and mastery over alien natural forces. The leaders of these early civilisations were ruthless warrior kings, aggressive, arrogant and defiant. In such conditions, the peak experience in art or religion was not to be expected. In time this exclusive concern with survival became somewhat mellowed in certain regions of the Mediterranean, particularly in and around Greece, whence a dawning sensitivity to other-worldly values spread, with intervals of conflict, chaos and decadence, into the region of Italy where the expertise of the ancient traders flowered in luxury and great wealth, enabling patronage of the arts and a high appeal barely known before. For the first time, in its music and painting and poetry, the West became aware of the splendour of the surreal.

Like art, the essential core of religion is symbolic, a symbolism that is in tune with the mystical lights of surreality rather than the demonic elements of the magical subconscious. Although there have been periodic outbursts of the mystical in the history of world religions, generally it is the more practical who have taken over religious activities and made use of the enormous worldly powers it offers. As the high mystical inspiration has waned, so the demonic and magical elements have increased and the arts have been affected accordingly. In the ancient New World, religion was almost completely dominated by the harassed, subconsciously overrun mind, with very little of the sublime aspect appearing in the arts. The massive and terrifying sacrifices of the Aztecs, their sensitive but demonically possessed sculpture and monumental religious architecture, point to a general state of psychosis. There are no angelic entities, no benevolent gods in the cosmology of the Mayas and Aztecs. These people, although they reached a high state of civilisation in many respects, brought with them a degree of psychological trauma more acute than that of the Eurasian West. This was undoubtedly attributable to their long and terrible pilgrimage from the East, down the glacially-ravaged American North. The Far East appears to have escaped this religious psychosis. Although the magical mind shows every sign of having been periodically active in the civilisation of China, the Taoist influence, with its refusal to become embroiled in a concrete theology, probably helped to spare it from the kind of infernal schisms and persecutions of religion, common in the West. The Taoist influence, so fertile in poetry, music, painting, pottery and porcelain, as well as in enamel and metal work, was more compatible with a humanly based science, and prevented the headlong rush into an anti-human industrialism, to which the West, because of its crude materialism, fell victim.

In India conditions appear to have been somewhat exceptional; possibly because what is now India and South East Asia were largely spared from both glaciation and intermittent desiccation. The earliest civilisations to appear there, which may have been contemporary with, or even earlier than those we have already discussed, show all the signs of a happy, benevolent existence. The children's toys, for example, were beautiful; unlike the gruesome objects depicting human sacrifice, common in the earlier phases of other civilisations. The arts of Indian civilisation have been particularly humanistic, joyful and exuberant, and its nature religions more benevolent and compassionate, than others.

Things went differently in Europe—the early civilisations were violent and ruthless, coming to a crisis of decadence with the collapse of the classical world. Roman civilisation brought order, if not very much inspiration, to the highlife of the mind; but this order was dismantled during the Dark Ages, probably due to a recurrence of near glacial conditions in Europe.

Whatever the particular conditions that coincided with the apogee of Greek civilisation, it favoured a greater clarity of the intellect than had ever been seen before. We should really try to discover much more about the exact conditions that brought this about for it is evident that this clarity of mind is now very rare, and most easily disturbed.

Today we show little sign of understanding the conditions that produced it or the true nature of this clarity. It was an inspired lucidity of vision that reappeared in the Renaissance; in the present century clarity is confused with mechanistic reason. This confusion can perhaps itself be seen as an aspect of the disturbance and clouding of the modern mind, for it should have been evident that reason, without a humanising predisposition, can but end as a dehumanising agency, as is proved by the humanly insensitive application of science.

Those few individuals, like Rousseau, who favoured a more sensitive attitude were ridiculed. The truth is that it is not possible to sustain a soft, sensitive, humanistic view under harsh conditions. To most people, to the politicians in particular, the Hobbsian view seemed more credible, more attuned to the facts of life. Materialism was thus the product of an angry age, one which preferred to see the human situation as accidental and meaningless, without any transcendental reference, for this implies that action could be taken against nature, in the name of human progress and emancipation.

Such a situation was bound to favour the more ruthless and violent, just as had glacial conditions and earlier civilisations. There has thus been a very long selection in Western civilisation from its very roots, for aggressive, predatory and violent assertiveness. There was no question of the meek inheriting the earth. There can be little doubt that this anger, and the aggressive materialism that went with it, was encouraged by the failure of the Christian world-view—resulting in the internecine struggles of one of the most terrible and pitiless wars in European history. But this was not the only cause; there were many other reasons, competitive, commercial, nationalistic and finally political. Science also acquired an aggressive, nature-assaulting streak.

Many of the tough minded men who acquired new industrial and scientific power, imposed appalling mental distress on the weaker or more sensitive majority of the population, as we can see in the soaring incidence of mental disease. Schizophrenia is the most serious of these symptoms for it affects especially the pubertal young, inducing a retreat from existence with often disastrous consequences on the psyche. We shall return to this, and to the almost general neurosis of civilisation; what needs to be mentioned here is that this situation has been the direct result of a humanly intolerable desensitisation of existence, worse than in any previous age, for now religion—the 'opium of the people' as Marx called it—has been removed.

The arts responded positively to this powerful dehumanisation. Although many sensitive people, denied creative expression, retreated into mental instability the genuinely creative protested by accentuating what was in fact being desecrated, that 'other world' of revelation. Battle was joined between the tough-minded and the sensitive, who managed to create imageries and music and poetry of protest, proclaiming to all who could feel that the materialistic age was a sham. The battle continues still, in the persecution of creative people by the dictatorships of right and left, the inheritors of the dehumanised age.

The result of this materialistic fallacy has been a stampeding rise in social violence and outrage against the human individual. This is highly significant, for it may well be the included mechanism whereby an unfit society is eliminated from the cosmic age. Since materialism is now the dominating force in all planetary societies, the elimination could well be planetary.

The serious extent of this deterioration is seen in the increasing incidence of acutely disturbed people among whom there are many who suffer from a growing incapacity to think clearly and rationally. Even among the better educated there is a confusion of thought, a readiness to accept the crudely irrational and fantastic and psychologically prurient, which was not evident, at least among the more stable middle-classes, half a century ago. The deterioration is therefore not merely progressive, but stampeding. What proportion of the public are so stricken and how much longer will it be before the entire population can be considered more or less acutely mentally deranged?

Among the unbalanced many are violent, life-hating and destructive and consequently hostile to art. This is increasingly evident in sexual opportunism and promiscuity—one of the means of dulling the sensitivities—and in the association of violence and sex evident in pornography. More recently this has taken a form that is particular to the present stage of civilisation: what might be called the 'Bonnie-and-Clyde' syndrome. By nature, the male is much more easily triggered into violence than the female; understandably so, for the male is specialised for the defence of family and society. Violent types are necessarily more sexually active and dominant, and this is determined by the male chromosomes. The human female, by contrast, is designed by nature to be compassionate and submissive for breeding and rearing purposes. This function can be cortically conditioned to male dependence, especially to the sexually dominant and violent male. Some women can become so attached to such males that they assume a violent, masculine role in a manner not witnessed in any other age or society. This is an indication of terrible auto-destructive forces at work in society. When the female mammal, on which the entire cerebral and mammalian experiment depends, becomes a life-rebel, the game would seem to be up.

Freud observed the close association of Thanatos, the death wish, with the demise of Eros or love, but his explanation of this association was incorrect. Love, in its humanising role and in its association with beauty and joy, has no possible connection with death, except in as far as love, beauty and joy may all transcend death. But when love becomes equated with self-seeking lust, there is an inbuilt obstacle to its full realisation which takes the form of guilt and the death-wish which has haunted civilisation and is undoubtedly on the increase. To a society in such a situation, art in any form is inconceivable. Even entertainment becomes corrupt and anti-human.

In such circumstances it is the magical mind, and its macabre and terrifying aspects, which governs existence to the point where living itself becomes sheer hell. Such a state is not one of continuous decline, but one which oscillates with increasing periods of horror. If in less harassed moments the tortured are allowed to suppose that things are not in fact as terrible as they seem, they are soon reminded of their terror by films of the cruellest moments of war and violence. Perhaps the greatest infirmity is the shortness of memory regarding pain and horror; in this hell on earth there is little evidence of beauty or harmony or order. These human beings seem designed not for love and creativity but for destruction and despair.

Freud rightly postulated that the inspired achievements of art, culture and civilisation in general, come from the sublimation of the sexual libido. But his interpretation of this aesthetically creative urge was faulty. The superego is not an artificial elaboration of social censure and sexual denial, but a biologically implanted humanising force originating in the higher aspects of the mind. As Freud saw it the arousal of the subconscious was a natural and inevitable part of man's animal nature, which was accentuated by the sexual frustrations imposed by civilisation. However if one takes the view that unchecked libidinal sexuality is not the human norm, but rather that civilisation based on sexual love, not lust, is the natural means of human enhancement, this in no way precludes the possibilities of inspiration achieved through cultural challenge and stimulus. In such circumstances, involving every positive aspect of existence both the 'feminine' humanising pole and the 'masculine' assertive and creative pole become more active, especially among the creatively endowed.

The sickness of civilisation is seen at its most acute in politics, which is the manifestation of a phenomenon that is probably inherent in the particular planetary deviations of earth; the strange terrible manipulation of power over human life. This often masquerades as something necessary to human progress and justice, but almost invariably it erodes human sensitivity and reduces perception virtually to a point of no return.

I have suggested that the arts which prosper in any period or place do not depend on the whim of artists, but reflect profound currents in the social psyche. This, however, is only true if the artist is sufficiently free to give expression to his intuitive response, and such freedom, alas, is rare. For the most part the artist is called in to serve the wielders of power—the magician or priest, prince or politician—and is persecuted or ignored if he fails to do their bidding.

There has always been a peasant-like underground art. It is often quaint and refreshing to the more sophisticated, but usually it can be described as simple, even childish. Art which involves the individual at a deeper level has usually been provided for an elite minority. At times this elite has allowed the artist considerable freedom. Such was the case with the painters and sculptors of the Renaissance; the poets and painters of the Tsung dynasty in China, and the Court musicians of Europe. It is a curious phenomenon that the more prosperous and powerful such an elite becomes, the more freedom it offers to creative artists. Indeed, it is virtually historical law that the harsher the conditions of power, and the tougher the elite, the greater the bondage of the arts, sometimes to the point of near extinction. At the other end of the scale, the easy-going life of the power-elite in prosperous times often fails to provide the artist with sufficient directive and sense of social purpose, so decadence sets in. It would seem that the most artistically profitable periods are those which come with the first flush of freedom following oppression.

In the present time, when it is widely believed that majority power is a practical possibility, and that elites can be eliminated, it is salutary to remember that great art, as defined here, has only flourished in the service of the more tolerant and benevolent of patrons.

Throughout the entire period of human history, the available resources have been in far too short supply to enable the majority to enjoy the good life, and so the elite has usually been brutal or cunningly avaricious. This means that great art has always been undemocratic, in that it has been reserved for a minority and inaccessible to the impoverished masses.

It is evident that it was not a fundamental difference between rich and poor which prevented wide appreciation of great art in the past, but rather that of an economic gap. And, as I have already emphasised, when life becomes sufficiently hard, brutish and inhuman, high art has no place. When the underprivileged have rebelled and taken power, they have, in due course, become as preoccupied with art as the aristocrats they displaced. It seems to be a universal principle that, given sufficiently easy conditions, art becomes passionately necessary. This is probably because people become more sensitive, less brutalised and more aware and possibly also because the arts offer some solace and comfort in the face of inhumanities that are unavoidable.

The breakdown of the elitist class systems of the past—brought about by the vast increases in resources made available through industry—has not automatically meant that the kind of art so cherished by the elite has become available to the masses. On the contrary, the level of art has dropped in every field—particularly in entertainment.

The effort of learning to appreciate great art has been rendered unecessary by easy, trivial, hedonistic art forms. The attempts of a minority to preserve the more demanding, more involving arts have failed because what satisfies the low-level tastes of the masses hangs like an immense opaque screen between the people and the true artist.

Is this inevitable? Must the fulfilment of the materialistic dream necessarily be accompanied by the death of great art? When attempting to answer this question one is confronted by the myth that power can be taken over by the masses. At present much of the civilised world is in a period of transition. The gullible believe this to be a transfer of power to the people; but the indications are that this is an illusion that disguises the ascendence of a new incomparably more ruthless elite, far worse in its manipulation of power, than were the worst tyrants of the past.

This world-wide revolution is essentially taking place under the Marxist banner, openly or surreptitiously, so that any critique of the times must necessarily focus on Marxist philosophy. No class that has held power, no system that has dominated human existence for as long as the capitalist system, can be expected to give way without ferocious resistance. This makes it difficult to examine Marxism at the present juncture without passion. On one side, there is biased condemnation; on the other, dogmatic imposition. The only reasonable starting point is to recognise the great advances in human social thinking instituted by Marx. Thus, Marxist condemnation of an age of intellectual and emotional confusion about problems which call for eminently practical solutions; the validation of scientific determinism; the mechanism of power manipulation inherent in class rivalry; the decisive importance of the environment on economic planning, and the need to transcend the profit motive are all certain to have a lasting influence on social thought and action. But the notable poverty of Marxism, its absence of an aesthetic, means that it does not qualify as a philosophy for all traditional philosophies embody an aesthetic; it is therefore no more than a branch of theoretical sociology. Magee is explicit about the irrelevance of Marxism to the arts: 'There is a great deal of Marxist art of all kinds, novels, plays, paintings, sculpture and so on—and I have to say I regard most of it as rubbish. It is rubbish because the impetus that created it has not been a genuinely aesthetic impulse at all'.[1]

The probable explanation of why Marx ignored such an important activity is that the arts point to quite a different world-viewing to that of the exclusively materialistic scientific viewing of his day. Deterministic attempts to justify this assumption a half century ago and more, make curious reading today, when the stranglehold of dogmatic materialism has weakened, at least in the non-Marxist camp.

This insecurity in its fundamental tenets accounts also for the dogmatic streak in Marxism, or rather its political implementation. Even science is not spared this fearful dogma, as is seen in the famous case of Lysenko, a humble plant breeder with little knowledge of science, who was awarded the highest Soviet scientific accolade because he contested the neo-Mendelian theory (that the essential traits of every living organism are determined by its genes). His refutation was invaluable to the preponents of Marxist theory and the proliferation of its policies, because it vindicated their claim that environmental influence, which is susceptible to manipulation and modification, is paramount.

But, in spite of its shortcomings and practical failures—in its economics its concepts have visibly impeded progress wherever they have been dedicatedly applied—

Marxism still has an enormous appeal, not only among the under privileged of the world but among intellectuals and many scientists as well. For the latter, the appeal is understandable, for Marx accorded to science the top role of cultural conditioner.

As for the intellectuals, one can only suppose that Marx's violent and radical proposals found a resonance in their deep and growing anger following the failures of contemporary society. There was common ground in their recognition of the frustrations involved in getting a complacent establishment to acknowledge legitimate demands for reform. But the overriding explanation of the Marxist appeal is its potent millennial myth, true to the Judeo-Christian tradition. This myth was formulated without the least support from reality and reality has proved it unreliable.

In no Marxist experiment tried so far has power been successfully shared by the people. In every case it has simply been taken over by a new and necessarily violent elite. Realists have always recognised that the wielding of power entails some degree of ruthlessness, and those who have held positions of power have generally adopted the attitude that the end justifies the means; but both princes and despots have taken care that the naked brutality of their power has been masked. This was rarely done out of human consideration or sensitivity but because it complied with man's profound demand for dignity and justice.

These demands must have been implanted in the human disposition from its genesis for, as we have seen, only a compassionate, shared and altruistic native disposition could have ensured an effective humanisation. Human beings will put up with terrible oppression, but if these genetic standards are abused for too long they will rebel. Indeed it seems that this biologically implanted demand for dignity, justice and freedom is so strong that people would rather destroy the planet than submit to the tyranny of life without these qualities.

The new Marxist elite, backed by revolutionary violence, and lauded by subsequent supporters of Marx—perhaps as a method of emotional release, have discarded such ancient camouflage, believing that the most ruthless means justify the Marxist ends. Unfortunately their ignorance of human nature ensures that the ends are never met. Violence continues and a profound, dissatisfaction frustrates the tidy plans of politicians.

Why, one may well ask, is human nature so averse to what seemed the epitome of possible progress? After all, if the millennium could be attained, even at the sacrifice of millions of individuals, would it not be justified? Millions have already been sacrificed for much less. The answer is that although the human being may well be indispensable as an agent in nature's schemes, humanisation has been defective on this particular planet. Knowing the way that nature works on a cosmic scale, heartlessly neglecting or eliminating all that does not comply with its developmental drives, it could well be that although humanisation has been achieved, things have subsequently gone very wrong. The Ice Ages may well be largely responsible, but the roots of failure lie in the replacement of instinct by cortical conditioning. This means that once habits have been acquired they tend to be perpetuated, even when they are harmful to the species.

If it is true that earth humans are cosmic outcasts, out of line with the main pilgrimage of humanisation as a universal cosmic drive, and if there is no transcendental reference to human existence, then the ruthlessness of the elite, and their deception of the masses, would be justified; if matter is the only reality, one must conclude that the rapacious prince, the ruthless politician and the robber baron would be the winners, and the decent, considerate and kind the losers. This presents a terrible possibility. It is just as well that it has been concealed from the masses, largely due to religion and social authority, for its only future must be the selfish acquisition of material goods, violence and slaughter, exploitation and torture.

Marxism, which came into being in terrible times, consciously or unconsciously accepts this situation. Where it has differed is in its belief that science and technology can solve all the planetary problems that man has created and solve them, moreover, through a purely artificial social order. This has seemed reasonable to many people, and Marxism has spread with the same ease as Christianity, to which it is the atheistic heir. Not only does the struggle for power persist, even in the midst of material plenty, but the legitimate aspirations of human nature have been ignored.

The absolute ruthlessness of totalitarian regimes is made worse through the widespread belief that there is no alternative. In a meaningless material universe, reactionary visions are the ultimate offence, and the inability of material plenty to satisfy deeper human needs is never recognised. When the deprivation of beauty, dignity and freedom causes disintegration in the human psyche, it is labelled insanity.

If Marxism continues to spread the prospects for the arts are grim. If they are to survive at all it will be in the form of severely persecuted rebel arts. Indeed, the prospects as a whole for a truly human condition are bleak. Given the terrible forms that power has taken on this planet, and its natural selection of violent types, no vision of hell as yet formulated is likely to compare with the future condition. Opposition to Marxism, which is considerable, can only be eliminated by the total dehumanisation of society, for the spur to freedom, individual dignity, a belief in transcendental realities beyond the common material sphere, are all deeply vested in human biology. Unfortunately there is enough validity in Marxism for it to continue to 'win friends and influence people', especially the young, so perpetuating the use of violence which this age seems to applaud. Even more tragically, the opposition is infiltrated by revivalist hopes; there is an unhealthy nostalgia for the past because there is no consistent alternative philosophy capable of amalgamating the rights for which Marxism stands, with those other imponderable yet vital human requirements which it condemns.

Although at the moment there is a considerable reaction against science, it cannot be denied that the modern world, and any possible orderly, progressive and humanistic future, is certain to depend on the humanisation of science and technology, rather than on some sort of return to simpler, more primitive conditions. The latter could possibly come about, however, and with a terror unimagined by its supporters, as the result of a planetary holocaust. But assuming that there is to be a tolerable humanised future, then power will have to be taken over by a humanised technocracy, guided by a humanised science, a revolution in which the arts are certain to have a key role. And in the meantime it would be wise for the artist to stay out of politics for, by definition, politics is a power game for which he is particularly ill-suited. The best service he can render in the reclamation of society is to pursue his creative, humanly felt, artistic direction in this dehumanised world.

CHAPTER NINETEEN

THE ROLE OF ART IN THE HUMANISATION OF SCIENCE

Any suggestion that the recovery of civilisation can come from a humanisation of the practical activities of modern life rests on the assumption that these activities are not fundamentally irreconcilable with the arts. What is irreconcilable is an exclusively materialistic view of reality, one which is hostile to the arts and to human sensitivity in general. There are signs that this is changing and it follows that reconciliation once again becomes possible.

Although superficially different in their approaches, the scientist and the artist have much in common. Although through training the scientist rigorously eliminates emotion from his work, studies of original work and scientific discovery indicate that intuition has often played an indispensable part. This is particularly true in the interpretation of experimental data and the build-up of theories and hypotheses, which in many respects resemble the making of a work of art and provides ample opportunity for intuitive enlightenment.

The late Professor Waddington, an eminent embryologist, made a pertinent observation about scientists and artists, when he said that while the majority of working scientists, who are merely exploiting fields that have already been opened up, can ignore or deny the intuitive process, those more original discoverers—on whom the progress of science depends—are invariably more open to intuitive guidance, resembling more closely the original artist. Waddington, himself a notable scientist with much original thinking to his credit, concluded that an aesthetically attuned sensitivity favoured the intuitive hunches on which original discovery depended.[1]

Intuitive guidance works through the artist's unconscious, as he experiments with his materials; the work develops and gains momentum. Although the scientist's methods of working are very different, inspiration can surface in much the same manner, provided aesthetic cues are present. Initially, inspiration comes in the form of ideas, subtle combinations of thought which precede all scientific endeavour. As Karl Popper[2] and others have made clear, the notion that the scientist can begin from blank impartiality is an illusion. Some sort of preconception is indispensable, although this is largely influenced by existing knowledge through a framed plan of investigation, or in the drafting of a new theory, there is always ample scope for intuitive intervention. In science as in art the approach and method, states of mind and body, and that of environment and background, are likely to account for the fact that original discoveries come to certain persons and not to others.

The freedom of the symbolic in the arts makes it much more likely that higher resources will be available than in the case of science; more immediately available, that is, but the entire endeavour of nature in space and time is replicated in the continuum. Although surreality only arises with the universal emergence of a humanising mind, long before the advent of such a mind nature had amassed a considerable continuum experience. Being purely functional it is conceivable that such an accumulation of experience would bring into being a quite new order in the physical universe, one subject to its own purely functional principles, so short-circuiting the delays and obstacles inherent in matter, space and time. In other words, in this continuum aspect of nature, functional problems have been resolved, and what could only be hinted at in the realm of space and time has become manifest and functionally effective in those specialised aspects of the continuum. It therefore follows that every aspect of nature—from the subatomic to the astronomical—has its replicative continuum aspects, available to the intuitively-guided scientist in the form of inspiration during his space-time investigations.

Besides the over-quoted example of the visionary discovery of the benzene ring, by the chemist Kekulé, there are many other examples of direct inspiration in science.[3] In some cases there would seem to be a virtually eidetic intensification, implying an involvement of the high mind plus a surreal approach. When this happens the purely physical replication of a particular aspect of nature becomes transfigured, made intensely vivid and convincing. This process does not necessarily reach the ordinary level of awareness. In fact, owing to the scientist's disciplined approach, this would be unlikely, but he would be strongly motivated toward some particular decision, some special co-ordination of available data, and have the urge to experiment in a definite direction, thus simultaneously achieving satisfaction on the emotional and intellectual levels.

G. S. Stent, a molecular biologist, has argued that a scientific discovery or theory, is more akin to a work of art than has been generally realised. Style, he contends, is as important as content.[4] Waddington suggested that Crick and Watson came upon the proper structure of the DNA molecule, on which all living functions including heredity depend, because it presented itself as an aesthetically satisfying structure. Other alternatives in the scientific air at the time, notably those of Linus Pauling, proved faulty because they were inelegant.

The scientist involved in research does not have to admit an art involvement. His mind works in the way it has been trained to work, and he believes in what he has been taught to believe. But an outsider can easily detect the streaks of artistic temperament in great original discoverers. Those who know Crick, and also understand the approach of the artist, agree that his verve and passion are closer to that of the artist than that of the scientist.

An interesting illustration of art and science coming together is provided by a recent theory which accounts for the plethora of 'particles' discovered in the last decade; a series of discoveries which have threatened our orderly view of nature. Just as the old idea that atoms were the ultimate units of nature had to be abandoned, so the idea that elementary particles are irreducible has been superseded by the recognition that they have properties which interchange and interact in a totally unexpected fashion. It is now supposed that elementary particles are composed of four *quarks* (recent evidence suggests that there may be more), each with different qualities. But if the qualities of the electrons discovered up to now have seemed mysterious, in that they possessed both material and insubstantial aspects, the properties which must be ascribed to the newly discovered quarks are even more fantastic. These properties are dealt with by ascribing to them particular mathematical symbols, this allows the physicist to deal with these mysterious entities by ignoring their material limitations. One method proposed for the handling of quarks is known as gauge theory. In this theory, the qualities of the quarks alter in such a way that they affect, in an orderly mathematical fashion, all the other quark properties in a particular situation. The best analogy one can find for such a situation is to imagine a grid of criss-cross elastic strings which can be coerced into producing different forms by being squeezed or pulled about. As the forms arise or disappear, every other aspect of the grid is affected. As we have seen, this is very much what happens in a work of art. Because of its absolute, holistic quality, the least alteration or addition affects the entire work.

This is a non-mechanical concept, for the force capable of bringing about such a unified, but differentiated change in the elastic grid cannot be an ordinary physical force; nor can the properties of the quarks be in any way conceived of in ordinary physical terms. In fact, to give some sort of verbal label to them physicists have ended up referring to their 'colours' and even their 'flavour'. Such a device is as symbolic as anything in the arts, and suggests that in moving away from ordinary, classifiable experience, the scientist is obliged to make use of much the same symbolism as the artist. The scientist, however, does not give form to this symbolism in paint or musical sound, but in the symbolic language of mathematics. Energy, it will be recalled, is used by the atom in a most specific manner, in very definite scales which, as the physicist Weiskopf suggests, has a musical equivalent.[5] This makes feasible application of the ancient Pythagorean notion of the 'music of the spheres', to the atomic world.

It is no coincidence that the basic sciences have become increasingly dependent on this kind of mathematics, for through such specialised symbols the human mind has been given a remarkable facility to attune itself to the most fundamental events in nature. The mathematics that deal with the ordinary world is inadequate because it deals in signs, but mathematics which penetrate beyond the appearance of reality are as absolutely symbolic as abstract painting or music. It is again no coincidence that many famous physicists and mathematicians have been lovers of music—notably Einstein.

Mathematics is effective in dealing with the basic functions of nature, because the mathematical equation is a dynamic device capable of symbolising the equally dynamic energy changes in nature. Looking through a textbook of advanced mathematics one gets the impression of a mass of jumbled hieroglyphics. Yet the equation, as it is deciphered, is as ordered and dynamic as the spin of an electron. If this were no more than an ingenious intellectual invention, it could not possibly have gone as far as it has in unravelling the mysteries of nature. The reason for the success of the mathematical equation is that the mind itself, like basic nature, is a ceaseless streaming process, a dynamic flux in which concepts arise, and new worlds are born. This property of mind has been recognised and drawn on by the important *stream of consciousness* movement in literature. The writer who can symbolise this fundamental streaming, touches upon the core of life's profound significance; for life itself is an outward and visible 'streaming' of the surreal world.

In devising his equations, in manipulating and modifying them to suit the data before him—or in pure mathematical speculation which undoubtedly has its own coherence—the mathematician, too, allows his intuition to function, so enabling him to attain transcendental sources of inspiration. The importance of elegance and beauty in mathematical procedure has been repeatedly stressed by a number of famous physicists and mathematicians; notably by Dirac of Cambridge, who has done so much original work on electron behaviour.[6]

How reliable this aesthetically-guided mathematics can be, is seen in the remarkable ability of theoretical mathematicians to work out independent systems without reference to other systems subsequently shown to be valid. It is a virtual law that only elegant and beautiful theories contain inner validity; those which are inelegant or unaesthetic are generally wrong or inadequate.

So reliable is this aesthetic criterion that some of the strange theories worked out by cosmologists are quite likely to be elegant references to other kinds of universes existing parallel to our own. As all the arts are said to aspire to the symbolic magnificence of music, so all the sciences aspire towards the mathematically elegant. Indeed, the power of aesthetic mathematics leads one to believe that under its influence the human mind has access to ultimate verities.

It follows then, that aesthetic sensitivity should be of enormous benefit to science, for as nature is loaded with aesthetic properties this widening of the scientific approach could be applied in any subject without the need of an external aesthetic. The scientist could become something of an artist in his own right. Such an intuitive sensitivity could be practically applied not only in research and theoretical work, but would help the individual scientist attain a higher level of fulfilment in his work, leading ultimately, as in alchemy, to an integrated personality. Backed by a meaningful model of nature there is no reason why the scientist, while retaining the rigid discipline of his particular field, should not widen his emotional horizon.

This hypothesis provides the means of allowing the broad cultural correlation, recognised by C. P. Snow, to be implemented through the development of sensitivity to art in scientists and technologists, as well as those involved in the creation and preservation of the environment. In other words, such an aesthetic would be pertinent to each and every field of enquiry and exploration.

It has to be realised that aesthetic cues exist in all forms of science, in all humanly worthwhile activity and labour, and that although usually ignored or regarded as unimportant or distracting, they could bring about a scientific and technological revolution if allowed to percolate into conscious awareness. Such an awareness would revitalise every branch of education, every profesion, every skill, and afford joy in place of monotony and boredom.

Such a flowering would confirm science as the preeminent cultural arbiter; it would be a science no longer culturally separated and impartial, but humanly involved. All artists cannot become scientists, but because they can grasp the symbolic significance of scientific concepts, they may be able to make obscure scientific theory available to those who deal with the practical world.

The broad data for such an integrational fusing of art, technology, architecture, planning and work organisation should be investigated. The outcome is far more than a question of preserving the already desecrated environment, it embodies the creation of a new synthesis; a synthesis of the naturalistic, the urban and the technological in terms of the full spectrum of human needs. Foremost among them are the aesthetic criteria of wholeness and purity. Once people's sensitivities were revived, they would find it inconceivable that the world could have been so desecrated, so unfeelingly exploited or ignored. Yet the contamination goes on. Every year thousands of new chemicals are added to our environment, substances of which animals and plant life have had no biological experience and which on the basis of this consideration alone, must be harmful, and often fatal.

The mystically inclined architect, poet or artist, as well as the great religious visionaries such as St Augustine, have sensed a sublime reference in the concept of the city.

In surreality, some equivalent of the city must exist in splendour and perfection, and if the spur towards environmental change is to make our environment a reflection of what exists in surreality, then the relevance of this vision can be appreciated. The city, strange as it may sound, becomes the focus of a possible reconciliation between nature and man-made artefacts, between art, science and technology. Through this the aesthetic potentiality of the machine can be detected. Not only are its forms integrated in meeting the needs of dynamic efficiency, but it also undoubtedly contains a new symbolism full of strange and fascinating connections to nature. There is no reason at all why a humanised, mechanised environment should not take on the role of stimulating human beings in a manner thought to belong only to nature. Indeed, the symbolical possibilities of the man-made environment, in collaboration with art and nature, could flower into a widening of a chance to reaffirm the relationship between cortical existence and that of the basic, biological mind. That is the challenge.

The attitudes necessary, and the sensitivities to be nurtured, have to be practised not only through a revised aesthetic and appreciation of the arts, but through a new relationship to nature, matter, object, work and entertainment. A course in natural philosophy, so popular with the Victorians, should once again have a place in every curriculum, so reconciling art, aesthetics and science. Virtually any subject pursued with an awakened awareness of its aesthetic potential can serve as a guide. The study of botany, mineralogy or geology—all within the grasp of the average educated person—are full of potential instruction along the lines of a reconciled intellect and intuition. Although it is not fashionable to praise them I believe personally that the Victorians with their sense of wonder at the strange urban and industrial world they were making, came close to finding the solution from which we have strayed so far.

Ecology is a particularly relevant subject, for in it the interrelatedness of art, science, nature and cosmos can be clearly perceived. The unravelling of the ecological web provides a high level of aesthetic and intellectual satisfaction making one aware, as no other subject can, of the relevance of the forces at work in Creation, and of the role of the humanised mind in this great work. The dynamic integration of creatures and environments is widespread and, as knowledge increases, it is beginning to be understood that this extends to the stars.

In this book I have tried to demonstrate how the process of humanisation is intrinsically tied to aesthetic sensitivity. It is my belief that people cannot properly be human unless this activity is manifest, and the measure of de-humanisation in any society, in any age, can be fairly accurately measured by the level of aesthetic sensitivity. The great social value of art is that even as a minority preoccupation it has a radiative influence, and there is no doubt that if even a few people truly accept the relevance of art and put it into practice, the present drift to the trivial, insensitive and increasingly inhuman, can be reversed and the long work of healing and recovery can begin.

CHAPTER TWENTY

THE DESTINY OF ART

I have suggested that the destiny of all arts, as the means of revelation of surreality, is to guide existence and effort, so that the environmental undertaking can be made to symbolise surreality as closely as possible. I have also suggested that this undertaking, like the civilising process itself, is a necessary aspect of the human role in the total scheme of things and one that must be met. For nature's summit creature to have remained in a simple arcadian condition would have made no sense at all. But whereas our past and present attitudes to nature and environment have been opportunistic they should at their most meaningful be aimed at the realisation of surreality in the midst of existence—as far as that is possible in terms of matter, space and time.

Our aim at the present juncture must be to find the means to break away from the prevailing threat of alienation and dehumanisation, caused by human failure to discover a satisfactory world viewing. Assuming that such a viewing is indeed possible—I shall end with this problem—the practical approaches remain to be resolved. In the first place, the ancient inclination to see in all man's extensive environmental undertakings, in temple or city, garden or industrial site, a reflection or symbolisation of cosmic relevance could be profitably revived. If man had always believed that the visible gives birth to the invisible, which in turn outshines the visible the present devastation of the planetary environment might have been avoided. Only a new vision of the surreal can now reverse the headlong flight to destruction. But before the environmental challenge *can* still be met, new disciplines are needed, able to repair the omissions in the present system of education. The prime subject should therefore be an integrated study pooling the teaching of art and science. All the specialist environmentally related subjects, engineering, architecture, planning, economics and sociology, medicine and agriculture should be involved. Such integrated courses will require highly versatile specialists able to co-ordinate the overall environmental undertaking; it will obviously need to be a very demanding study, which must include the indispensable experimental aspects of all its disciplines.

The way in which the overall environment can be integrated, made humanly meaningful and aesthetically valid, is shown in the way the problem has been met in nature. Even in its aesthetically successful aspects, not all the components in nature can be fully aesthetically resolved; some elements remain relatively neutral, a few perhaps can never be assimilated. Nature is effective because it has managed to produce aesthetic foci of enormous power, able to radiate out and reclaim the surroundings. This interrelationship of active foci and less aesthetically active components is so complex that it is only likely to be soluble by adequate attunement and intuitive sensitivity. But as in all things, study and experiment can ensure that intuition is effectively used. Clearly these high foci, thoroughly integrated into the environment cannot be conceived as individual works of art; they must be an intrinsic part of the active, functional environment, they must therefore be provided by the more aesthetically endowed in the various environmental disciplines, under the guidance of the integrated studies experts.

The assumption that the arts can guide all who are engaged in creating a particular civilisation—in our case especially those who control our environment—rests on the thesis that the arts respond to and articulate the emotional, aesthetic, psycho-social and spiritual needs of an age. This response is extremely complex and in no way mechanical. It is evident that some kinds of art suit a particular period better than others. Gregorian chant, for instance, for all its greatness and profundity, is less appropriate today, just as are El Greco's paintings or those of Fragonard.

The particular value of painting in this respect is that it provides a visual reference to such a climate. Impressionism, for instance, displays a much more evident reaction to the outrage of industrialism and urbanism than did the music of the same period. Images can be experimented with and modified more easily than musical form, while literature tends to become so preoccupied by the turmoil of contemporary existence, that the underlying causes of events may be obscured.

It may be possible for an exceptional person, whether architect, engineer, planner or some other controller of our lives, to ignore this emotional guidance and yet produce a significant contribution, but if the adaptive role of art is accepted, he will be more likely to think and work in the best way if he is emotionally and aesthetically attuned to the needs of his time. For those engaged in the challenge of the present day the emotional background that the related arts can provide, should perform much the same service that was formerly fulfilled by faith and religion. For a secular age, it is the only transcendental guidance still available.

All the senses should be involved in the process as they have all been involved in our relationship with nature. That we have largely lost the sublime olfactory involvement, except in an occasional whiff of floral scent or perfume—only underlines our insensitivity. Light, in all its sublime magic, now extended by new techniques such as lasers, is also poorly exploited. Evidently it is not only a question of synthetic environmental contributions; the naturalistic can, and indeed must, be incorporated. Large expanses of fully naturalistic expressiveness should be created within and between urban and industrial sites. Here also integration is the prime consideration; this rules out the present park-mentality, the growing of trees along city streets, flowers in windowboxes and the usual urban gardens. A quite revolutionary concept, making expressive use of the naturalistic in terms of the synthetic, is called for. This is a subject that has so far received very little attention and therefore requires experiment and study.

The human presence, as nature's greatest art, should be an inherent component of this environmental undertaking. Just as bodies have been evolved for the benefit of nervous systems, so the man-made environment is primarily for human use and expression, and the utilitarian should be subordinated to this, a reversal of present attitudes. This also requires a redefinition of what one is to mean and incorporate as a human being. Sick, ugly, violent and depraved people can be no part of this inspiration. Here compassion would appear to clash with aesthetics. Evidently the environmental effort must adapt compassionately to the fact that a considerable number of people are sick, deformed, handicapped, mentally disturbed, violent and destructive. But an effective environment can only be conceived in terms of the hale, the pure and the beautiful. Such an environment would undoubtedly have a recuperative and reclaiming influence, totally lacking in the present disintegrated and frequently hideous man-made condition.

The environmental challenge, conceived as the supreme work of art, is so demanding and so complex that it can only be met by inspired vision, verve and passion, fired once again by a belief in mankind and transcendental life. Without this vision, the unavoidable and increasing human impact on the environment can but lead to ever increasing folly and desecration, which will bring in its wake an irreversible dehumanisation, until the earth will be a hell beyond present imagining. The lingering belief and hope that in some as yet undiscovered way reason and common sense can save mankind, is denied by the increasing deterioration of these characteristics throughout the world.

The artist is no more qualified than most people to discover a meaningful world-view, even though he must find such a view to enable him to work effectively. Such a concept can only be proposed by a new generation of philosophers, drawing from both the sciences and the arts and attuned to the contemporary situation. This does not mean that what they may offer must be blindly accepted, but that they may serve as guidelines. On the other hand there does seem to be an inbuilt capacity in most people to accept what is offered if this is instinctively—or intuitively—felt to be true and right. Such is the basis of faith which is as old as mankind. As I have tried to indicate in this book, some aspects at least of an alternative world-view are within the grasp of those who wish to find them, and carry enough conviction to make them satisfying and acceptable.

It is encouraging that science is beginning to grope for

such alternative concepts. One of these, based on new evidence, is the concept that the universe is an anthropic venture, with life and mind in view from the first steps in the formation of matter some six billion years ago. But we must not be complacent—there is so little time and but the smallest reason for optimism. Success is too precarious, chance too omnipresent in all aspects of the universe. When a glimmer of hope is offered the human mind tends to jump to the conclusion that our particular world is safe and that, from this small and rather miserable planet, mankind can manage the universe.

This is a view to which those in the basic sciences are especially exposed, but it is extremely difficult and indeed contradictory, to suppose that the universe is precisely planned or expertly managed. That it has an extremely weak organisational direction is obvious. On the other hand confronted with the contradictions of theology, the non-scientific may be inclined to jump to the other extreme and rule out any teleological principle.

New concepts are evidently called for. An interesting approach to this problem was made recently by Dr Paul Davies, lecturer in applied mathematics at Kings College, London. After surveying the anthropic idea, he came to the following conclusion:

> In all these speculations, the remarkable nature of the observed Universe can be explained as a kind of biological selection. Observers will only be found in those very rare places where the highly improbable conditions necessary for life just happen to occur by chance. On this view . . . the world is still an accident, but one which is chosen by us to witness.[1]

The fact that we are the observers follows from the anthropic principle; we simply have to accept that it has required such a fantastically vast, possibly infinite Creation to provide these extremely rare circumstances where the anthropic principle in fact succeeds, against preposterous odds. Choice or teleology are in man's favour, but chance reigns very nearly supreme.

The dominance of chance is seen in the very near disasters of earth history, any of which might have brought the work of Creation here to a halt. This evidence has come from the computed interpretation of all that is now known of the earth's geological past.[2] On several occasions life was very nearly extinguished; that it was not, is because this planet evidently provides one of those very rare environments in the universe favourable for life. About 3.7 billion years ago, a runaway green-house effect, due to large amounts of liberated carbon dioxide, nearly turned the earth into a Venus-like condition, totally hostile to life. If it had been a little closer to the sun, disaster would have been inevitable.

To talk of 'purpose' in such a situation, or to bring in some creator or managerial agency outside the universe, is stretching credulity to unacceptable limits. Chance is too decisive, disaster too frequent. As the anthropic principle can be easily confused with such purposive creation, one can understand the scientists' suspicion of it. This point is made clear in an article in *Nature* by R. J. Carr and M. J. Reese in which the authors observe that the anthropic principle is scientifically unsatisfactory because it rests on coincidences.[3] However they go on to say that the concept can be made more palatable by certain cosmological concepts such as those of H. Everett. The 'many worlds' proposal of this cosmologist is in perfect accord with the quantum theory. In spite of their scientific caution, Carr and Reese comment, '. . . the discovery of every extra anthropic coincidence increases the *post hoc* evidence of it.' Although the concept is not yet a part of a new scientific world view, it is so important for the arts, indeed for existence in general, that we must accept it intellectually and prepare the way for the intuitive process. The evidence for the surreal world is all about us, clearly available through the absolute reassurance, the sense of enlivened wonder and the ineffable joy which the peak experience whether revealed through a work or art, or the art aspects of nature, can provide. It is enough for us to know that such revelation is genuine, it is enough that we know ourselves to be an integral part of Nature's purpose, sharing with it the inherent capacity to transcend time.

If I have stressed a particularly intense and demanding kind of art experience, it is because it has for too long been regarded as out of place in the materialistic view of reality which has dominated our civilisation. Common in earlier civilisations, and in a few rare phases of our own, the peak experience is today greatly neglected. Few people are aware of the transforming joy and reassurance it can provide, and some of those few, though convinced by its intensity, may yet believe themselves to be cultural outsiders. Because this hyperaesthetic experience is one of the most powerful and effective of humanising agencies, I believe its revival to be of immense significance to the survival of mankind.

Because there are so very few transcendental references left to modern man the hyperaesthetic is more important than ever before. It is everywhere evident that human beings are ill equipped for the spiritual aridity of modern life. Rising anger and violence is the reaction to deep despair and impoverishment. It is a dangerous reaction, one that will inevitably lead to the destruction of civilised existence if it is allowed to run rife. There is room in life for fun and diversion, entertainment and frolic, but let us find space too, for the sense of wonder, of reverence for beauty, harmony and purity in nature's own art, and in any human art that extolls and hallows and praises nature. For herein lies the only hope of human recovery.

REFERENCES

Chapter 1 Art, Science and Reality

1 A. Toynbee. *A Study of History* London 1977
2 J. Silk in a letter to *Nature* Vol 265 February 1977
3 S. L. Saki. *Science and Creation* London 1974
4 M. Capec. *The Philosophical Impact of Contemporary Physics* Princeton 1961
5 E. E. Harris. *The Foundations of Metaphysics in Science* London 1963
6 F. A. Wilson. *Nature Regained* Boston 1976; *Crystal and Cosmos* London 1977

Chapter 2 Varieties of Aesthetic Experience

1 M. Laski. *Ecstasy* Indiana University 1962
2 A. Koestler & R Smythies Eds. *Beyond Reductionism* London 1968
3 R. Clarke & C. Hindley. *The Challenge of the Primitives* London 1975

Chapter 3 Aids to the Peak Experience

1 A. Huxley. *The Doors of Perception* London 1954

Chapter 4 The Humanising Process
1 A. Maslow. *Motivation and Personality* New York 1970
2 H. Read. *Education through Art* London 1958

Chapter 5 Inspiration and Revelation
1 H. Waddington. *Behind Appearances* Edinburgh 1969
2 Kandinsky. *On the Religious in Art* London 1914

Chapter 6 Art and the Public
1 F. A. Wilson. *Alchemy as a Way of Life* London 1976
2 R. W. Fuller & J. A. Wheeler. 'Causalty and Multiple-connected Space-time' *Physical Review*, Vol 228, 15 October 1962

Chapter 7 A Two Level Model of Reality
1 Carter, Dicke, Dyson, Bonnor, Everett and others referred to in 'How Special is the Universe' *Nature* Vol 249, 17 May 1974
2 J. A. Wheeler. 'Our Universe: The Known and the Unknown *Scientific American* April 1968
3 For further explanation of Boltzman's theory see: P. Davies. *The Runaway Universe* London 1978
4 S. W. Hawking. 'The Quantum Theory of Black Holes' *Scientific American* January 1977
5 B. d'Espagnet. 'The Quantum Theory of Reality' *Scientific American* November 1979
6 A. N. Whitehead. *Process and Reality* Cambridge 1929

Chapter 8 Art as Revelation
1 T. Leary. *The Politics of Ecstasy* London 1970
2 In *Phaedo*: for further discussion see F. A. Wilson *Crystal and Cosmos* London 1977

Chapter 9 The Creative Process
1 French mathematician and philosopher see: E. P. Northrup, *Riddles in Mathematics* London 1945

Chapter 10 The Limits of Communication
1 J. A. Wheeler & C. M. Patton in *The Encyclopaedia of Ignorance*, Eds. R. Duncan & N. Weston-Smith, London 1945

2 Editorial 'Science and the Citizen' in *Scientific American* July 1978
3 A. Hardy, R. Harvie & A. Koestler. *The Challenge of Chance* London 1973
4 H. Carrington. *Telepathy* London 1945
5 H. Bergson. *Matière et Memoire* Paris 1925

Chapter 11 Art and Eros
1 F. A. Wilson. *Alchemy as a Way of Life* London 1976

Chapter 12 The Evaluation of Art
1 N. Chomsky. *Aspects of the Theory of Syntax* Cambridge, Mass 1965

Chapter 13 Confusion and Direction
1 H. Jennings. *The Biological Basis of Human Nature* London 1930
2 E. O. Wilson. *Sociobiology* Harvard 1963

Chapter 14 Art in Nature and Matter
1 S. Langer. *Philosophy in a New Key* New York 1948
2 W. H. Thorpe. *Purpose in a World of Chance* Oxford 1978
3 F. A. Wilson. *Nature Regained* Boston 1976
4 J. Silk in a letter to *Nature* Vol 265 February 1977
5 W. Reese. 'The 13 Million Year Bang' *New Scientist* 2 December 1976
6 M. Calvin. *Chemical Evolution* Oxford 1969
7 F. A. Wilson. *Crystal and Cosmos* London 1977

Chapter 15 The Aesthetics of Life
1 A. Hardy. *The Living Stream* London 1965
2 R. E. Benveniste & J. J. Todaro in a letter to *Nature* Vol 261 13 May 1976
3 F. A. Wilson. *Art into Life* London 1963
4 E. M. Simons. 'Ramapithecus' *Scientific American* May 1977
5 R. F. Kay in a letter to *Nature* Vol 268 18 August 1977

6 P. Andrews in a letter to *Nature* Vol 268 25 August 1977
7 M. Pickford. 'Prehuman Fossils from Pakistan' *New Scientist* 8 September 1977
8 R. Gorczynski & T. Steele, Proc. U.S. Academy. Sciences Vol 72: 1980
9 P. B. Taylor. 'Lamarkist revival in immunology' *Nature* Vol 286, 28 August 1980

Chapter 17 Art as an Aid to Integration

1 C. Jung. *The Archetypes and the Collective Unconscious* London 1930
2 Thomas Traherne. *Centuries of Meditation* Cent iii
3 For Ruskin on this subject see F. A. Wilson *Nature Regained* Boston 1976

Chapter 18 Art, Society and Politics

1 B. Magee. *Men of Ideas* BBC, London 1978

Chapter 19 The Role of Art in the Humanisation of Science

1 H. Waddington. *Behind Appearances* Edinburgh 1969
2 K. Popper & J. C. Eccles. *The Self and Its Brain* London 1978
3 B. Ghiselin. *The Creative Process* California 1952
4 G. S. Stent. 'Molecular Evolution and Metaphysics' *Nature* Vol 348 26 April 1974
5 V. S. Weiskopf. *Knowledge and Wonder* New York 1962
6 P. A. M. Dirac. 'The Evolution of the Physicist's Picture of Nature' *Scientific American* May 1973

Chapter 20 The Destiny of Art

1 P. Davies. 'Chance or Choice; Is the Universe an Accident?' *New Scientist* 16 November 1978
2 'Monitor' *New Scientist* 15 March 1979
3 R. J. Carr & M. J. Rees. 'The Anthropic Principle and the Structure of the Physical World' *Nature* Vol 278 12 April 1979

Appendix

AN INTERPRETATION OF THE NEW PHYSICS

The transcendental level in nature referring to a space-time continuum beyond our own, is discernible in certain aspects of both relativity theory and quantum theory, although from a different standpoint in each case.

In relativity theory, matter (m) is equivalent to energy (E) as set by the squared speed of light in the familiar equation $E = mc^2$. The speed of light or radiation sets the limit to energy in the form of matter. Other equally intense expressions of energy would serve the same end, for instance, in the gravitational collapse of certain types of stars, matter becomes so compressed that unimaginably vast amounts of energy are released, which can exceed the limits of existence of matter in space and time. In such *black holes* matter continuously disappears out of the universe. If a black hole is reversed matter pours from a *white hole* into the universe of space and time.

To the inevitable question as to what happens to matter in such an event, the only possible answer is that it passes over into some energy state, related to matter, while no longer manifesting itself in space and time as we know it, it continues to exist in some other aspect of nature. As the speed of light, or a black hole, is approached, very strange things begin to happen—strange, that is, to ordinary common sense perception. Time dilates and matter shrinks. It is at least theoretically possible that suitable mechanisms could dematerialise themselves and subsequently become rematerialised, in which case travel throughout the universe, in the space of a single lifetime, becomes a conceivable possibility. This idea has been revived recently by Dr J Gribbin in his book *Time Warps* (Dent 1979). But H. G. Wells long ago saw the possibilities.

In relativity theory matter is created by a very special feature of space called its *curvature*. As long as space is assumed to be an emptiness separating objects, this does not make sense—but space is *not* empty, it is a ceaseless pulsating creativity. What Einstein referred to as curvature describes the way this universal creativity squeezes energy into its material form. This creative stamp also causes matter to *bend* radiation in its vicinity, this is another proposition of relativity theory which has been proved by observation. This proposition also accounts for the pegging of space to the existence of universe-time, which we call space-time. Compared to the ordinary Euclidean geometric parameters of material existence this is a new dimension whose properties refer to quite another order of nature. In relativity theory new geometries have been required which go much further than Euclid or Newton. The evidence is as yet incomplete and somewhat distorted, which may be the reason that it has so far proved impossible to reconcile relativity and quantum theories.

The quantum approach can be traced to Nils Bohr who, in 1922, found it necessary to conjecture that radiation was discontinuous, to account for some of the evidence then available. The fact that energy, in the form of radiation, does manifest itself in pulses—or quanta—rather than continuously is fortunate, for had the manifestations of energy in space and time been continuous, experimental science would have faced an impenetrable wall. The existence of quanta means that basic events in nature can be treated *as if they were particulate.*

Not only does radiation have this property of pulsating, but the elementary particles themselves are discontinuous entities. They vibrate billions of times per second, and in intervals during this vibration they appear and reappear in and out of space, time and time again. It is quite impossible to explain what is happening in terms of an exclusively one-level material universe, but if a two-level universe is postulated, one in space and time and the other transcendent to it, this in-and-out of space-time existence can be seen as a vibration between two worlds. The interval of non-existence in space and time is known as the *quantum time gap*. It has a spatial aspect, the *quantum space gap*, set at 10^{23}cm. That is the unimaginably small size of the 'hole' between the material world and the interacting other world in nature.

Some non-material particles, like photons, have no need to maintain such an oscillatory connection with the other world for they are almost entirely a part of that world. One particle, the neutrino, may have a very special role to play in the functioning of nature. Until very recently it was assumed to have no mass at all. The only way in which it could be detected was by its spinning. So non-material is this particle that it can pass right through the earth as if it did not exist. Physicists have therefore had much trouble trapping it. Once believed to be rare, it is now thought that the neutrino may be one of the most common entities in the universe. Recent experiments indicate that it can change from a bodiless 'nothing' that spins, into a mass-possessing particle and that many grades of neutrinos can exist between these two poles (see: 'Neutrinos; Do they rule the universe?' by Dr Christine Smith *New Scientist* 19.6.80 p308). It seems likely that neutrinos have a very significant role to play as messengers between the non-material and the material aspects of nature.

Mass is as strange as any of the other properties of particles, although it is the one most closely connected with our ordinary notion of materiality. The mass of a particle is the energy from which it is formed, behaving in a very particular way which, magnified billions of times in, for example, a grain of sand, gives to it the common property we call density or weight. But one must emphasise that basically this property is not material at all; it is energy transformed so that the mass of the particle may seem to disappear. Although such particles can be destroyed or changed experimentally, there is reason to believe that in their in-and-out, Cheshire cat existence, they are not broken down at each pulsation, but are in some way transposed from one level of existence to another. The quantum gap can thus be seen as the means whereby the transcendental aspect of nature is exposed in every pulsation of every particle in the universe.

Because the transcendental level is atemporal and non-spatial events that have once occured must, in some sense, persist. It therefore seems probable that matter, at its most basic level, is programmed to function in this replicating manner, and that from the Big Bang onwards every event occuring in every atom has been duplicated and thus a replicate of the entire evolution of the universe persists at the transcendental level in nature. In this way, as it evolves, the universe provides itself with both memory and the expertise to profit from it.

For the human being, whose senses and intellect can only deal efficiently with an aspect of reality somewhere between the two extremes of the astronomical and quantal, this replicate organisation is not apparent. This is largely due to the materialistic way in which we are conditioned to look at things. As should be evident from the text such phenomena as light and colour and the aesthetics of nature, as well as the vitality we see in nature, are all evidence of another world. What is both important and exciting is that now it is science itself, as it becomes more penetrative, in both the astronomical and quantal scales, which is retrieving this lost vision.

The new evidence in science provides hints as to how the other world in nature is able to influence the evolution and functioning of the cosmos. In the first place there must have been an initiating directive which ensured that the Big Bang went in a very special direction. The necessary concepts have been provided, mathematically, in the pre-geometry described by the renowned astrophysicist, J. A. Wheeler and referred to in chapters 7 and 10.

Now that it has become possible to feed the required information into computers we can begin to appreciate how desperately narrow were the limits within which the universe could have succeeded. Minor differences or divergences in the first few milliseconds of the Creation would have resulted in a different universe, one probably quite uncongenial to the eventual evolution of life and mind.

Soon after the Big Bang another guiding system probably came into operation. As matter evolved it accumulated an ever increasing bank of information and expertise in its transcendental aspect, which could be played back into the events of space and time. There is evidence, for example, that the first stars were crude and clumsy, but because they were linked to this inbuilt guidance, they subsequently became more efficient. Our sun is a late generation star. With the evolution of matter into life and mind this transcendental influence increases, becoming a decisive force in space and time.

Returning to the quantal events in the atomic realm, such a transcendental replicate level enables phenomena to be accounted for which are otherwise inexplicable. For instance quantum theory and experiment indicate that electrons receive and emit radiation in very definite amounts, a kind of musical notation characteristic for every one of the ninety-two naturally occuring kinds of atom. In the course of this emission or reception of radiation energy, electrons shift orbit in an orderly manner. Such events cannot be imagined as happening in any material sense. Only some sort of pre-geometry, some protostructuring in a transcendental level of matter can account for them.

Although a transcendental level in matter is being proposed this does not in any way imply anything *supernatural*. The transcendental aspect of nature is an intrinsic part of the physical order; from all the evidence thoroughly self-consistent and totally independent of outside intervention.

It is also evident that this control over the events of space and time is discrete and requires very long stretches of time to become apparent. As evolution progresses the guidance becomes more evident due to the accumulation of experience in the transcendental aspect of nature, and to a progressive improvement in the inbuilt faculty for communication between the material and the non-material, which the quantum gap provides. One may suppose that the key aim of molecular evolution has been to exploit this faculty, and that the most evolved forms of matter—the human brain and nervous tissue—have the most fully and successfully exploited it.

In the past these ideas have been dismissed by scientists who reject the least hint of the supernatural in the workings of nature. But recent developments in quantum physics suggest that such a sidestepping of the natural laws is provided for in the quantum functioning of matter. In certain somewhat rare circumstances particles can circumvent the principle of conservancy of energy, by borrowing from the limitless sources of the energy substratum of the universe. This borrowed energy is paid back very quickly, but for a fraction of a moment it makes possible a near miraculous event. In the evolution of matter certain structures, in the brain for example, may have been able to exploit this rare possibility.

In the material world objects are separated by an apparently empty space. Relativity theory replaces the concept of emptiness with a dynamic medium—space-time. Quantum mechanics has had to go much further. It has been obliged to unify objects or events as aspects of a universal quantum field which overcomes space altogether. How difficult this has been to accept is indicated by a recent polemic following an article in *Scientific American* ('The Quantum Theory and Reality' B. d'Espagnet, November 1979) between the author and the distinguished physicist Professor Weiskopf. In a letter to *Scientific American* (May 1980) Weiskopf points out that his colleague has misunderstood the significance of quantum theory which, by abolishing the need for space, made the interaction of particles, irrespective of distance, natural and unavoidable. He refers to a recent experiment in which it was found that electrons passing through parallel slits in a suitable instrument formed a pattern on a screen which indicated that those passing through one of the slits were instantaneously aware of the state of those passing through the other slit, and adjusted their behaviour accordingly. In a common-sense world such a claim seems nonsensical, which is exactly why traditionally-minded scientists have encountered such difficulties in accepting recent quantum physics. But the experimental evidence is there, and once the concept of the quantal organisation of nature is accepted, such phenomena can be seen as perfectly natural.

Quantum theory is so self-consistent that it has not only dismissed the notions of space and the separability of events—a subject known as non-locality in quantum mechanics—but has also made superfluous such concepts as force and continuum. The earlier physicists like Weyl and Dirac, working in the thirties, were aware that an aspect of nature transcending space and time was required; they referred to this as the *substratum continuum*. Quantum mechanics, in its development of *field* concepts has already made these earlier terms superfluous, although in this book I have retained the term continuum, for it does make it easier for non-physicists to follow the ideas I am putting forward.

The only classical force of nature which refuses to be encompassed by quantum theory, is gravity. The probable reason is that it refers so much to the other world in nature, and requires such vast amounts of matter to make itself felt, that its very subtle quantal properties have so far been missed. However some experiments performed early in 1980 do indicate that gravity interacts with neutron fields, suggesting that it is likely to have some quantal property.

The development of the field concept accounts for the greatest successes of quantum theory. The notion goes back to Clarke Maxwell in the nineteenth century. By plotting electric charge and magnetic moment as points in a unifying mathematical matrix or field, he found the wonderful equation which consistently unites electricity and magnetism. Such mathematical devices appear to deal exclusively with events occuring in space and time, but neither electricity nor gravity are fundamentally material. Maxwell's field theory therefore, was already relating non-material events in terms of space and time.

In quantum mechanics the elementary particle itself can

be considered as a field, its wave aspect being a non-material (but physical) property. By dealing with electron wave packets as the co-ordinates in the field, their interaction with other particles can be calculated. If, for instance, two electrons approach each other, at a certain point in the field they will repel each other because of their similar negative charge, the energy necessary for this being conveyed by a quantum of the field, in this case a photon. The photon is a mathematical necessity; had it not been discovered it would have been necessary to invent it. Such a field simulates actual physical events so closely that it can predict the existence of particles and processes not previously detected. This suggests that such mathematical inventions as the field, although remote from every day reality touch upon some very real and important quality in nature. Better mathematical devices may yet be found, meanwhile quantum field theory remains successful.

Mathematicians and scientists have long believed that a valid system is always elegant and symmetrical. Everyone knows what symmetry means in the ordinary world, from the image of an object in a mirror, to the hexagonal symmetry of a snow crystal. But far more complicated symmetries are possible; for instance electric charges, or the spin of elementary particles, can be expressed symmetrically. The absence of symmetry in any system is the alarm signal that all is not well. Mathematicians therefore go out of their way to look for symmetrical solutions. In quantum field theory, if symmetry is absent it can usually be brought about by adding further fields—i.e. other particles. In this way new particles have been predicted and, in most cases, found.

Gauge theory is a special kind of field theory. The term was invented by Weyl in 1920, when he likened the choice of a scale for a particular field to the polished blocks of steel of different, but related, sizes, which are called 'gauges' and are used by machinists as standards. At the time Weyl was attempting to relate electro-magnetism to relativity theory, by varying the entities in a field so that while they could vary within set limits, their relationship remained symmetrical and consistent. This device allows the mathematician to deal with events of great complexity and to find symmetrical relationships in apparently diverse situations.

Particles like the electron are probably fundamental; they cannot be dismantled. But the protons and neutrons of the nucleus are evidently made up of more basic entities—the *quarks* and *antiquarks* of the present day. These are such odd entities that no ordinary terms can deal with them. Indeed R. P. Feynmann, the eminent American physicist who is renowned for his work on quantum electro-dynamics, believes that quarks have not been found because every quark encompasses the entire universe. To pick out a single quark would therefore involve dismantling the universe! Because of their extreme oddness physicists have chosen to label them with colours in order to describe their interactions and the way in which they build up from protons and neutrons. Red, green, blue and their complementaries cyan, magenta and yellow are the chosen colours, and one of the curious things about this is that just as in the ordinary world, if these colours are all mixed, or any is mixed with its complementary colour, white results, so in quantum chromodynamics, the mixing of the quarks in the same way creates white, equivalent to the creation of protons and neutrons. Clearly quarks are not themselves coloured, but it seems that the properties of quarks are in some way related to the colour evoking process in nature. This does not seem preposterous when one remembers that colour is formed by vibrating electrons interfering with light waves, and, as we have seen, light waves and vibrating atoms are not restricted to this world but interact with the replicate world. The creative process in the arts thus has much in common with field theory. The various constituents in a work of art, ceaselessly changing under the artist's intuitive guidance, remain integrated and symmetrical in a profound sense. The success of quantum chromodynamics is due to its qualities of integration and symmetry. However disjointed the universe may appear in, for example, the vast scatterings of stars, at its fundamental level it must be united. If this were not so evolution and continued existence would have been impossible.

So far physical theories have not been holistic. But, as physics has been forced to confront the unity of the universe, so theory and speculation have tended to become more concerned with holistic phenomena, which, while not strictly mechanical, can be dealt with by such inventions as gauge theory. Further insights into the new thinking can be found in *Wholeness and the Implicate Order* by Dr David Bohm, a physicist working in London, (Kegan Paul 1980).

An aspect of wholeness with which physicists have been confronted quite recently, and which caused dismay in scientific circles, is the experiment described in chapter 10, which suggests that an elementary particle does not 'know' which of two possible choices to make until some factor related to the observer's presence, causes it to make a decision. This is the factor normally referred to as 'chance', but, if chance it is, then chance must have a consistency and logic of its own, for it is such microphysical decisions which have determined the course of the universe's evolution. Seen without bias the framework provided by quantum theory should make such phenomena acceptable, for in this theory particles, as wave functions and fields, are not separate but can be conceived of as aspects of a sustaining state which is universal and instantly available. There is no need for signals between such particles, nor is the observer separate from them. If, as I have suggested, the mind is an aspect of the transcendental level in nature organised by the brain, then the human mind, and the decisions taken in nature, occur at the same level, and the influence of the human mind is natural and inevitable. This does not mean that nature does not take decisions without the presence of the human mind. Obviously it has been doing so for five thousand million years or more, but the advent of mind upon the scene, brings in another dimension to the functioning of nature.

Compared to the complexity of developments in quantum theory the requirements of the replicate model of reality proposed in this book, are elementary, and if, as I have suggested, the evolution of the universe is the result of both initial and sustained pregeometry, followed by an increasing feedback of experience accumulating in the transcendental aspect of nature, then one can conclude that the pregeometry of Creation has, from the start, been humanly congenial. The abundant evidence of past struggle and failure prevents one from assuming that this anthropic universe was in some way pre-ordained. All one can say is that against enormous odds the dice seem to have been loaded in our favour, otherwise we would not be here. There may be no certainty, but there is hope. In the words of the well known mathematician and physicist Freeman Dyson:

> 'I do not feel like an alien in this universe; the more I examine the universe and study details of its architecture, the more evidence I find that the universe in some sense must have known that we were coming.'

INDEX